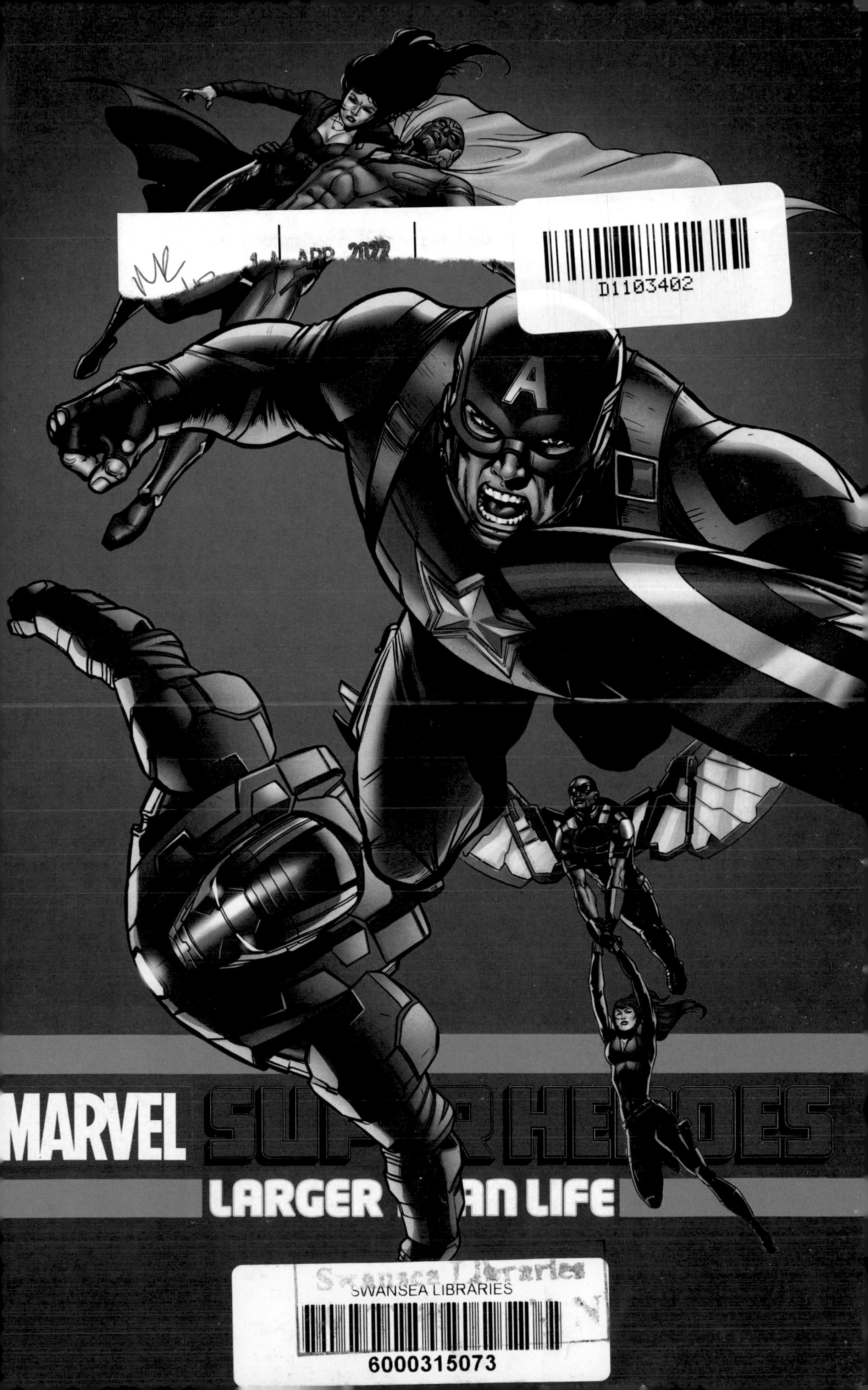
MARVEL
LARGER
LIFE

AVENGERS: OPERATION HYDRA

WILL CORONA PILGRIM
WRITER

ANDREA DI VITO
ARTIST

LAURA VILLARI
COLOR ARTIST

VC's CLAYTON COWLES
LETTERER

MICHAEL RYAN & JAVIER MENA
COVER ARTISTS

EMILY SHAW
CONSULTING EDITOR

BILL ROSEMANN
with MARK BASSO
EDITORS

ANT-MAN: LARGER THAN LIFE

WILL CORONA PILGRIM
WRITER

ANDREA DI VITO
ARTIST

VERONICA GANDINI
COLOR ARTIST

VC's CLAYTON COWLES
LETTERER

JUNG-SIK AHN
COVER ARTIST

MARK BASSO & EMILY SHAW
EDITORS

CAPTAIN AMERICA: ROAD TO WAR

WILL CORONA PILGRIM
WRITER

ANDREA DI VITO
ARTIST

LAURA VILLARI
COLOR ARTIST

VC's TRAVIS LANHAM
LETTERER

RON LIM & GURU-eFX
COVER ARTISTS

EMILY SHAW
EDITOR

MARVEL SUPER HEROES: LARGER THAN LIFE. Contains material originally published in magazine form as AVENGERS: OPERATION HYDRA #1, ANT-MAN: LARGER THAN LIFE #1, CAPTAIN AMERICA: ROAD TO WAR #1, DOCTOR STRANGE: MYSTIC APPRENTICE #1, GUARDIANS OF THE GALAXY: DREAM ON #1 and SPIDER-MAN: MASTER PLAN #1. First printing 2017. ISBN# 978-1-302-90889-8. Published by MARVEL WORLDWIDE, INC., a subsidiary of MARVEL ENTERTAINMENT, LLC. OFFICE OF PUBLICATION: 135 West 50th Street, New York, NY 10020. Copyright © 2017 MARVEL. No similarity between any of the names, characters, persons, and/or institutions in this magazine with those of any living or dead person or institution is intended, and any such similarity which may exist is purely coincidental. **Printed in the U.S.A.** DAN BUCKLEY, President, Marvel Entertainment; JOE QUESADA, Chief Creative Officer; TOM BREVOORT, SVP of Publishing; DAVID BOGART, SVP of Business Affairs & Operations, Publishing & Partnership; C.B. CEBULSKI, VP of Brand Management & Development, Asia; DAVID GABRIEL, SVP of Sales & Marketing, Publishing; JEFF YOUNGQUIST, VP of Production & Special Projects; DAN CARR, Executive Director of Publishing Technology; ALEX MORALES, Director of Publishing Operations; SUSAN CRESPI, Production Manager; STAN LEE, Chairman Emeritus. For information regarding advertising in Marvel Comics or on Marvel.com, please contact Vit DeBellis, Integrated Sales Manager, at vdebellis@marvel.com. For Marvel subscription inquiries, please call 888-511-5480. **Manufactured between 10/6/2017 and 11/6/2017 by** QUAD/GRAPHICS WASECA, WASECA, MN, USA.

MARVEL SUPER HEROES
LARGER THAN LIFE

DOCTOR STRANGE: MYSTIC APPRENTICE

WILL CORONA PILGRIM
WRITER

ANDREA DI VITO
ARTIST

LAURA VILLARI
COLOR ARTIST

VC's TRAVIS LANHAM
LETTERER

MICHAEL RYAN & JAVIER MENA
COVER ARTISTS

MARK BASSO
EDITOR

GUARDIANS OF THE GALAXY: DREAM ON

MARC SUMERAK
WRITER

ANDREA DI VITO
ARTIST

LAURA VILLARI
COLOR ARTIST

VC's TRAVIS LANHAM
LETTERER

MICHAEL RYAN & JAVIER MENA
COVER ARTISTS

MARK BASSO
EDITOR

SPIDER-MAN: MASTER PLAN

ROBBIE THOMPSON
WRITER

NATHAN STOCKMAN
ARTIST

JIM CAMPBELL
COLOR ARTIST

VC's TRAVIS LANHAM
LETTERER

NATHAN STOCKMAN & JIM CAMPBELL
COVER ARTISTS

MARK BASSO
EDITOR

FRONT COVER ARTISTS **MICHAEL RYAN & JAVIER MENA**

BACK COVER ARTISTS **RON LIM & GURU-eFX**

COLLECTION EDITOR **MARK D. BEAZLEY** ◇ ASSISTANT EDITOR **CAITLIN O'CONNELL**
ASSOCIATE MANAGING EDITOR **KATERI WOODY** ◇ SENIOR EDITOR, SPECIAL PROJECTS **JENNIFER GRÜNWALD**
VP PRODUCTION & SPECIAL PROJECTS **JEFF YOUNGQUIST** ◇ SVP PRINT, SALES & MARKETING **DAVID GABRIEL**
BOOK DESIGNER **JAY BOWEN**

EDITOR IN CHIEF **AXEL ALONSO** ◇ CHIEF CREATIVE OFFICER **JOE QUESADA**
PRESIDENT **DAN BUCKLEY** ◇ EXECUTIVE PRODUCER **ALAN FINE**

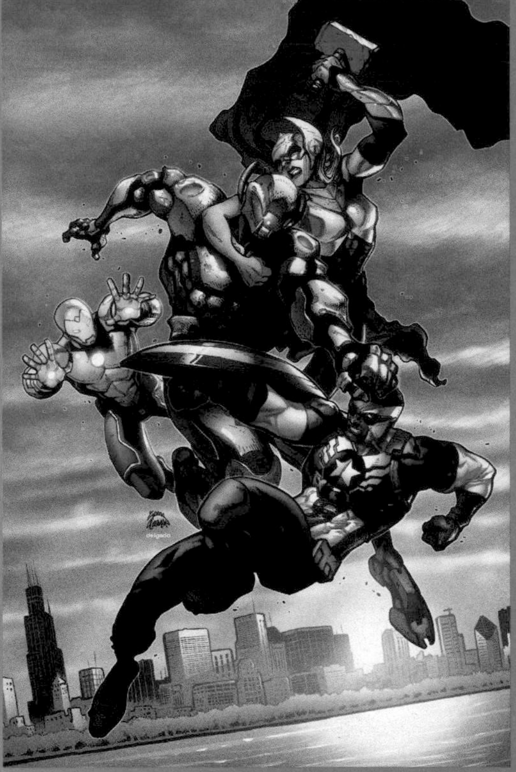

AVENGERS: OPERATION HYDRA #1
VARIANT BY **RYAN STEGMAN & EDGAR DELGADO**

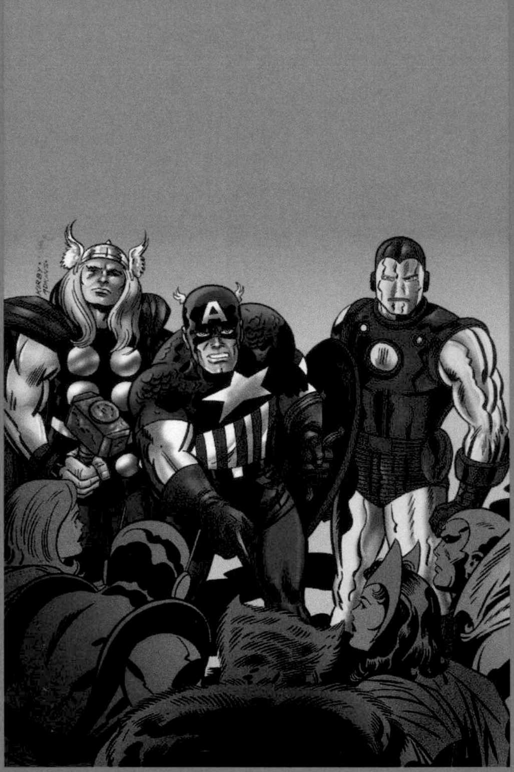

AVENGERS: OPERATION HYDRA #1
VARIANT BY **JACK KIRBY, DAN ADKINS & TOM SMITH**

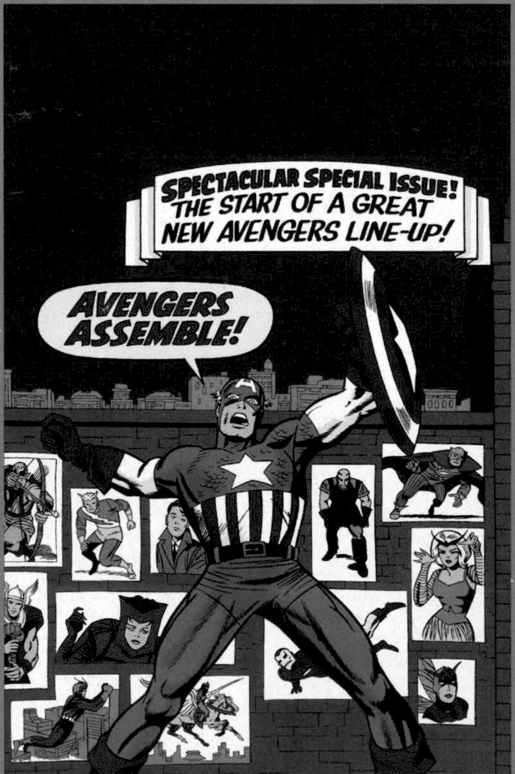
SPECTACULAR SPECIAL ISSUE! THE START OF A GREAT NEW AVENGERS LINE-UP!
AVENGERS ASSEMBLE!

AVENGERS: OPERATION HYDRA #1
VARIANT BY **JACK KIRBY**

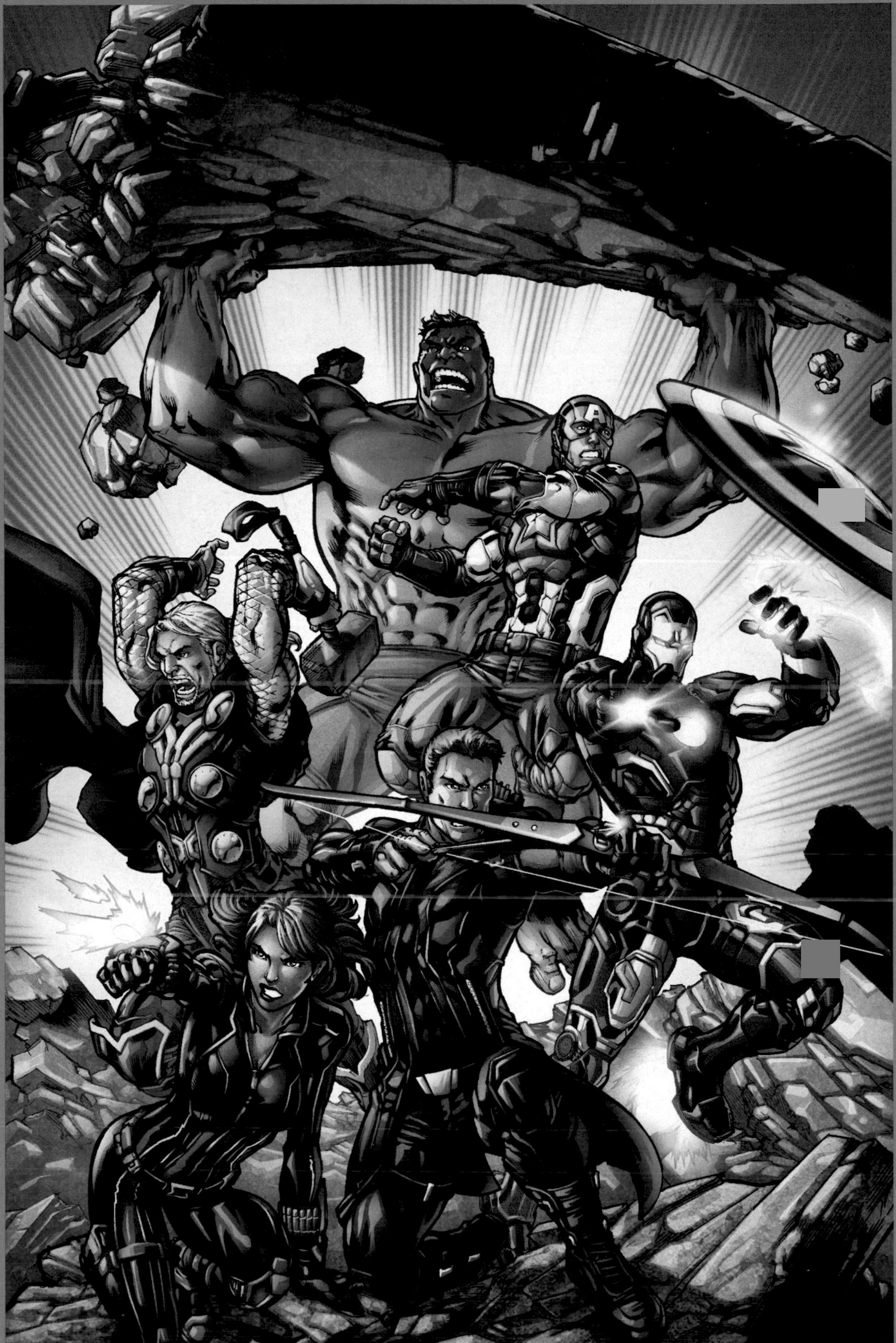

AVENGERS: OPERATION HYDRA #1

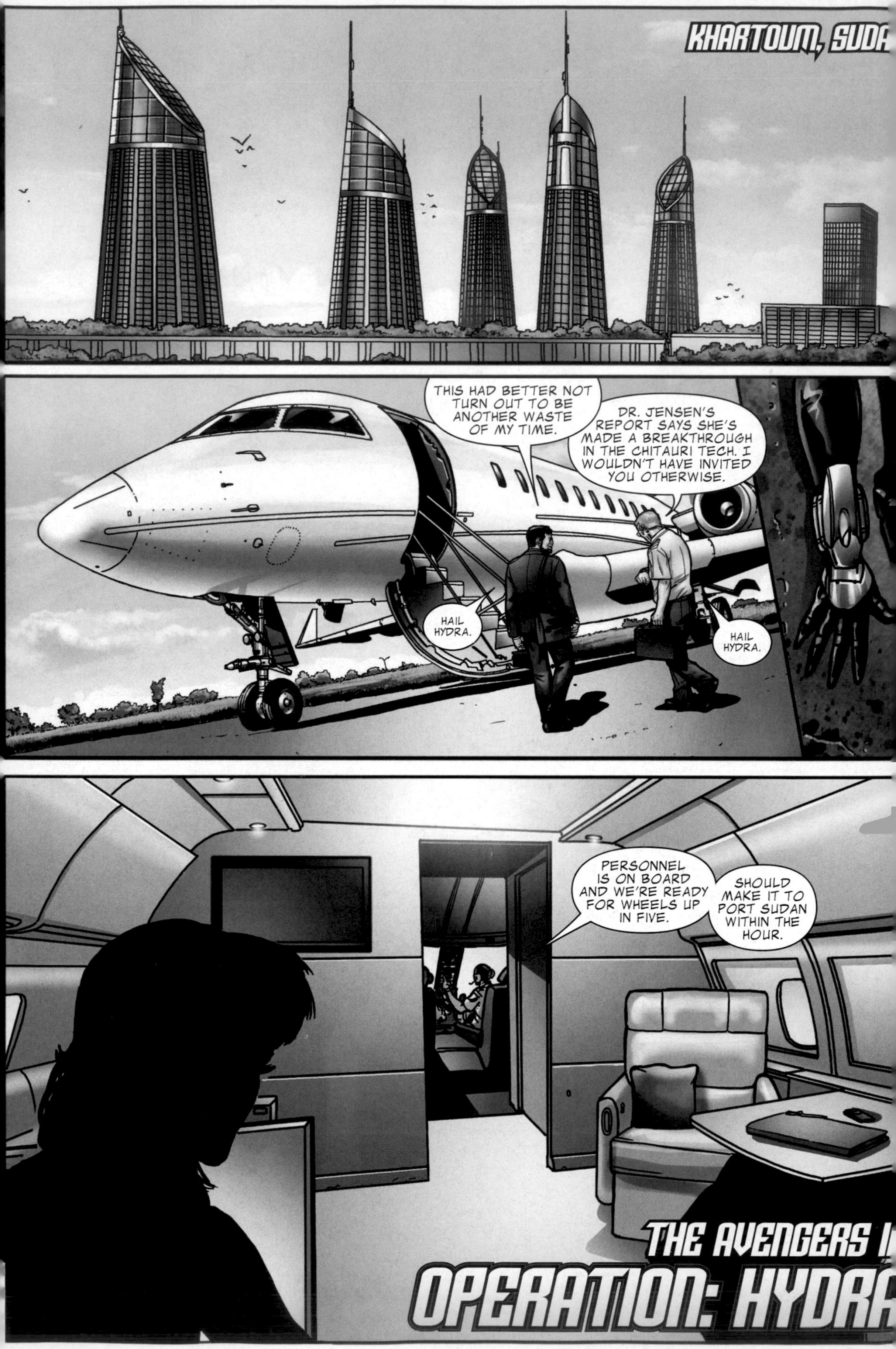
KHARTOUM, SUDA
THIS HAD BETTER NOT TURN OUT TO BE ANOTHER WASTE OF MY TIME.
DR. JENSEN'S REPORT SAYS SHE'S MADE A BREAKTHROUGH IN THE CHITAURI TECH. I WOULDN'T HAVE INVITED YOU OTHERWISE.
HAIL HYDRA.
HAIL HYDRA.
PERSONNEL IS ON BOARD AND WE'RE READY FOR WHEELS UP IN FIVE.
SHOULD MAKE IT TO PORT SUDAN WITHIN THE HOUR.
THE AVENGERS I
OPERATION: HYDRA

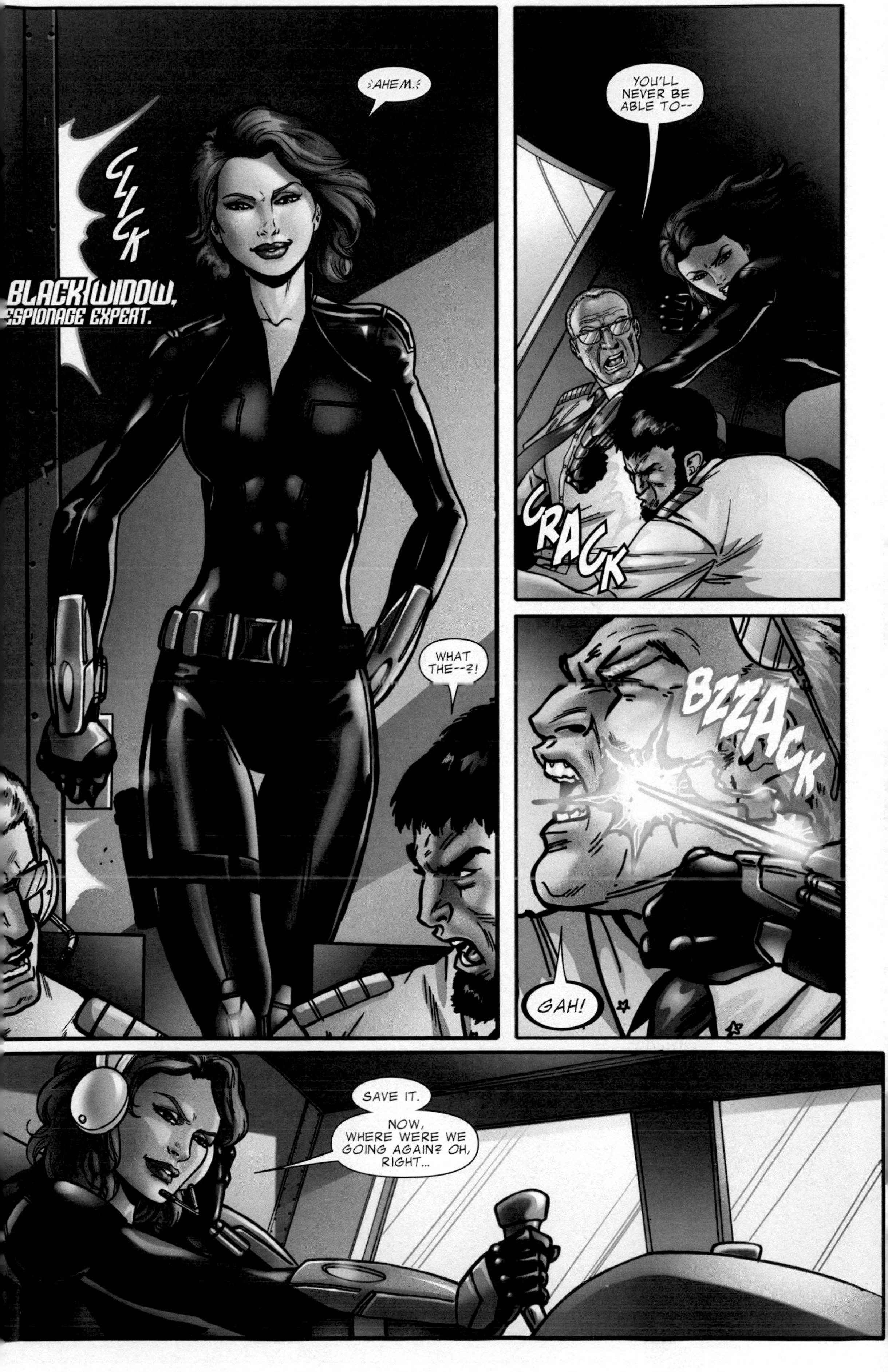
AHEM.
CLICK
BLACK WIDOW,
ESPIONAGE EXPERT.
WHAT THE--?!
YOU'LL NEVER BE ABLE TO--
CRACK
BZZACK
GAH!
SAVE IT.
NOW, WHERE WERE WE GOING AGAIN? OH, RIGHT...

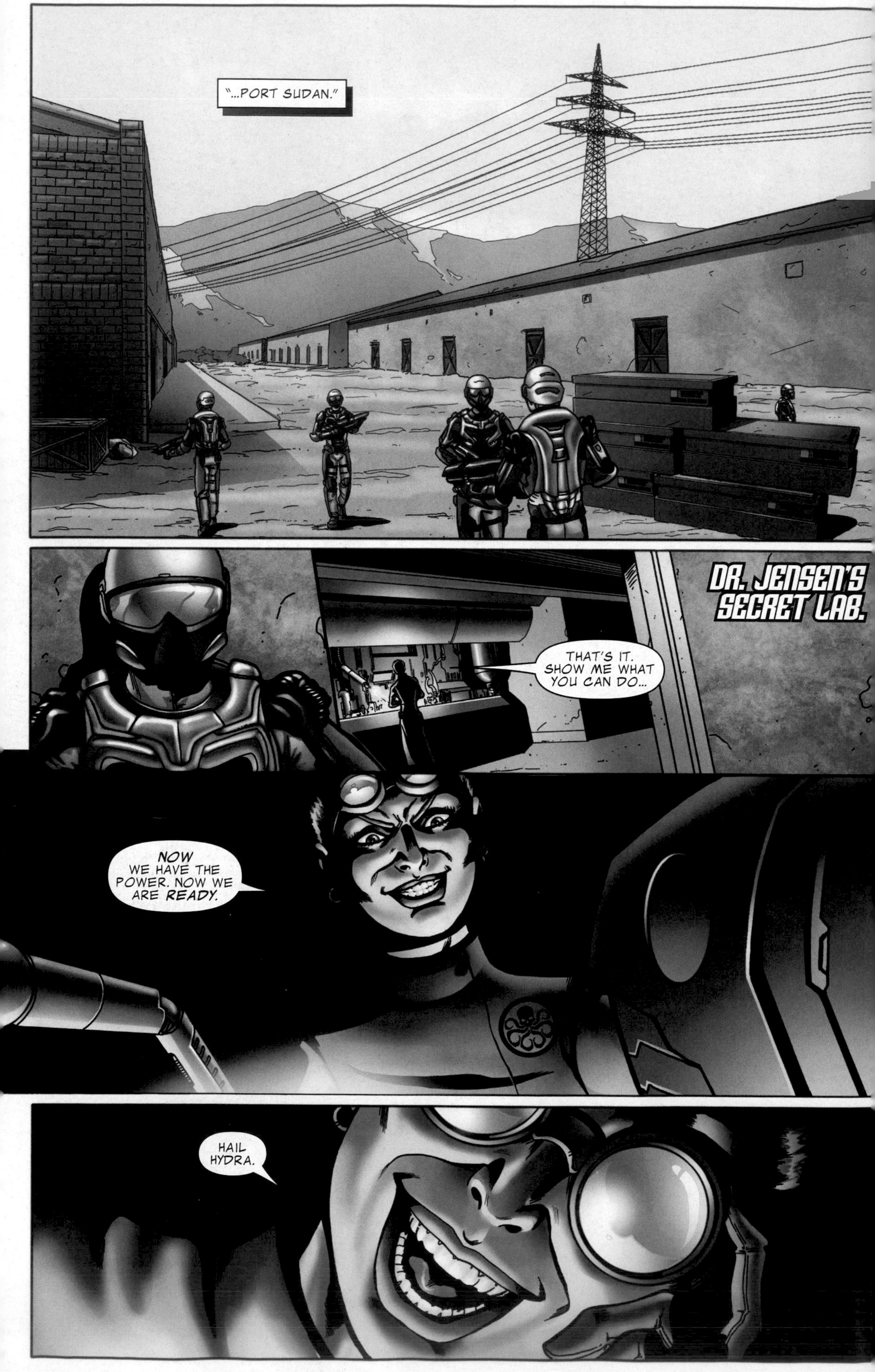
"...PORT SUDAN."
DR. JENSEN'S SECRET LAB.
THAT'S IT. SHOW ME WHAT YOU CAN DO...
NOW WE HAVE THE POWER. NOW WE ARE READY.
HAIL HYDRA.

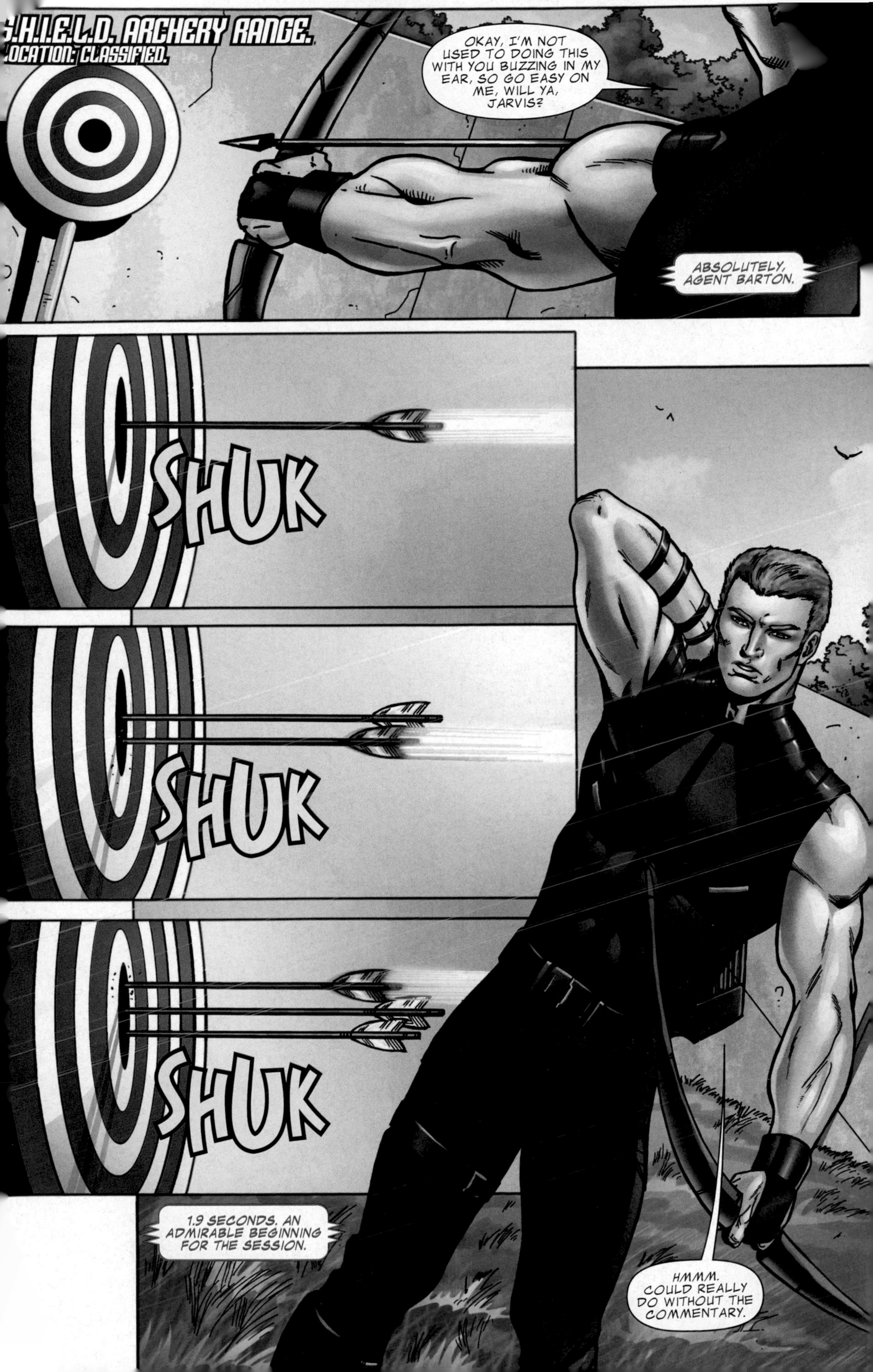
S.H.I.E.L.D. ARCHERY RANGE.
OCATION: CLASSIFIED.
OKAY, I'M NOT USED TO DOING THIS WITH YOU BUZZING IN MY EAR, SO GO EASY ON ME, WILL YA, JARVIS?
ABSOLUTELY, AGENT BARTON.
SHUK
SHUK
SHUK
1.9 SECONDS. AN ADMIRABLE BEGINNING FOR THE SESSION.
HMMM. COULD REALLY DO WITHOUT THE COMMENTARY.

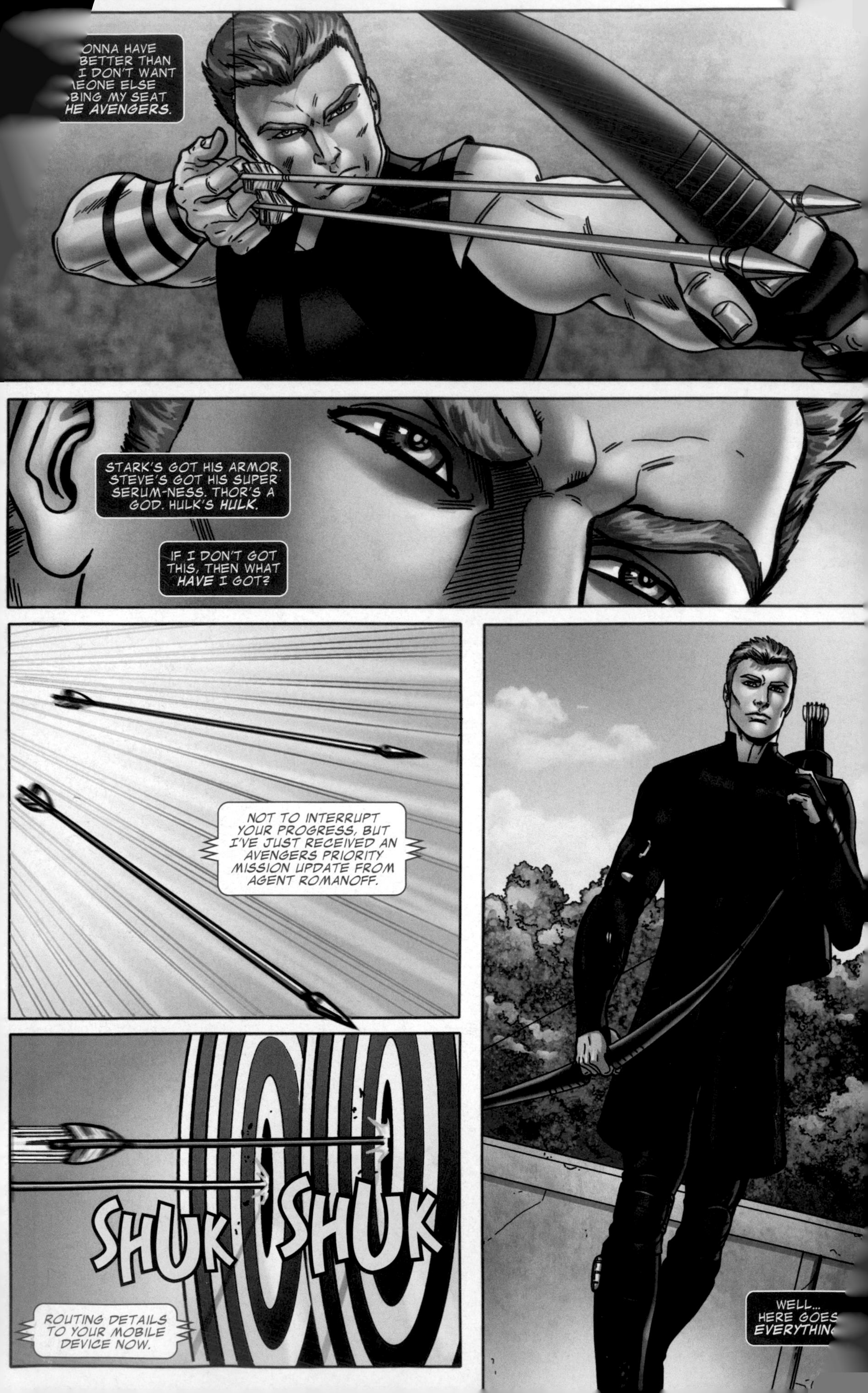
ONNA HAVE
BETTER THAN
I DON'T WANT
EONE ELSE
BING MY SEAT
HE AVENGERS.
STARK'S GOT HIS ARMOR. STEVE'S GOT HIS SUPER SERUM-NESS. THOR'S A GOD. HULK'S HULK.
IF I DON'T GOT THIS, THEN WHAT HAVE I GOT?
NOT TO INTERRUPT YOUR PROGRESS, BUT I'VE JUST RECEIVED AN AVENGERS PRIORITY MISSION UPDATE FROM AGENT ROMANOFF.
SHUK SHUK
ROUTING DETAILS TO YOUR MOBILE DEVICE NOW.
WELL... HERE GOES EVERYTHIN

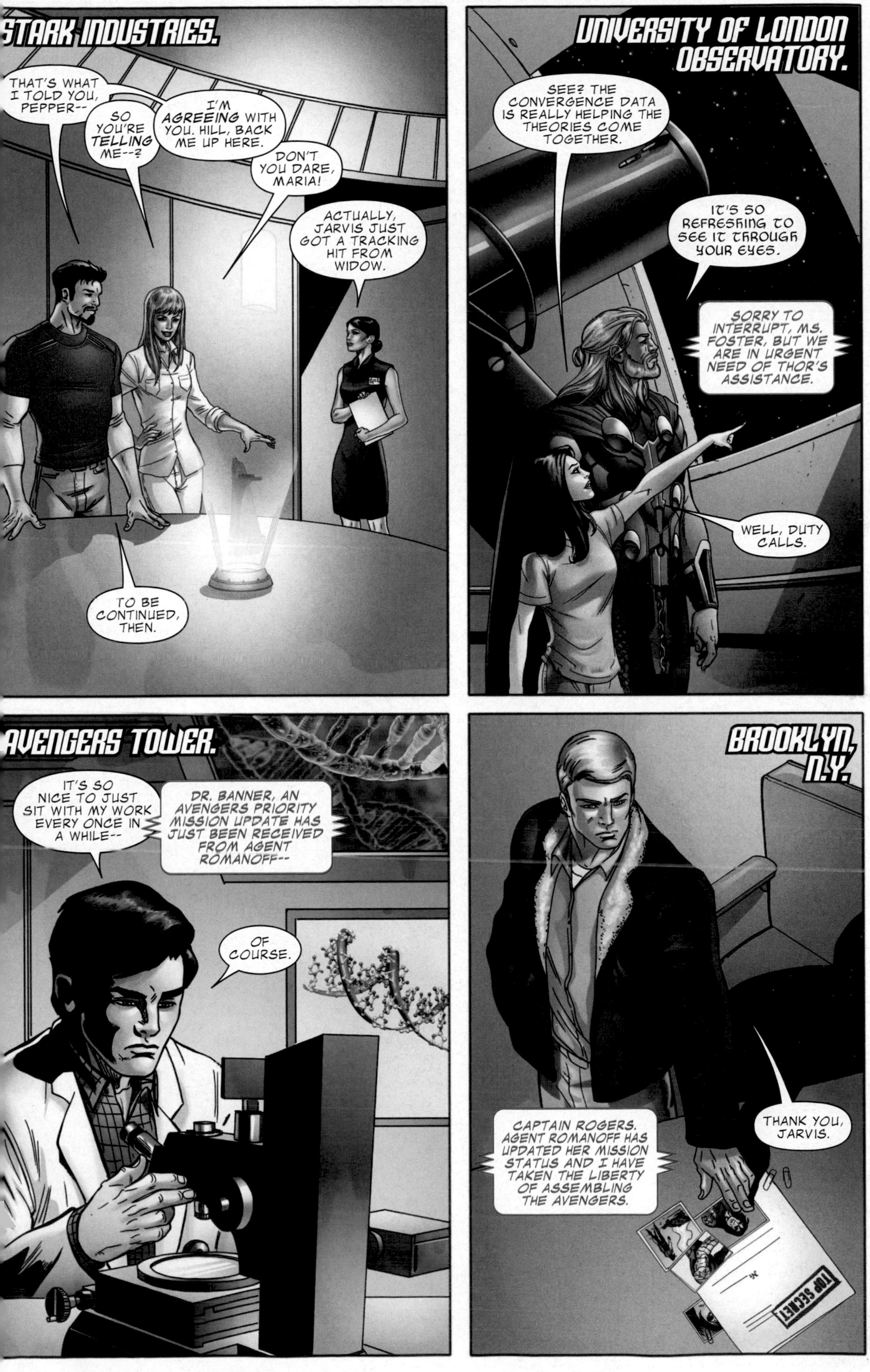
STARK INDUSTRIES.
THAT'S WHAT I TOLD YOU, PEPPER--
SO YOU'RE TELLING ME--?
I'M AGREEING WITH YOU. HILL, BACK ME UP HERE.
DON'T YOU DARE, MARIA!
ACTUALLY, JARVIS JUST GOT A TRACKING HIT FROM WIDOW.
TO BE CONTINUED, THEN.
UNIVERSITY OF LONDON OBSERVATORY.
SEE? THE CONVERGENCE DATA IS REALLY HELPING THE THEORIES COME TOGETHER.
IT'S SO REFRESHING TO SEE IT THROUGH YOUR EYES.
SORRY TO INTERRUPT, MS. FOSTER, BUT WE ARE IN URGENT NEED OF THOR'S ASSISTANCE.
WELL, DUTY CALLS.
AVENGERS TOWER.
IT'S SO NICE TO JUST SIT WITH MY WORK EVERY ONCE IN A WHILE--
DR. BANNER, AN AVENGERS PRIORITY MISSION UPDATE HAS JUST BEEN RECEIVED FROM AGENT ROMANOFF--
OF COURSE.
BROOKLYN, N.Y.
CAPTAIN ROGERS. AGENT ROMANOFF HAS UPDATED HER MISSION STATUS AND I HAVE TAKEN THE LIBERTY OF ASSEMBLING THE AVENGERS.
THANK YOU, JARVIS.
TOP SECRET

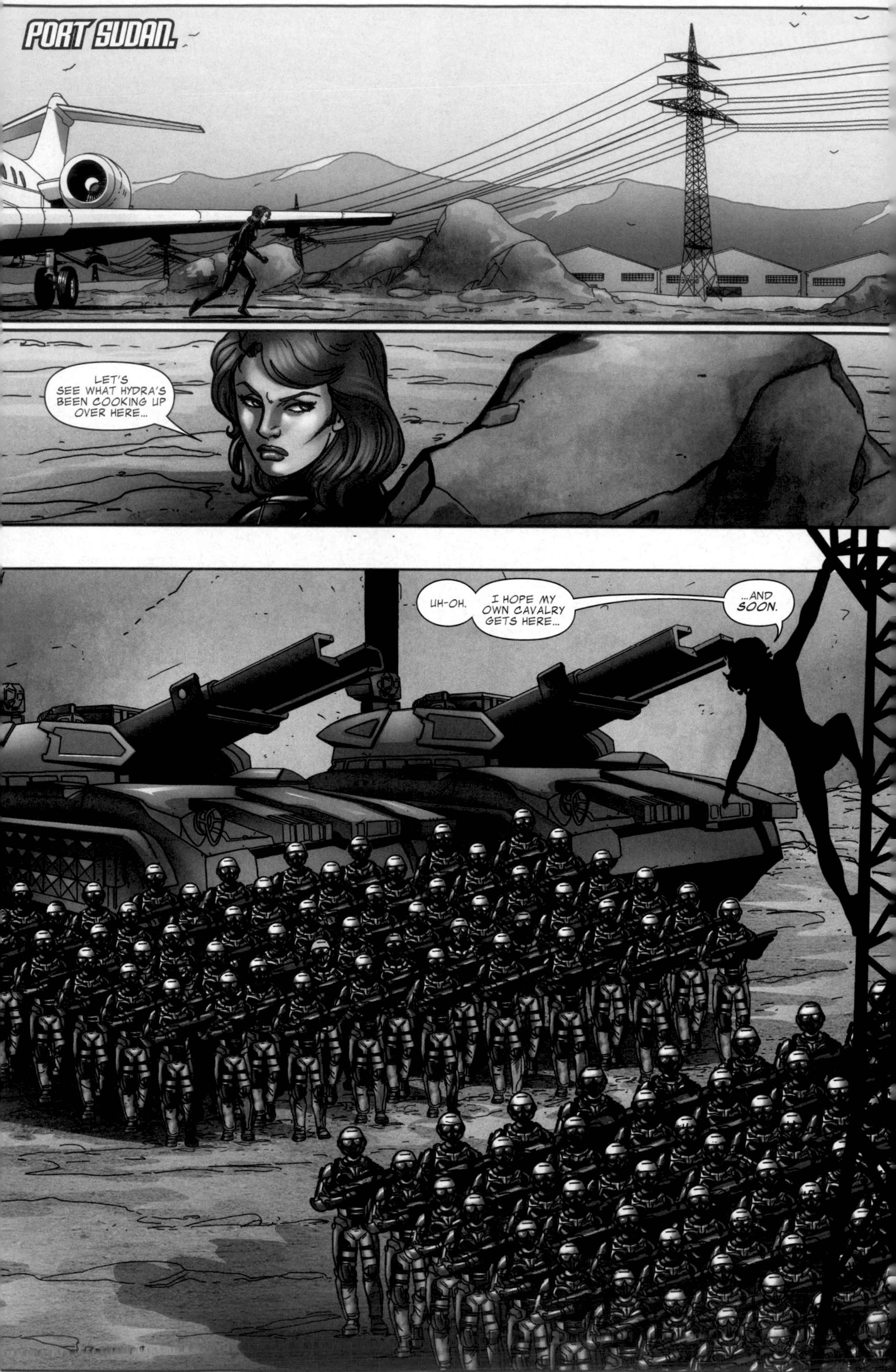
PORT SUDAN.
LET'S SEE WHAT HYDRA'S BEEN COOKING UP OVER HERE...
UH-OH.
I HOPE MY OWN CAVALRY GETS HERE...
...AND SOON.

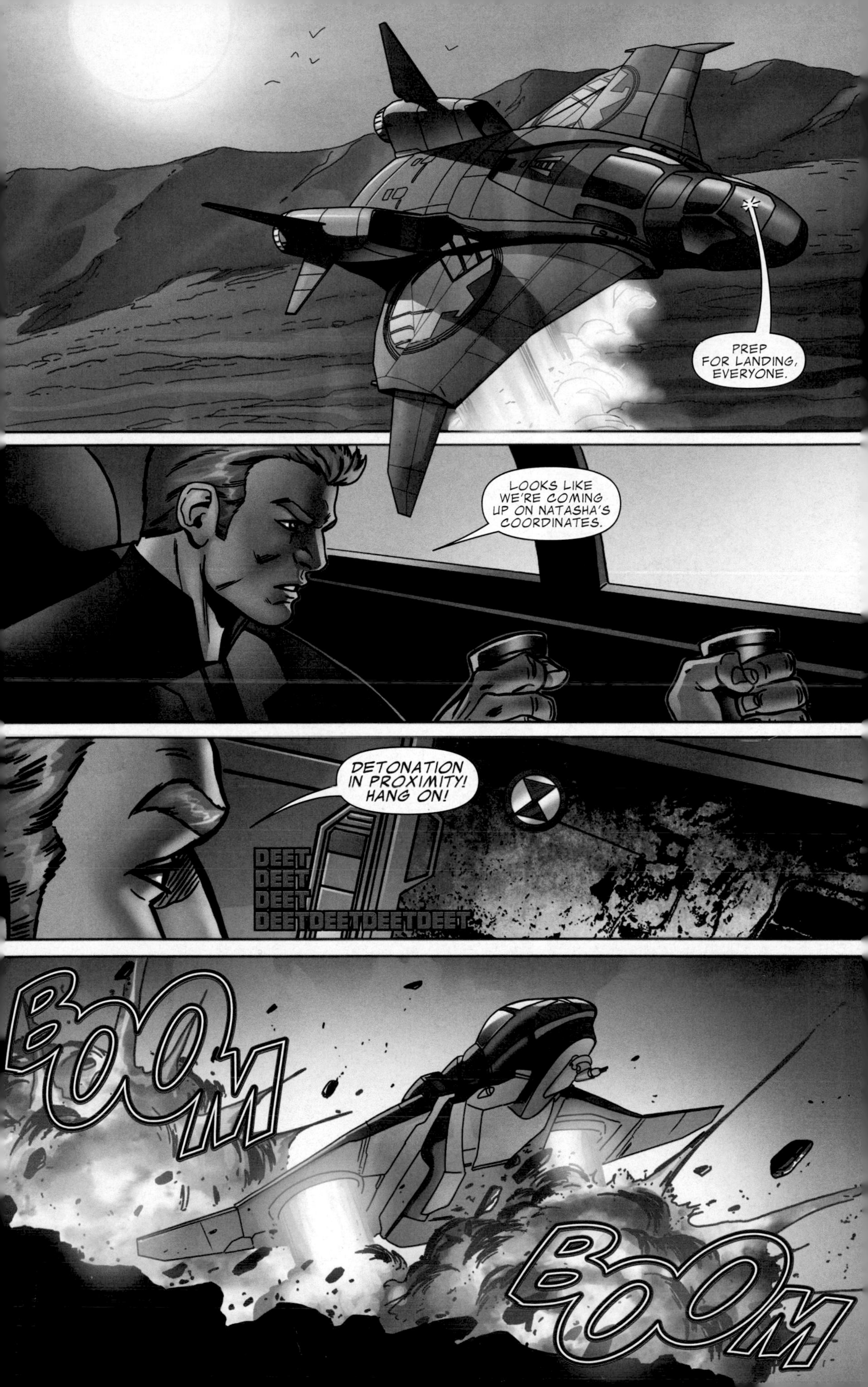
PREP FOR LANDING, EVERYONE.
LOOKS LIKE WE'RE COMING UP ON NATASHA'S COORDINATES.
DETONATION IN PROXIMITY! HANG ON!
DEET DEET DEET DEETDEETDEETDEET
BOOM
BOOM

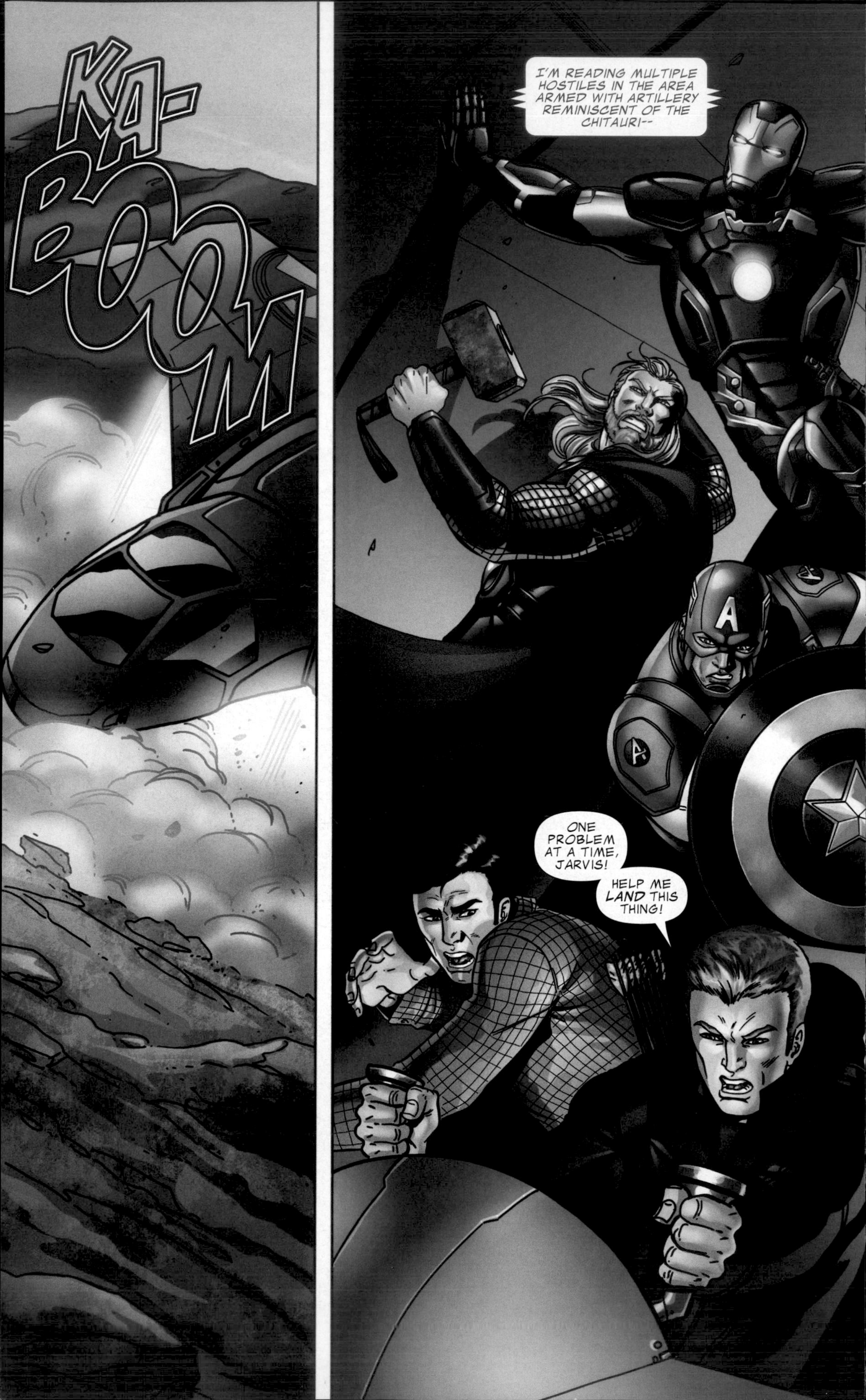
KA-BOOOM
I'M READING MULTIPLE HOSTILES IN THE AREA ARMED WITH ARTILLERY REMINISCENT OF THE CHITAURI--
ONE PROBLEM AT A TIME, JARVIS!
HELP ME LAND THIS THING!

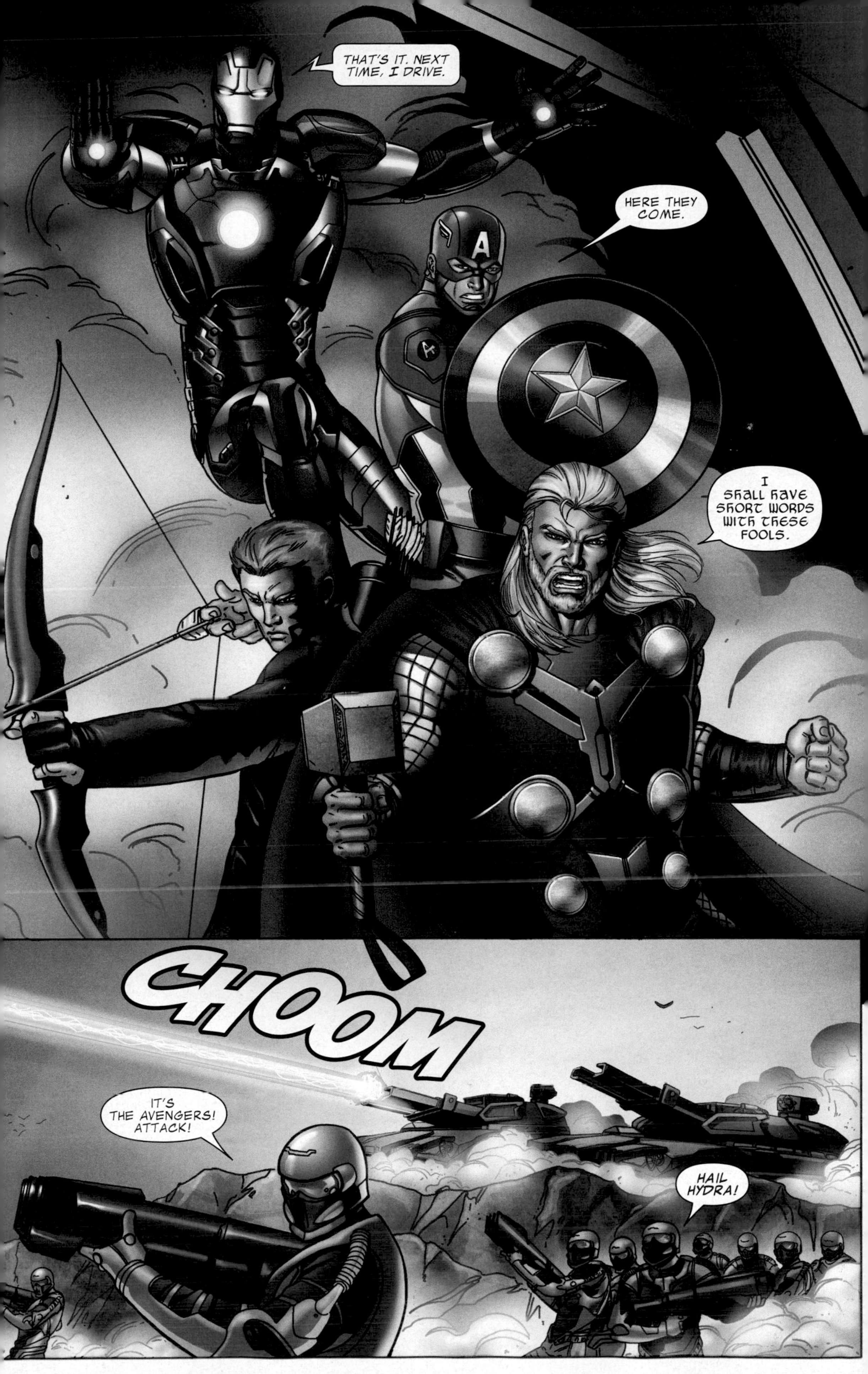
THAT'S IT. NEXT TIME, I DRIVE.
HERE THEY COME.
I SHALL HAVE SHORT WORDS WITH THESE FOOLS.
CHOOM
IT'S THE AVENGERS! ATTACK!
HAIL HYDRA!

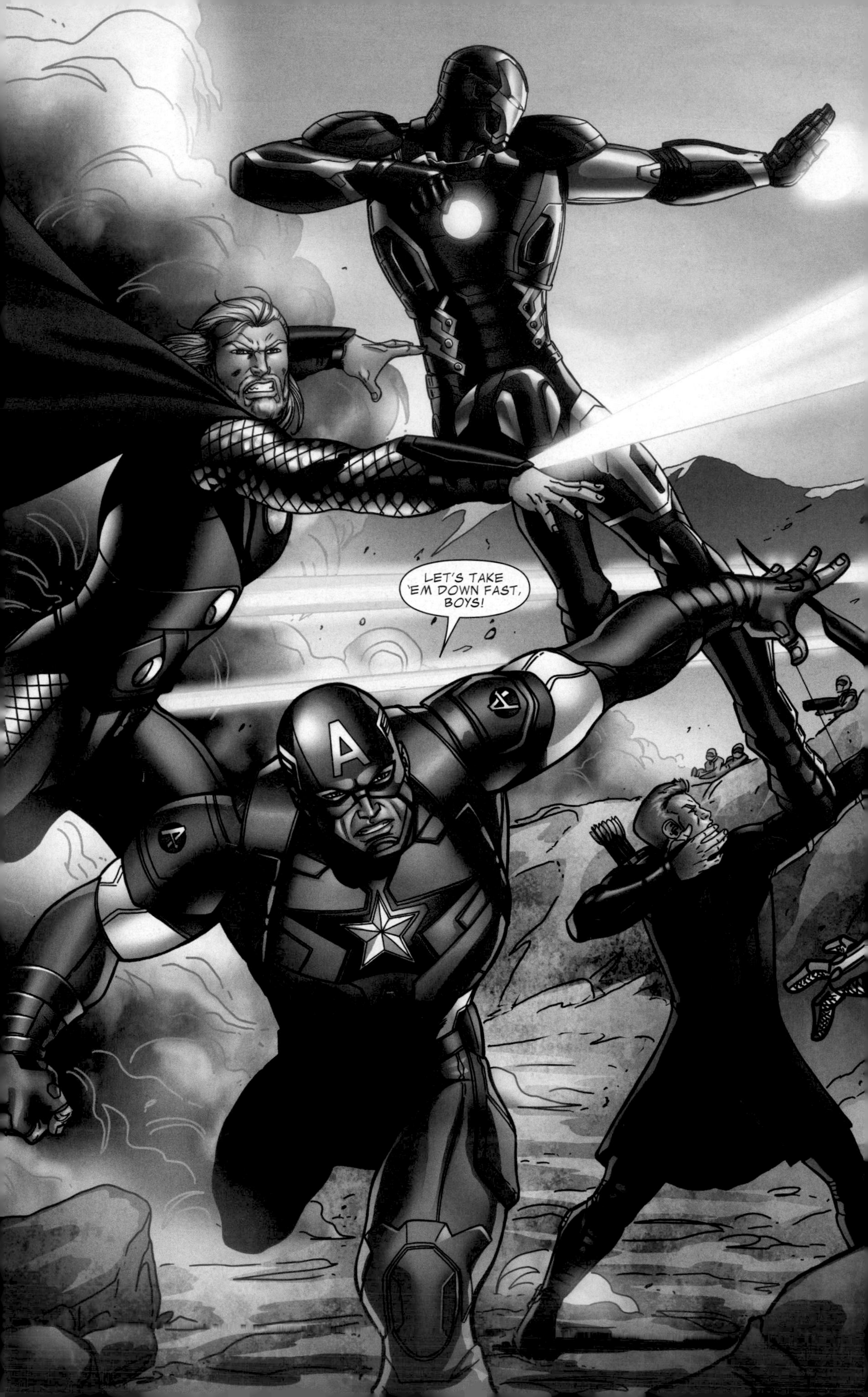
LET'S TAKE 'EM DOWN FAST, BOYS!

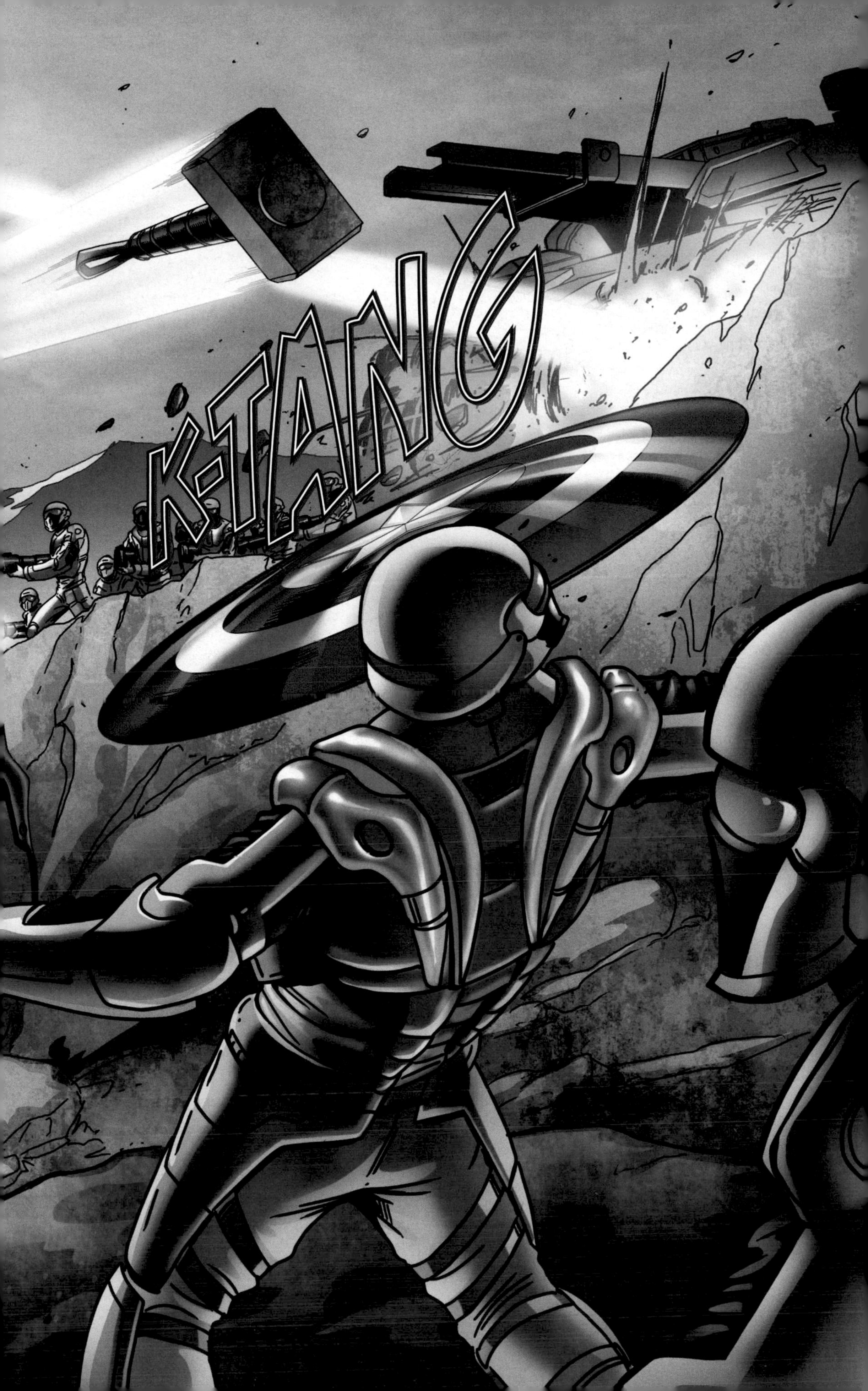
K-TANG

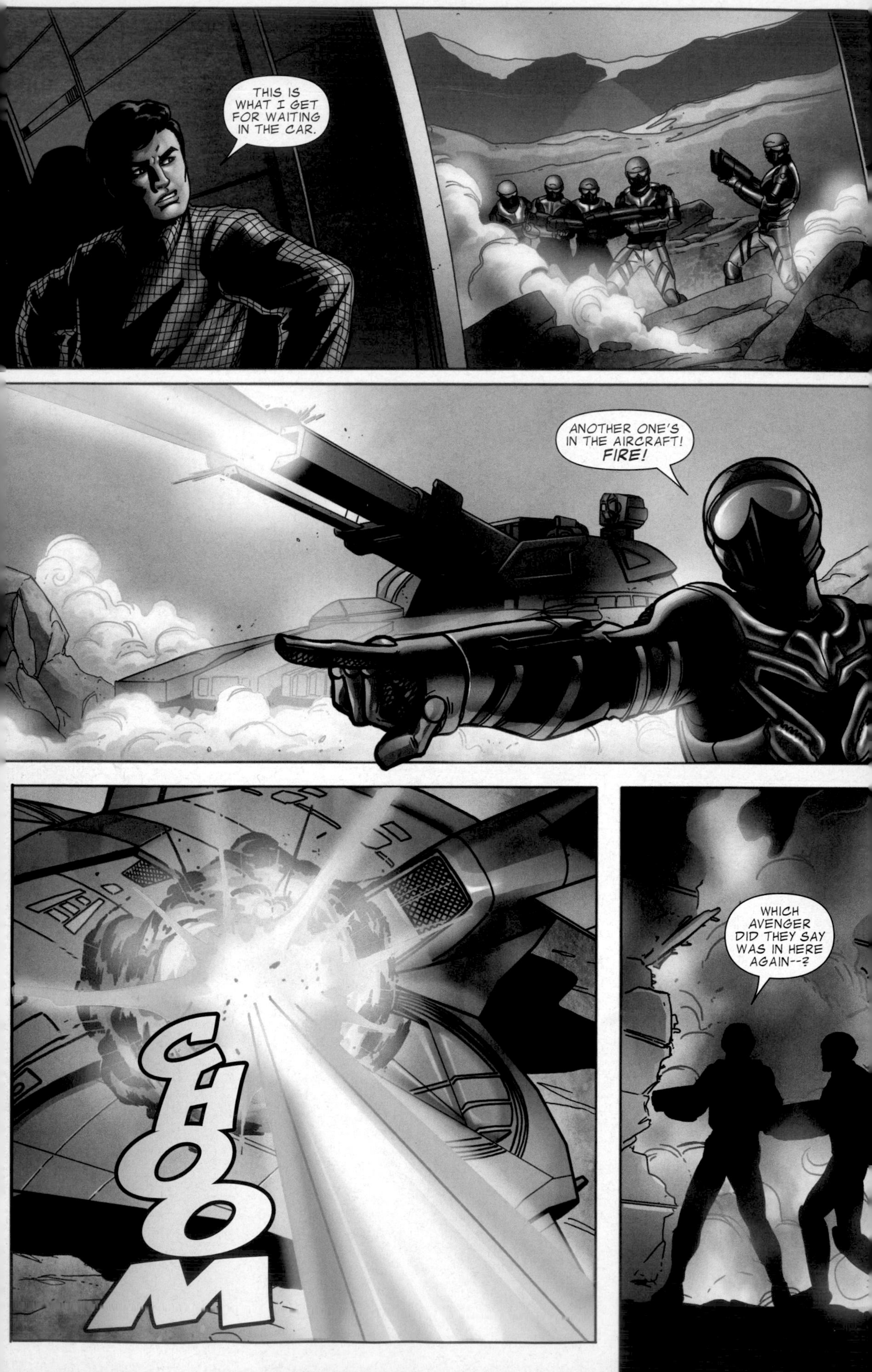
THIS IS WHAT I GET FOR WAITING IN THE CAR.
ANOTHER ONE'S IN THE AIRCRAFT! FIRE!
CHOOM
WHICH AVENGER DID THEY SAY WAS IN HERE AGAIN--?

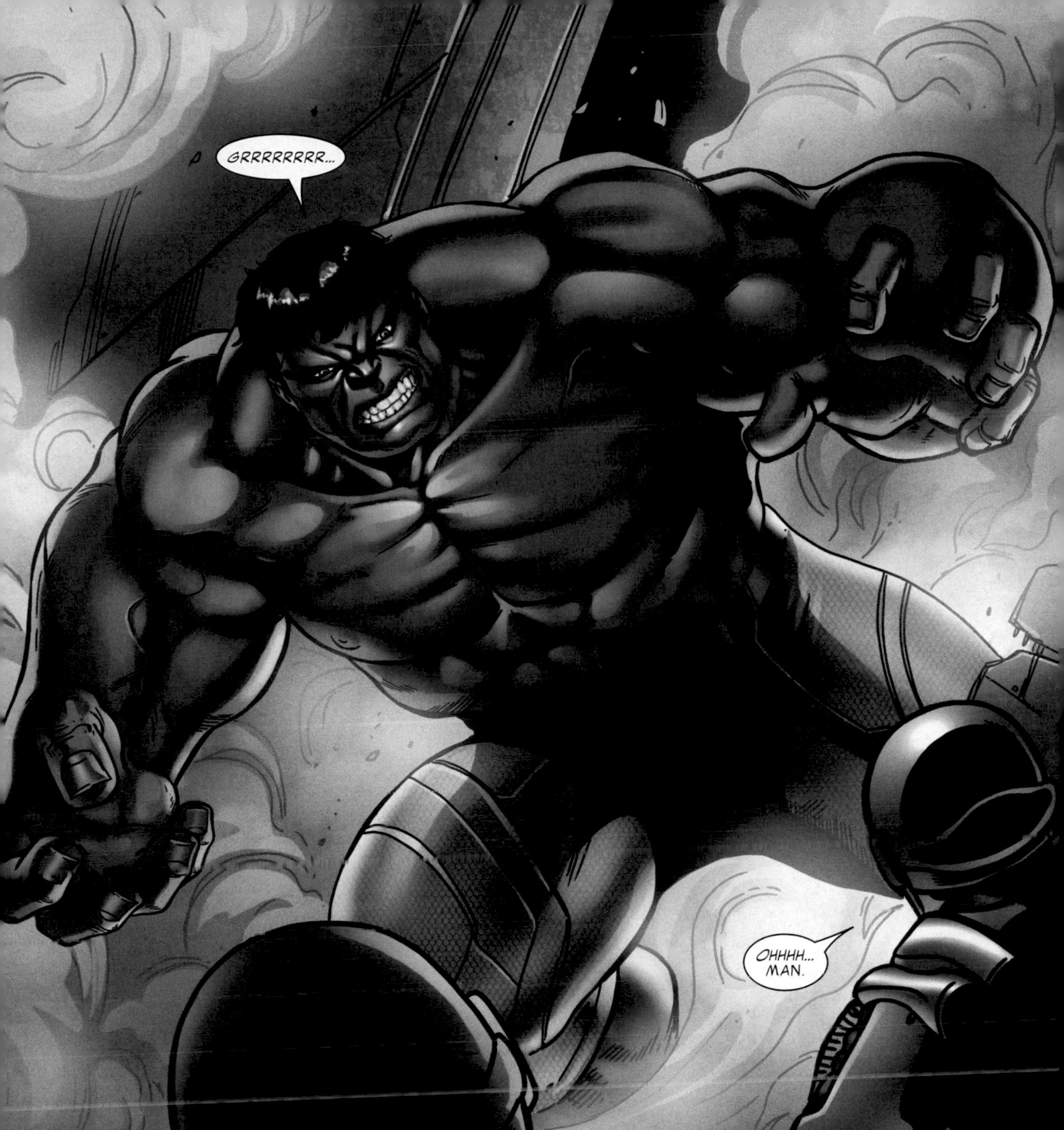
GRRRRRRRR...
OHHHH... MAN.
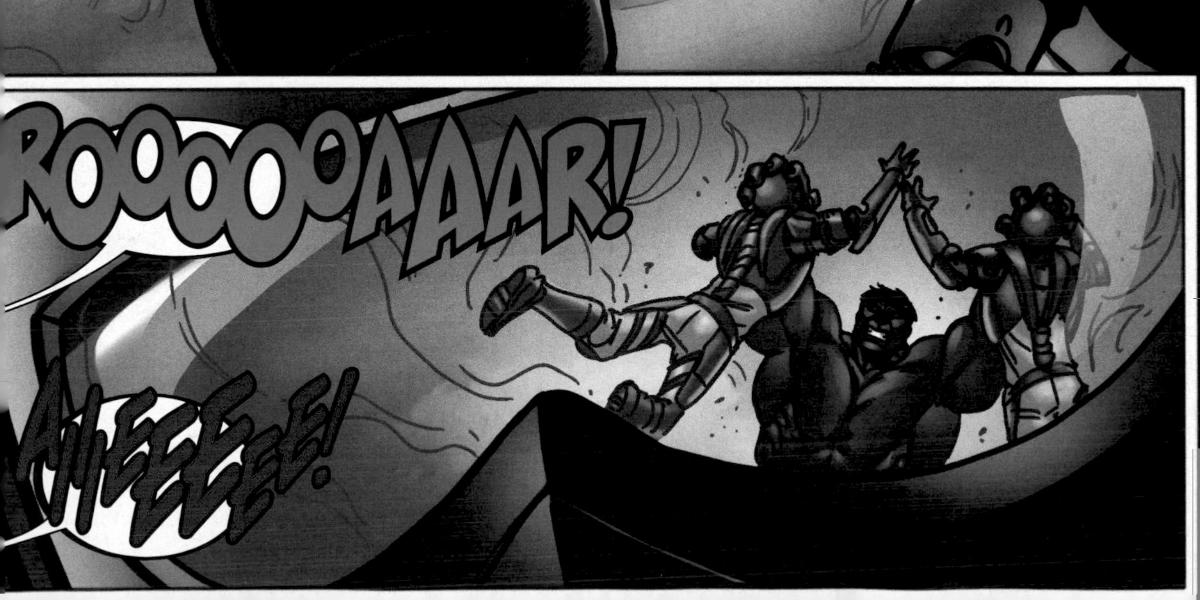
ROOOOOAAAR!
AIIEEEEEE!

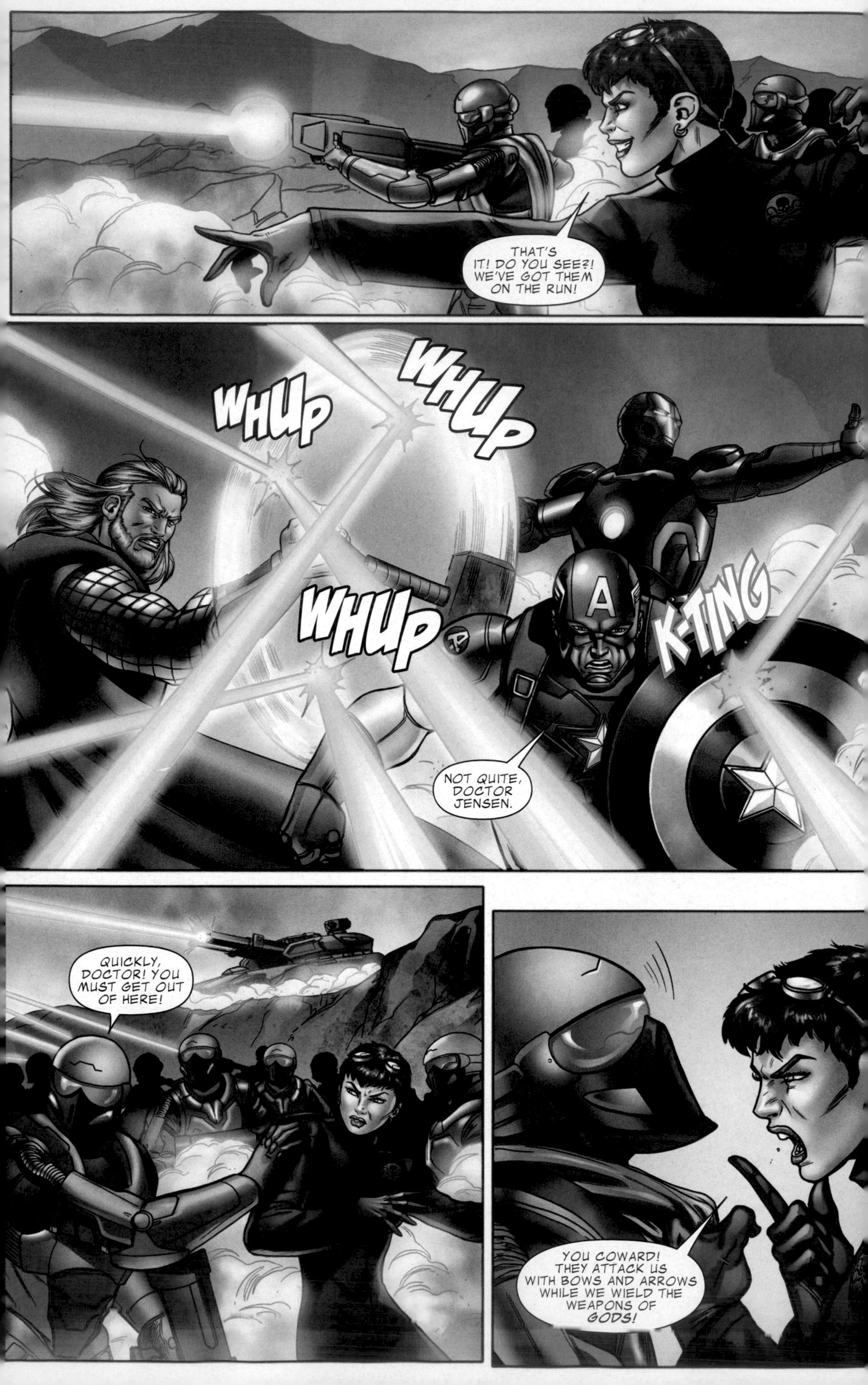
THAT'S IT! DO YOU SEE?! WE'VE GOT THEM ON THE RUN!
WHUP
WHUP
WHUP
K-TING
NOT QUITE, DOCTOR JENSEN.
QUICKLY, DOCTOR! YOU MUST GET OUT OF HERE!
YOU COWARD! THEY ATTACK US WITH BOWS AND ARROWS WHILE WE WIELD THE WEAPONS OF GODS!

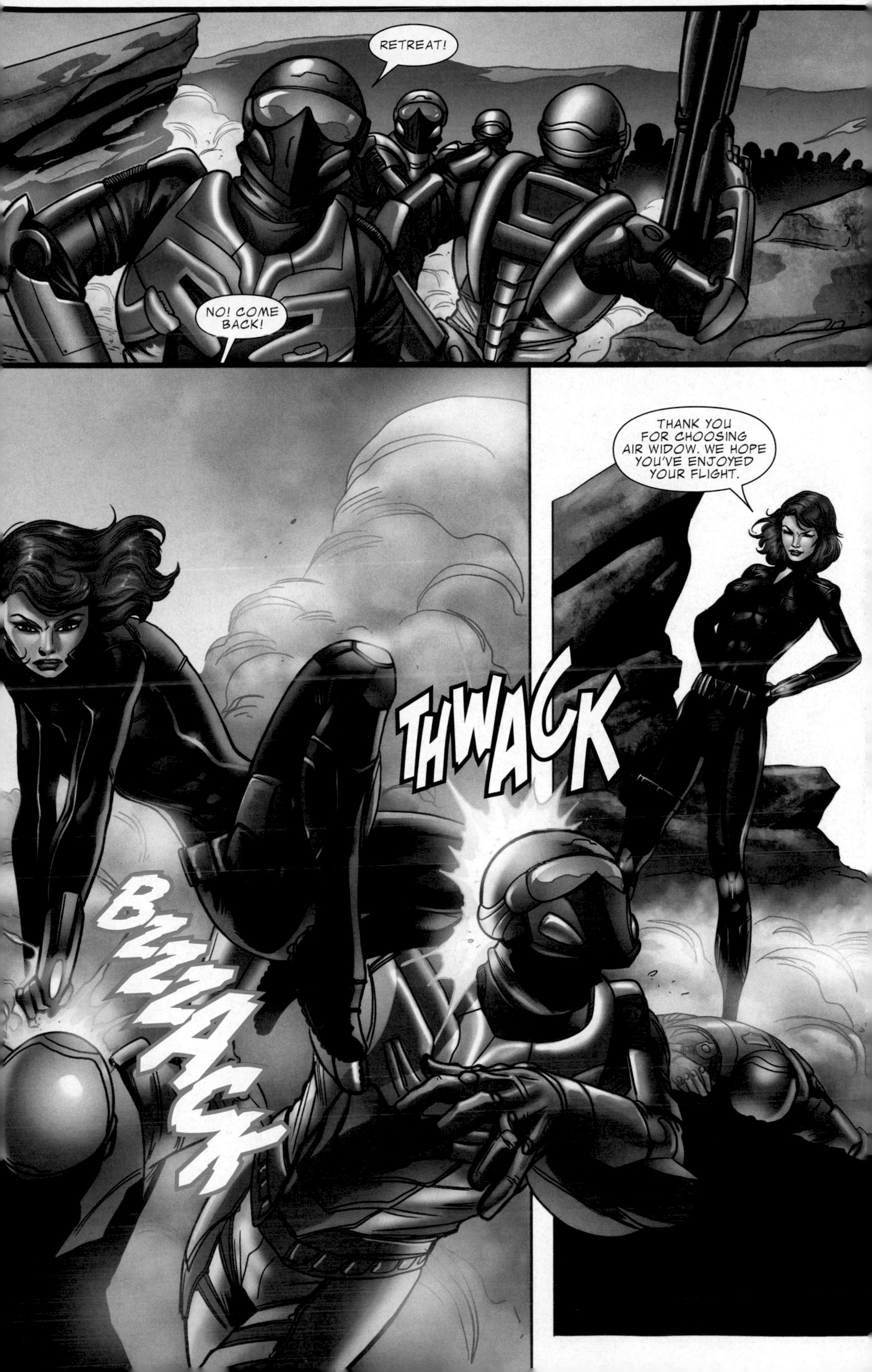
RETREAT!
NO! COME BACK!
THANK YOU FOR CHOOSING AIR WIDOW. WE HOPE YOU'VE ENJOYED YOUR FLIGHT.
THWACK
BZZZACK

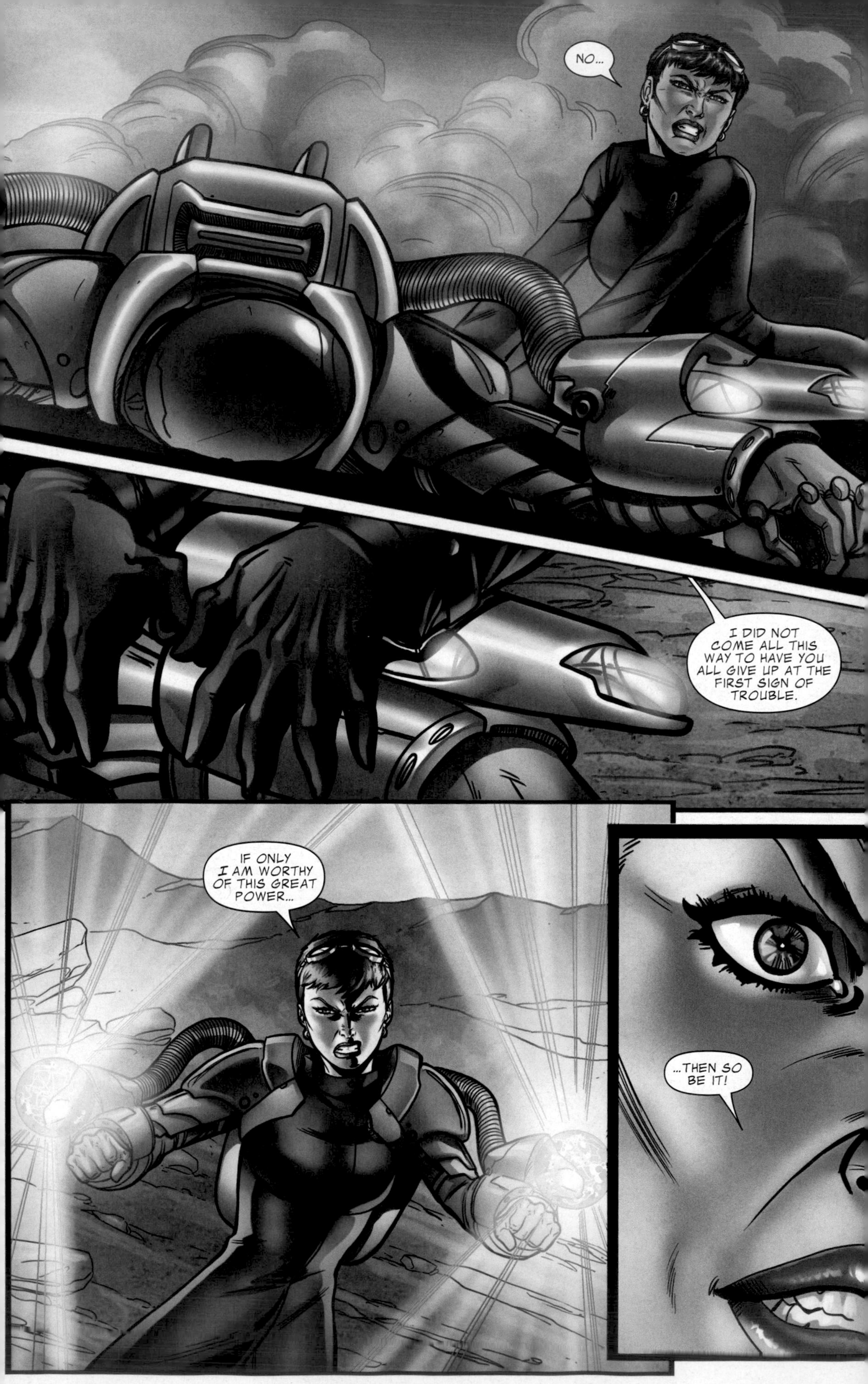
NO...
I DID NOT COME ALL THIS WAY TO HAVE YOU ALL GIVE UP AT THE FIRST SIGN OF TROUBLE.
IF ONLY I AM WORTHY OF THIS GREAT POWER...
...THEN SO BE IT!

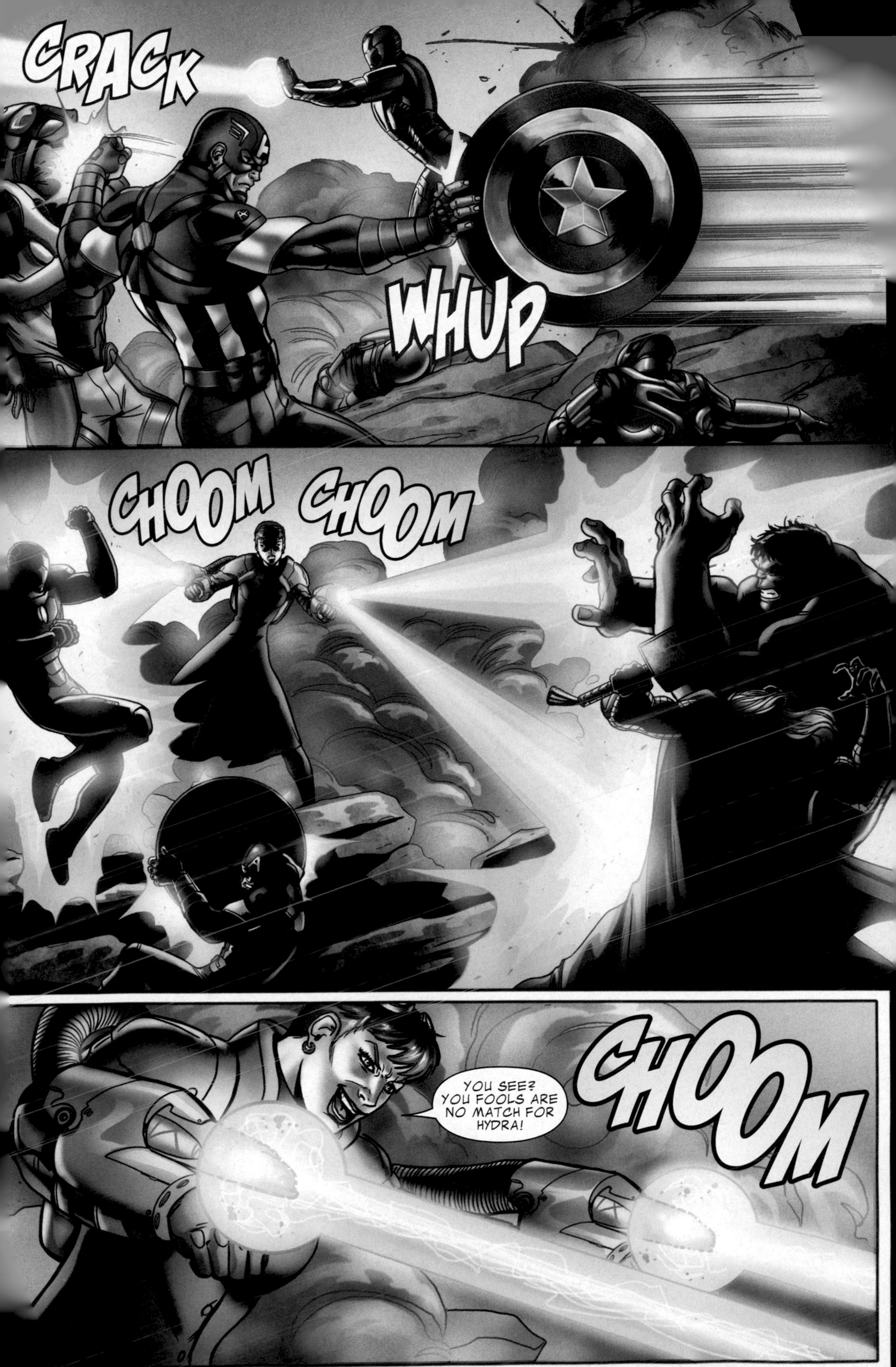
CRACK
WHUP
CHOOM
CHOOM
YOU SEE? YOU FOOLS ARE NO MATCH FOR HYDRA!
CHOOM

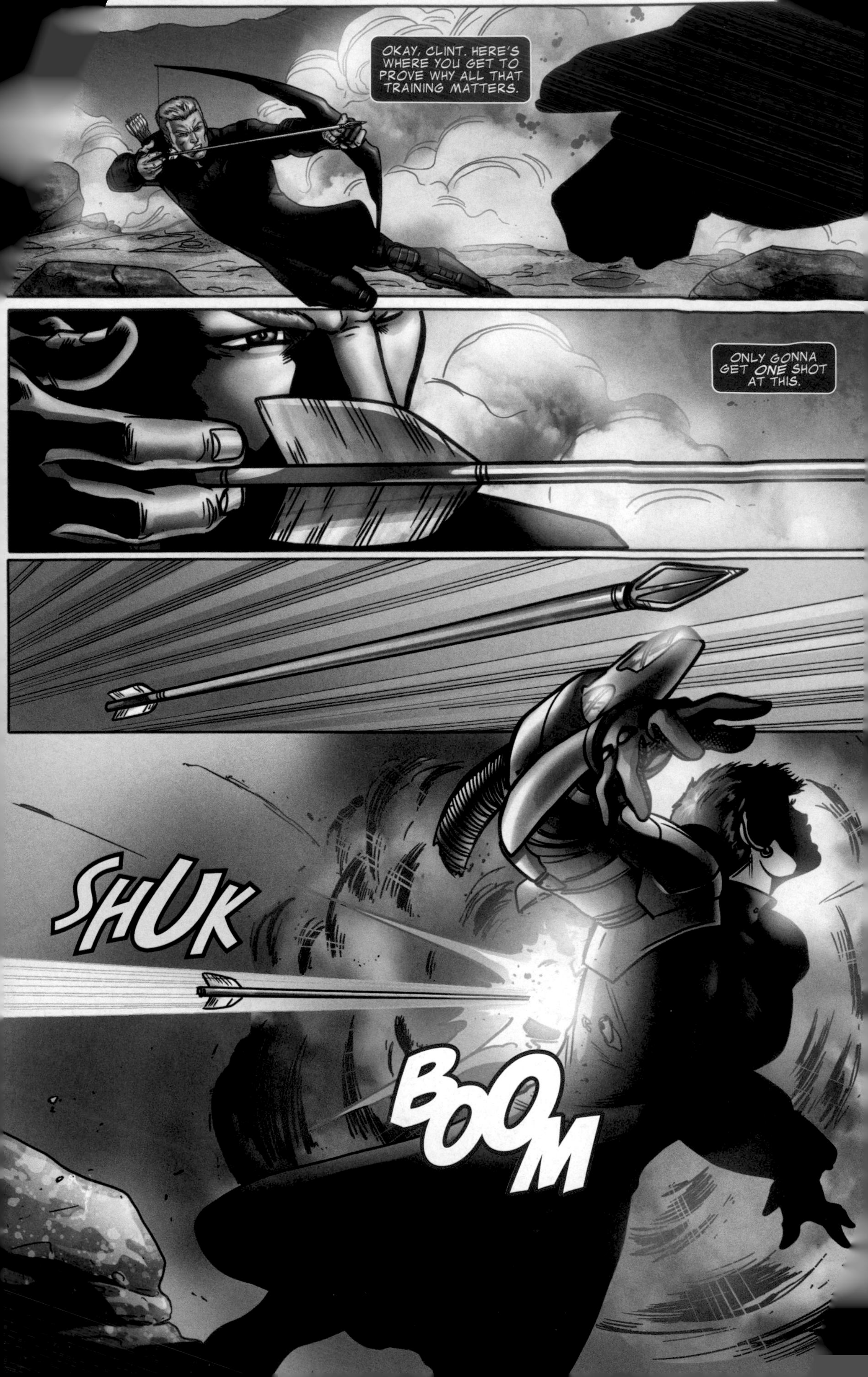
OKAY, CLINT. HERE'S WHERE YOU GET TO PROVE WHY ALL THAT TRAINING MATTERS.
ONLY GONNA GET ONE SHOT AT THIS.
SHUK
BOOM

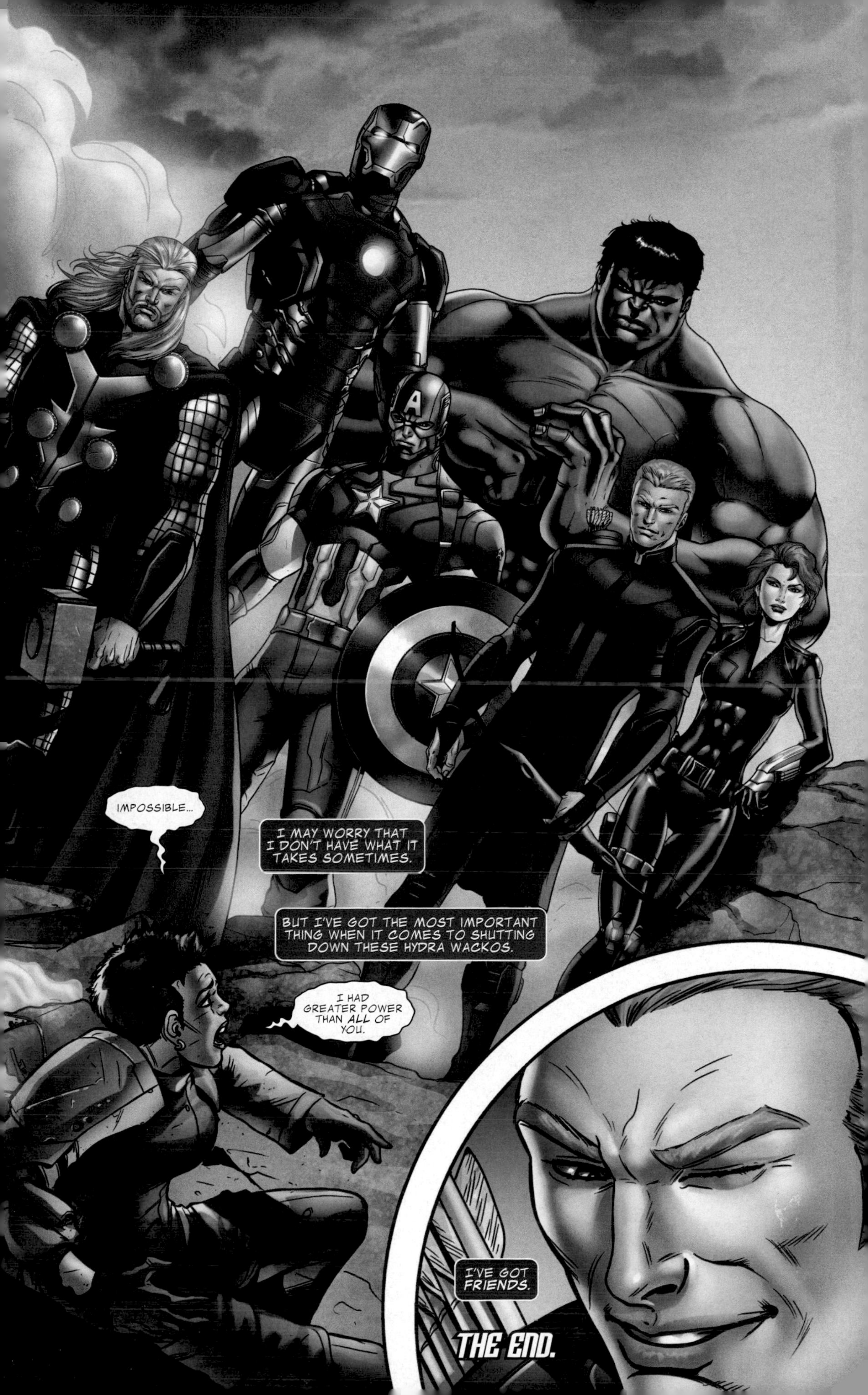
IMPOSSIBLE...
I MAY WORRY THAT I DON'T HAVE WHAT IT TAKES SOMETIMES.
BUT I'VE GOT THE MOST IMPORTANT THING WHEN IT COMES TO SHUTTING DOWN THESE HYDRA WACKOS.
I HAD GREATER POWER THAN ALL OF YOU.
I'VE GOT FRIENDS.
THE END.

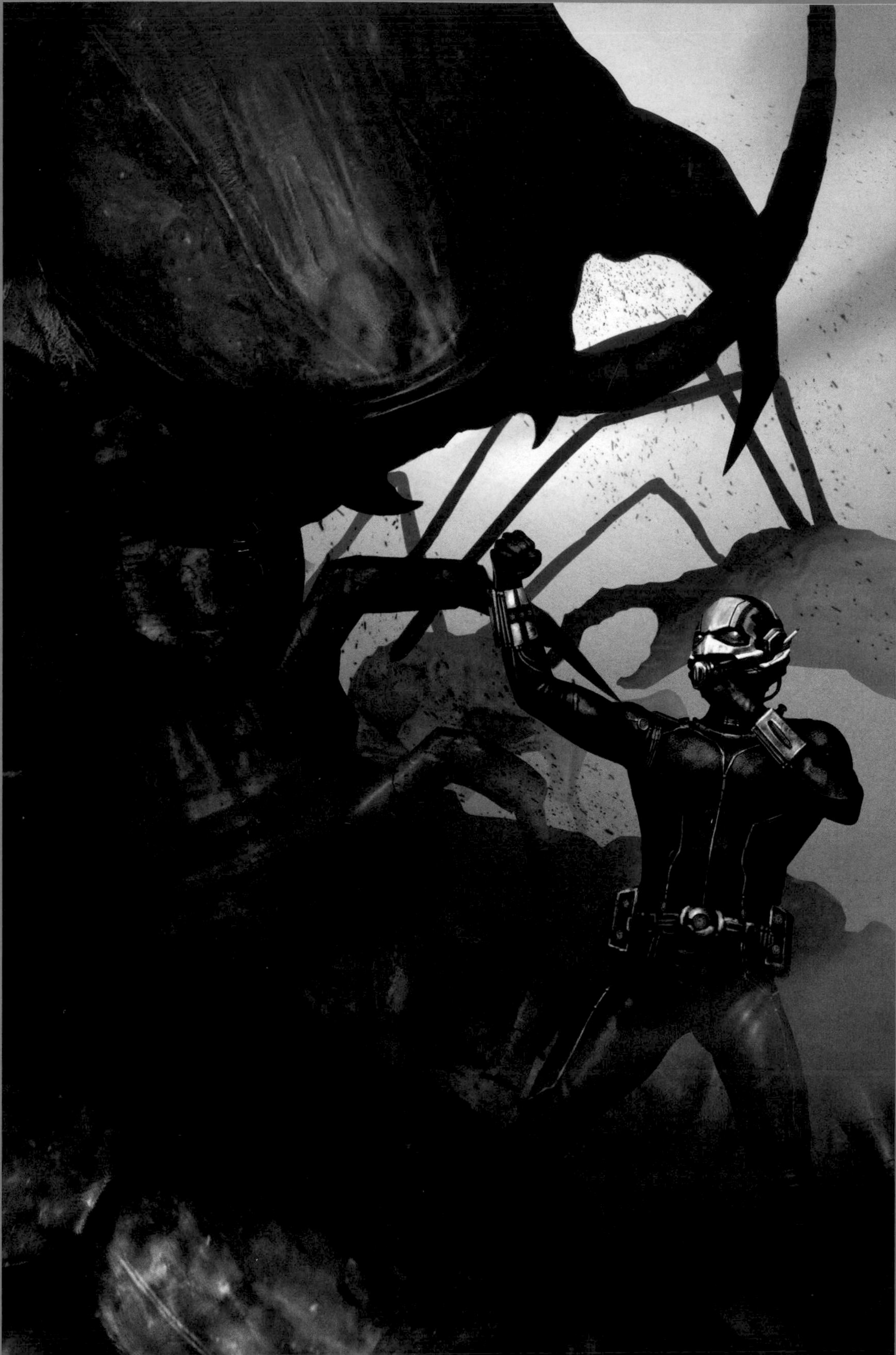

ANT-MAN: LARGER THAN LIFE #1

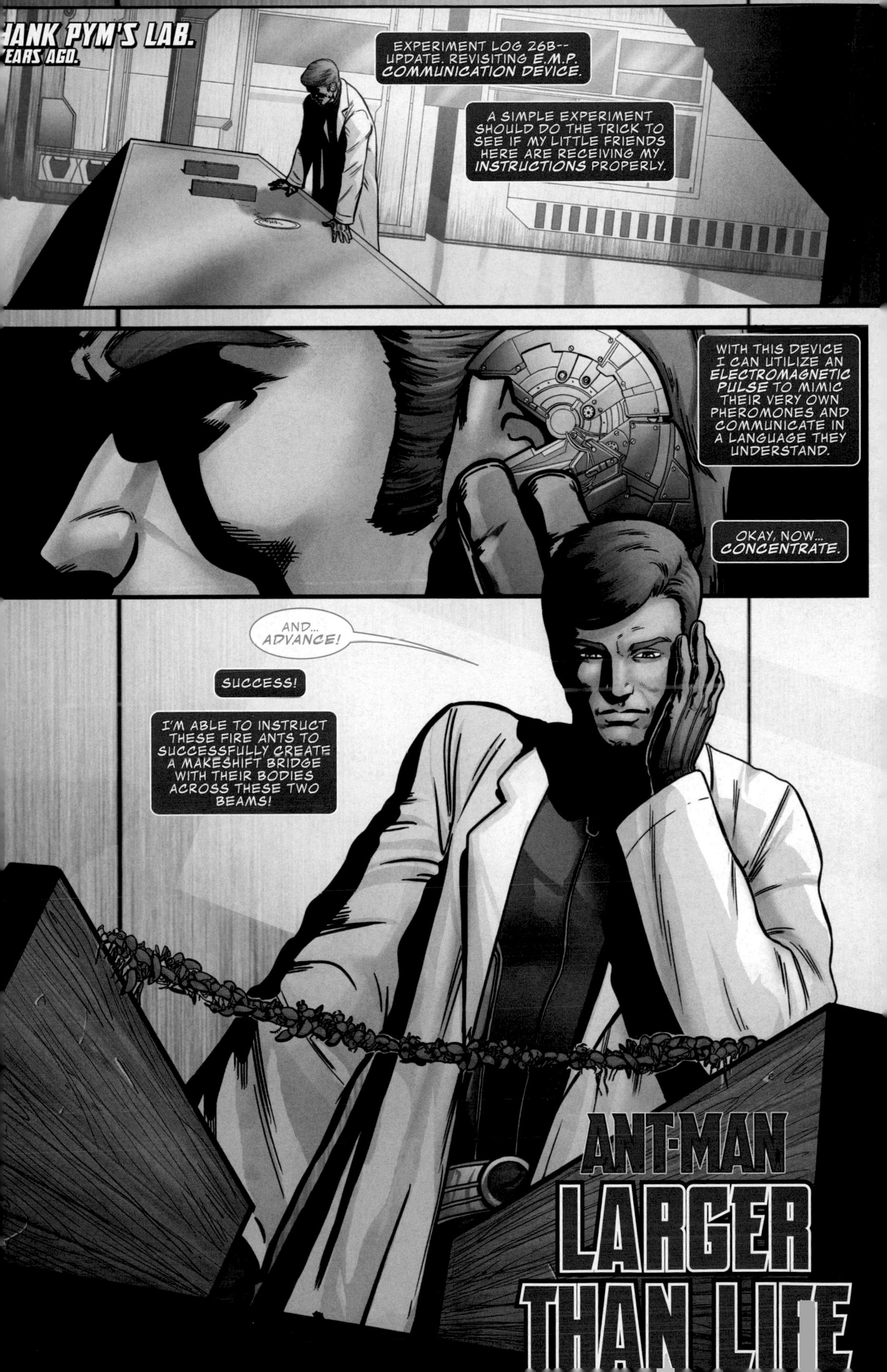
HANK PYM'S LAB.
EARS AGO.
EXPERIMENT LOG 26B-- UPDATE. REVISITING E.M.P. COMMUNICATION DEVICE.
A SIMPLE EXPERIMENT SHOULD DO THE TRICK TO SEE IF MY LITTLE FRIENDS HERE ARE RECEIVING MY INSTRUCTIONS PROPERLY.
WITH THIS DEVICE I CAN UTILIZE AN ELECTROMAGNETIC PULSE TO MIMIC THEIR VERY OWN PHEROMONES AND COMMUNICATE IN A LANGUAGE THEY UNDERSTAND.
OKAY, NOW... CONCENTRATE.
AND... ADVANCE!
SUCCESS!
I'M ABLE TO INSTRUCT THESE FIRE ANTS TO SUCCESSFULLY CREATE A MAKESHIFT BRIDGE WITH THEIR BODIES ACROSS THESE TWO BEAMS!
ANT-MAN
LARGER THAN LIFE

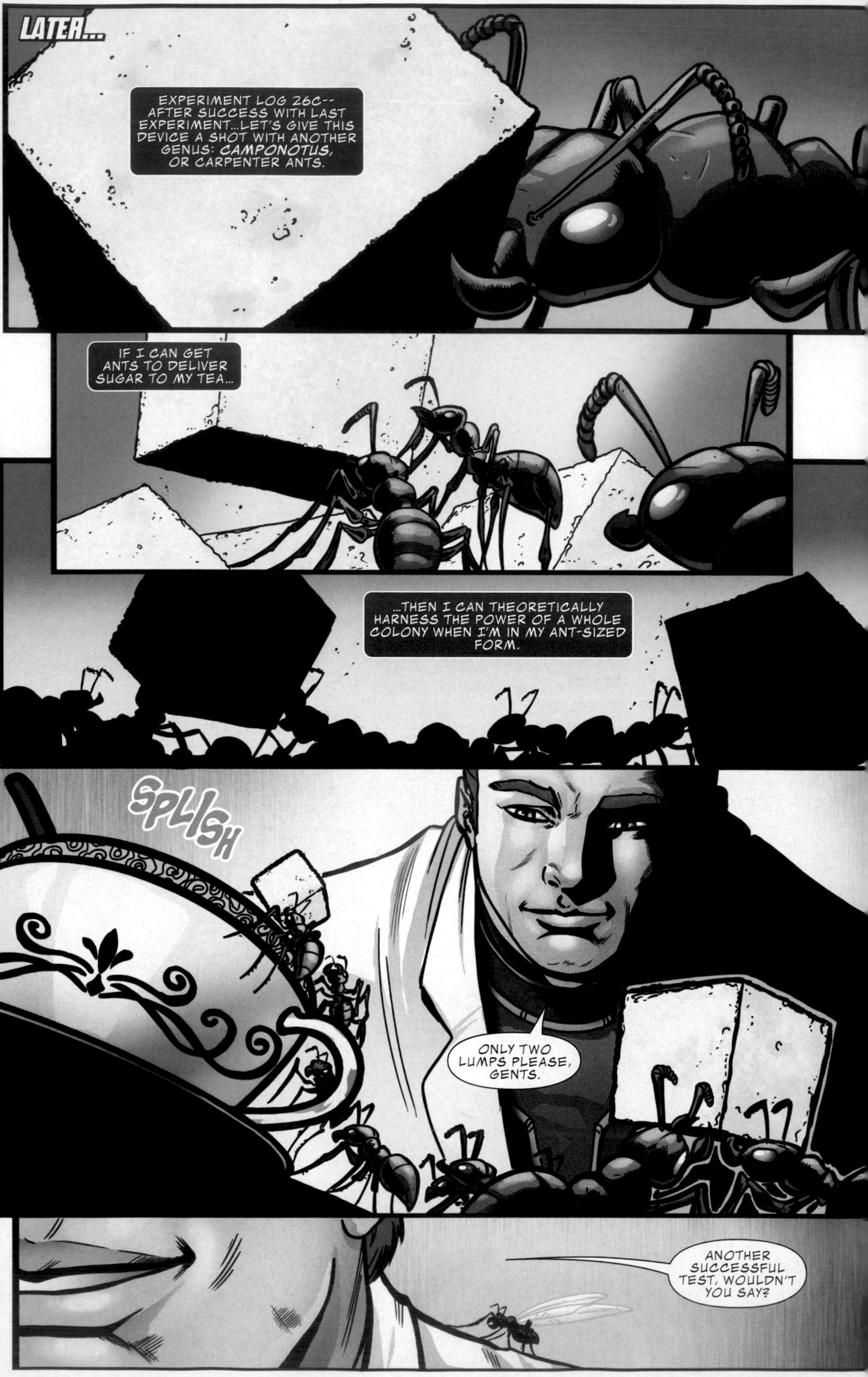
LATER...
EXPERIMENT LOG 26C-- AFTER SUCCESS WITH LAST EXPERIMENT...LET'S GIVE THIS DEVICE A SHOT WITH ANOTHER GENUS: CAMPONOTUS, OR CARPENTER ANTS.
IF I CAN GET ANTS TO DELIVER SUGAR TO MY TEA...
...THEN I CAN THEORETICALLY HARNESS THE POWER OF A WHOLE COLONY WHEN I'M IN MY ANT-SIZED FORM.
SPLISH
ONLY TWO LUMPS PLEASE, GENTS.
ANOTHER SUCCESSFUL TEST, WOULDN'T YOU SAY?

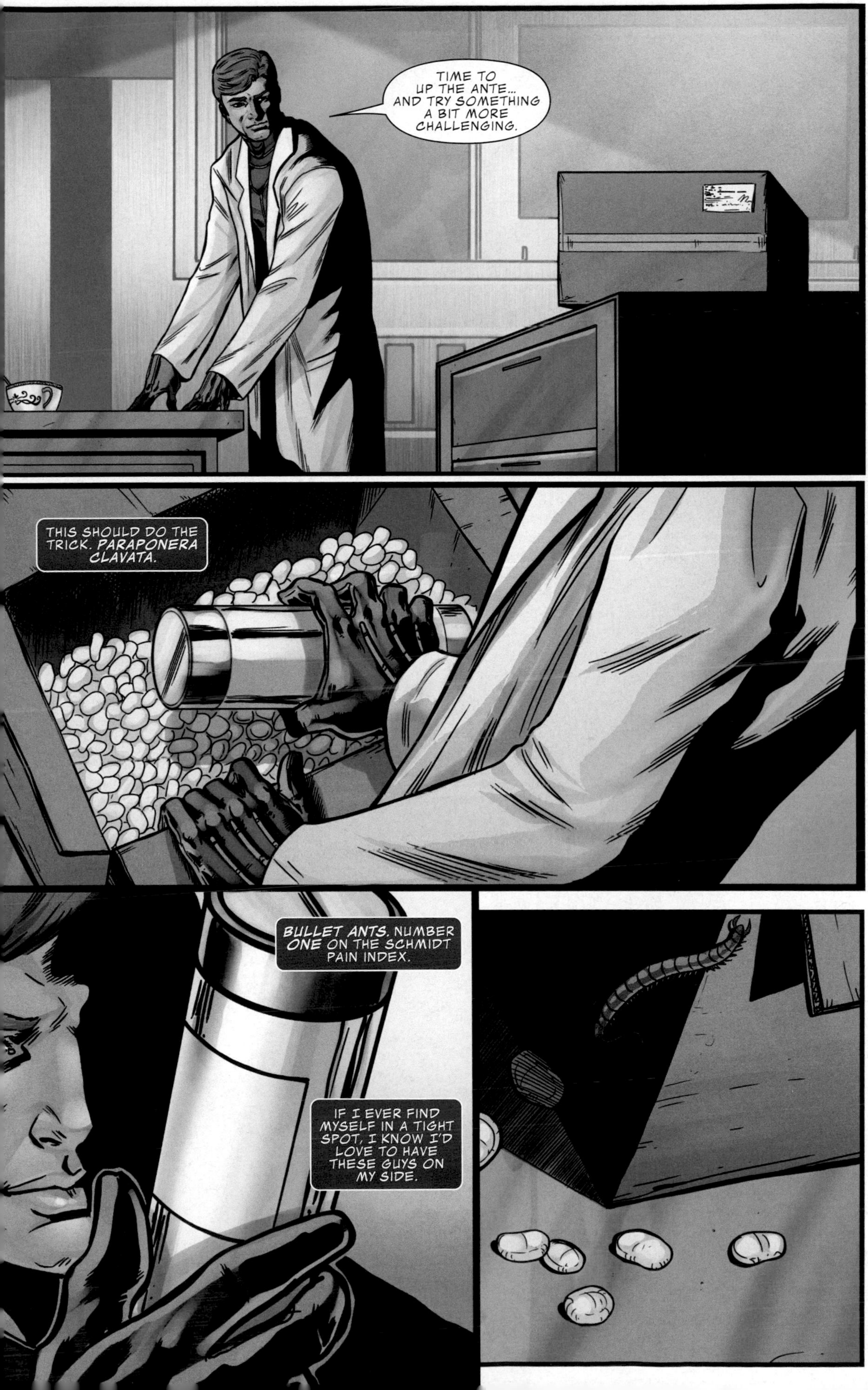
TIME TO UP THE ANTE... AND TRY SOMETHING A BIT MORE CHALLENGING.
THIS SHOULD DO THE TRICK. *PARAPONERA CLAVATA.*
BULLET ANTS. NUMBER *ONE* ON THE SCHMIDT PAIN INDEX.
IF I EVER FIND MYSELF IN A TIGHT SPOT, I KNOW I'D LOVE TO HAVE THESE GUYS ON MY SIDE.

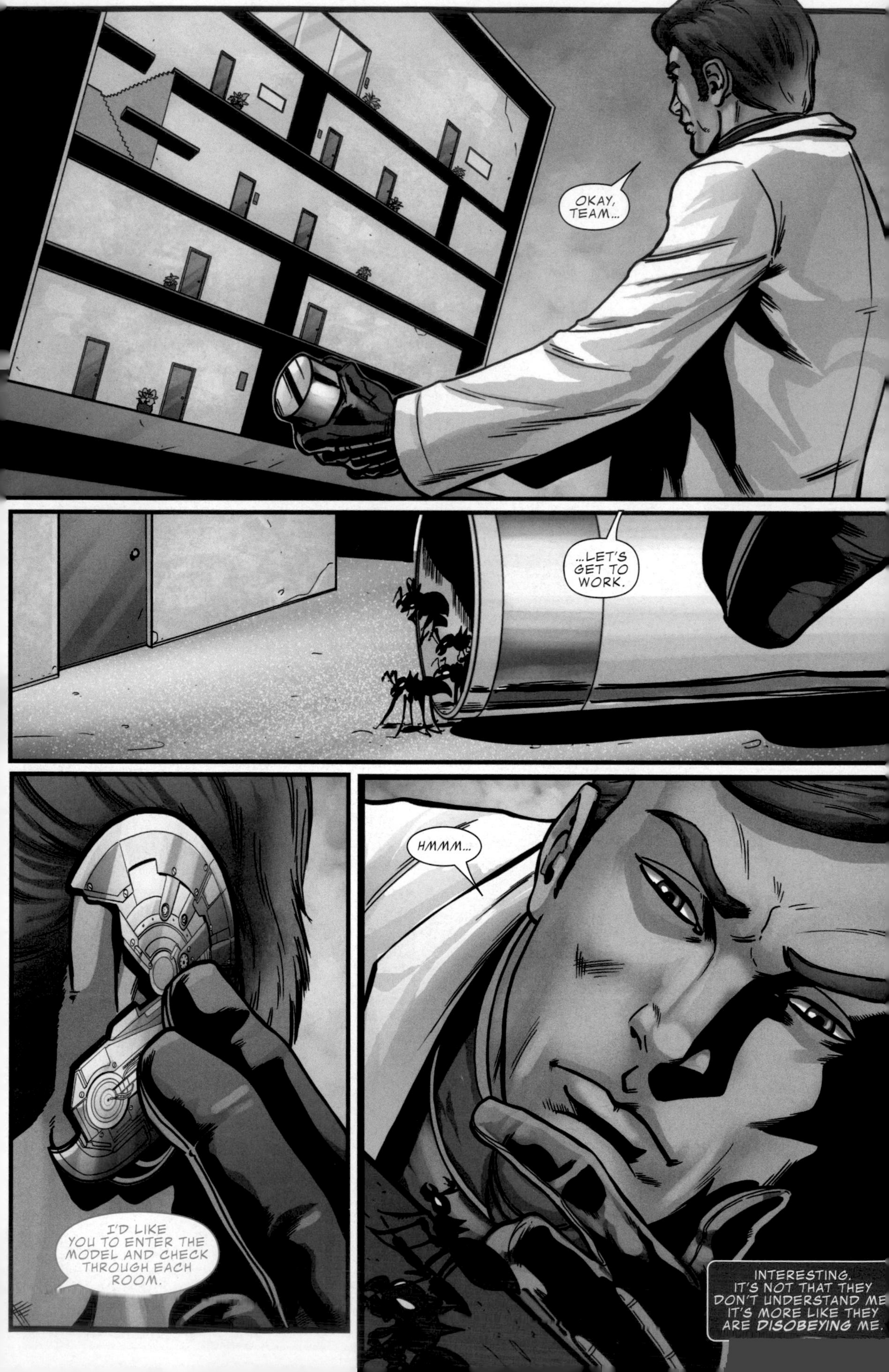
OKAY, TEAM...
...LET'S GET TO WORK.
I'D LIKE YOU TO ENTER THE MODEL AND CHECK THROUGH EACH ROOM.
HMMM...
INTERESTING. IT'S NOT THAT THEY DON'T UNDERSTAND ME. IT'S MORE LIKE THEY ARE DISOBEYING ME.

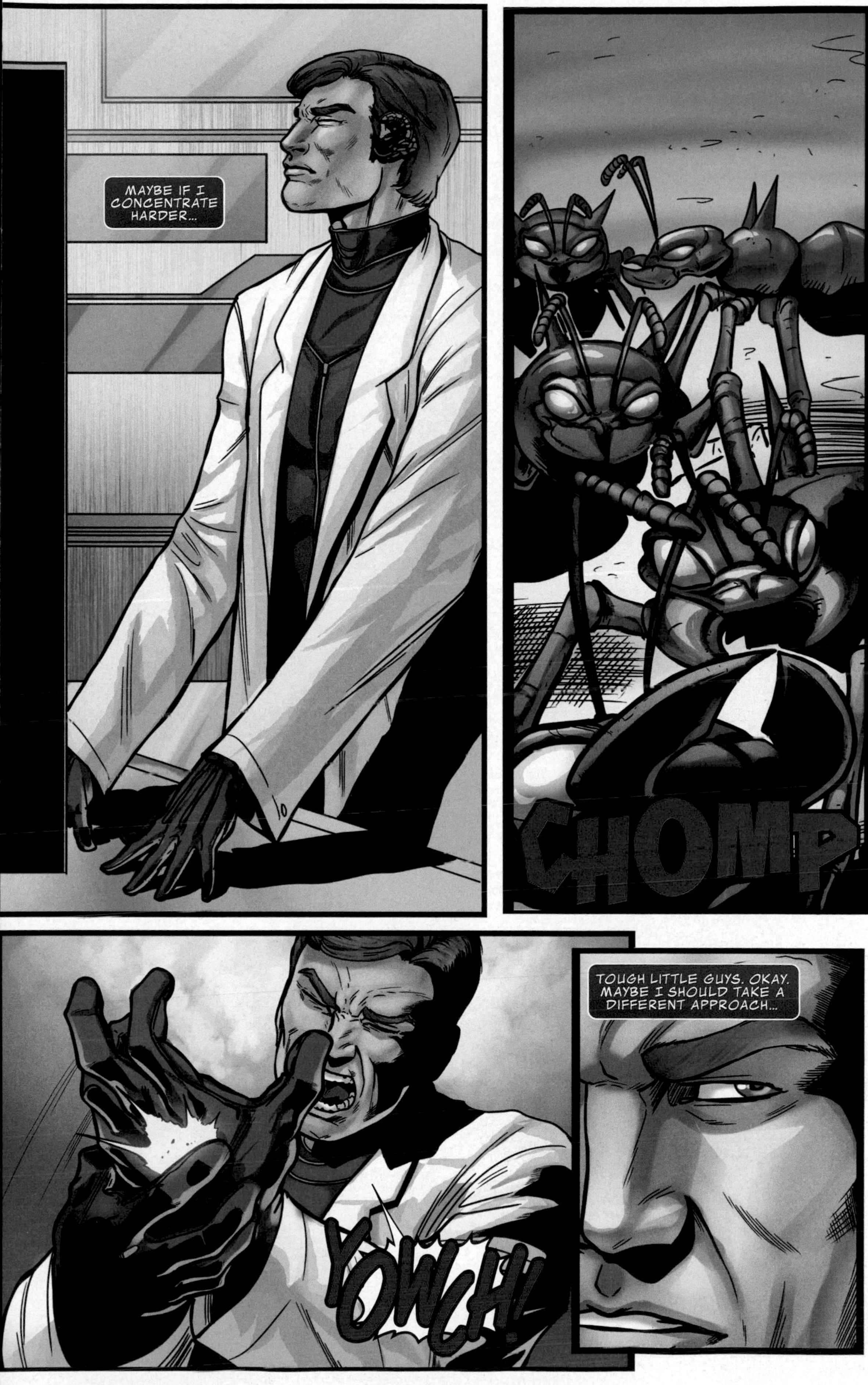
MAYBE IF I CONCENTRATE HARDER...
CHOMP
YOWCH!
TOUGH LITTLE GUYS. OKAY. MAYBE I SHOULD TAKE A DIFFERENT APPROACH...

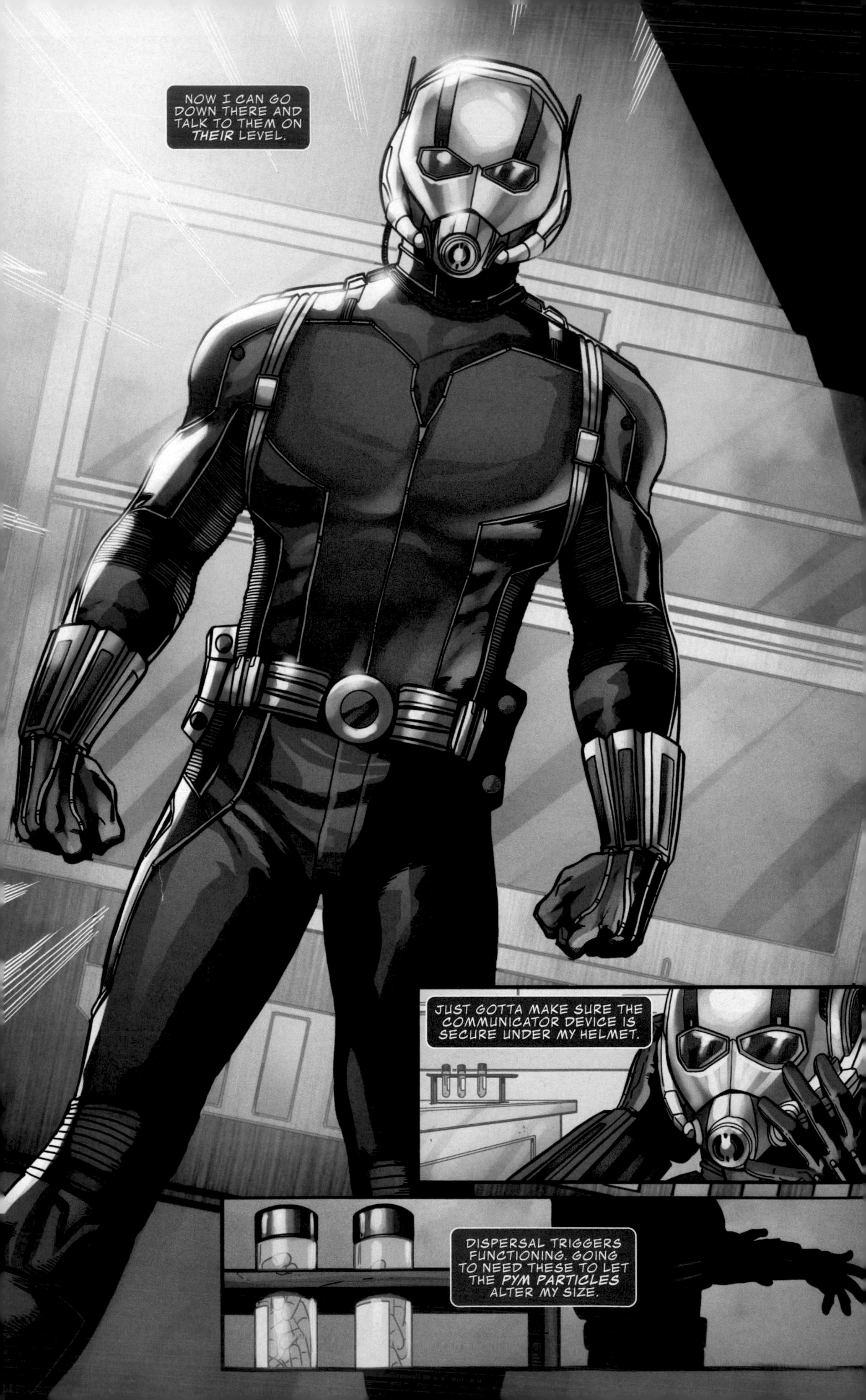
NOW I CAN GO DOWN THERE AND TALK TO THEM ON THEIR LEVEL.
JUST GOTTA MAKE SURE THE COMMUNICATOR DEVICE IS SECURE UNDER MY HELMET.
DISPERSAL TRIGGERS FUNCTIONING. GOING TO NEED THESE TO LET THE PYM PARTICLES ALTER MY SIZE.

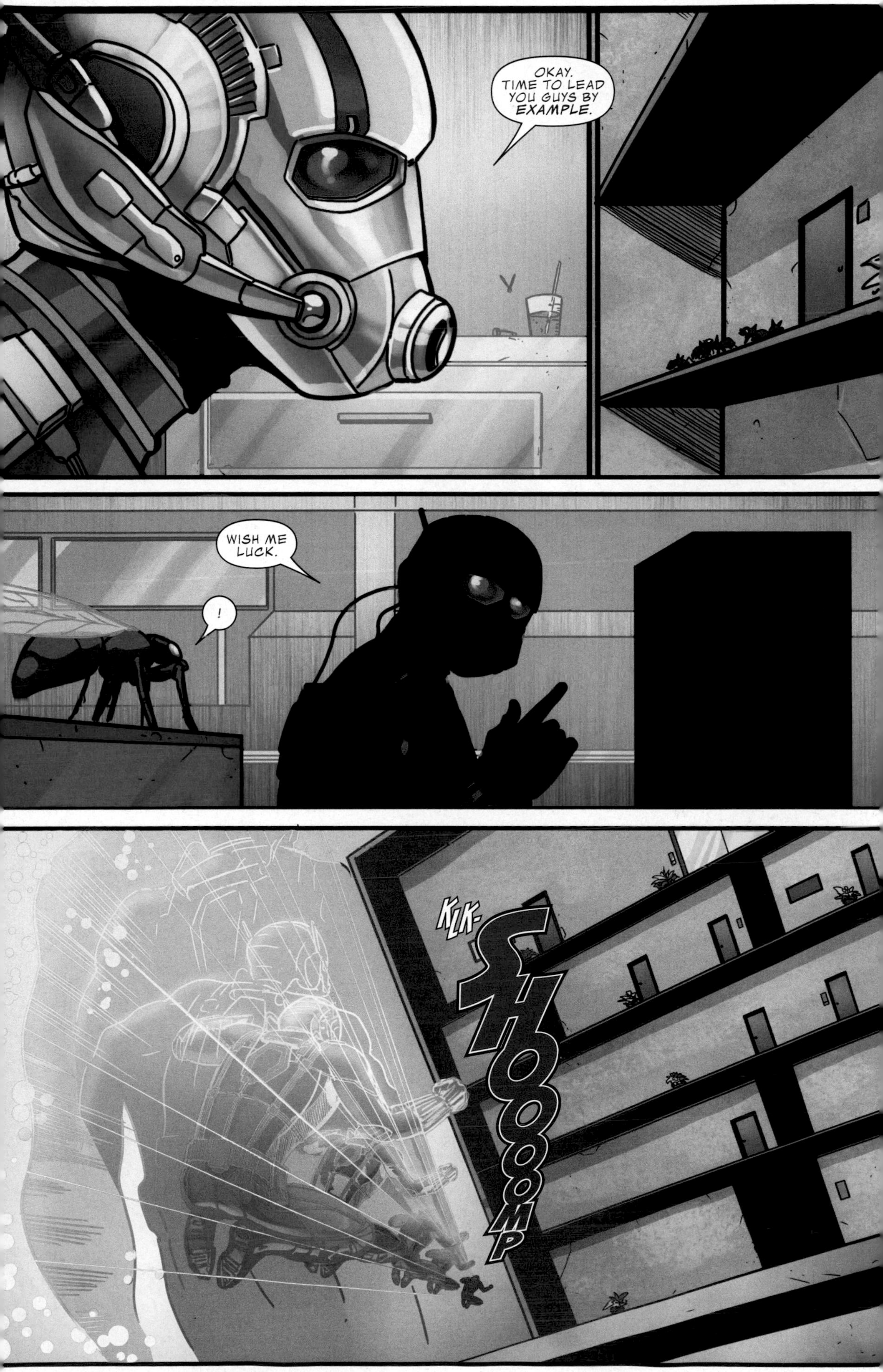
OKAY. TIME TO LEAD YOU GUYS BY EXAMPLE.
WISH ME LUCK.
!
KLK-SHOOOOMP

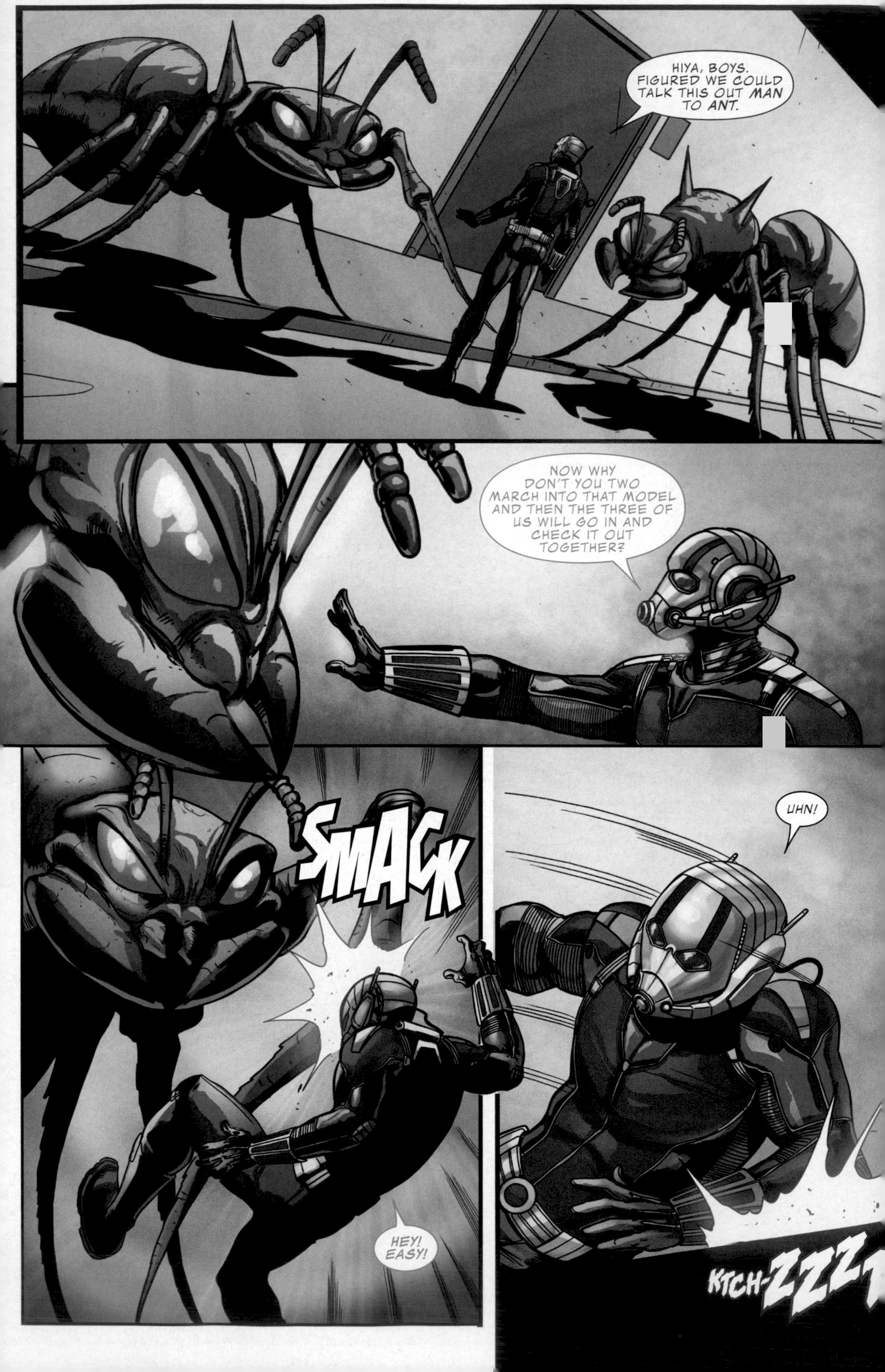
HIYA, BOYS. FIGURED WE COULD TALK THIS OUT MAN TO ANT.
NOW WHY DON'T YOU TWO MARCH INTO THAT MODEL AND THEN THE THREE OF US WILL GO IN AND CHECK IT OUT TOGETHER?
SMACK
HEY! EASY!
UHN!
KTCH-ZZZT

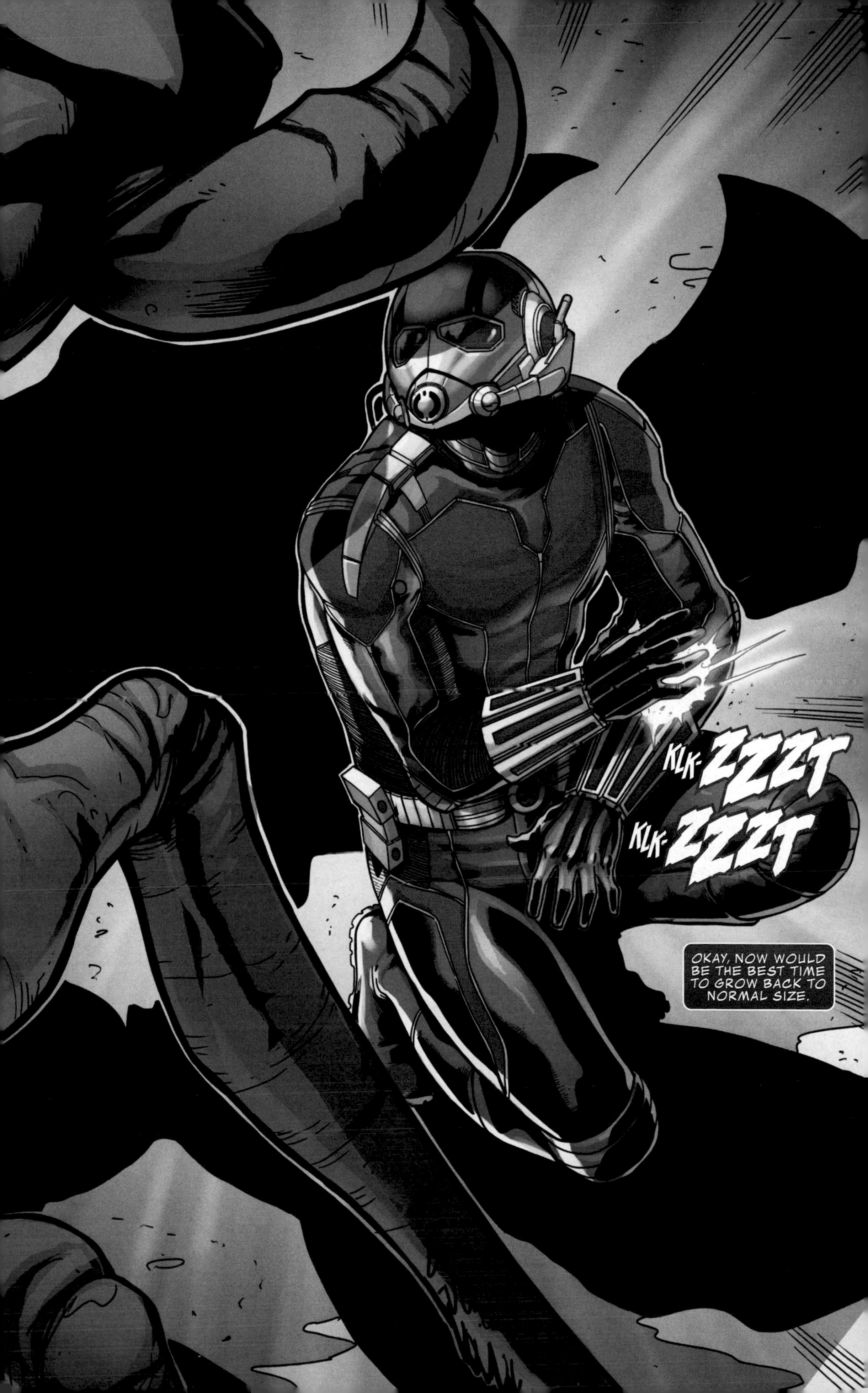
KLK-ZZZT
KLK-ZZZT
OKAY, NOW WOULD BE THE BEST TIME TO GROW BACK TO NORMAL SIZE.

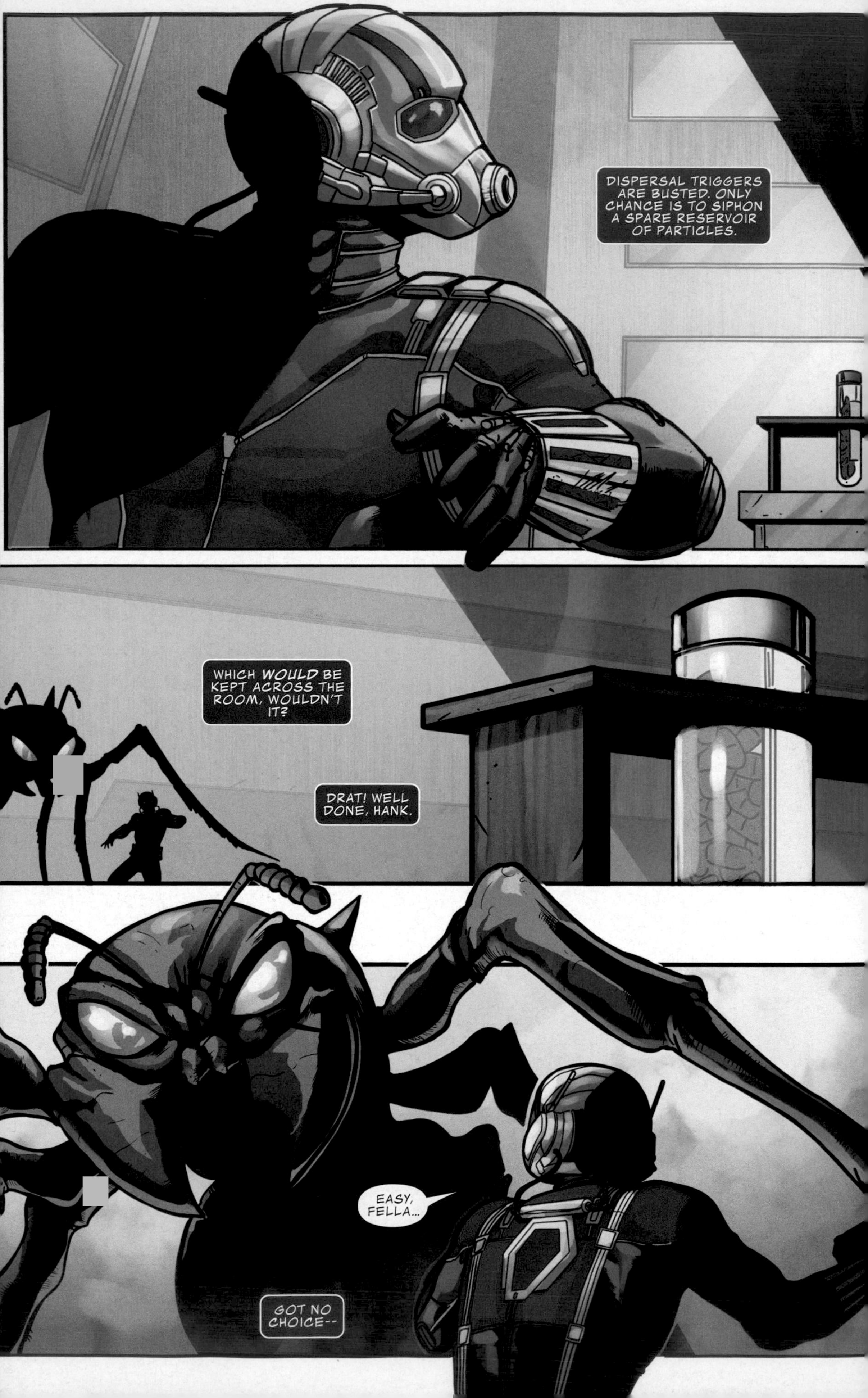
DISPERSAL TRIGGERS ARE BUSTED. ONLY CHANCE IS TO SIPHON A SPARE RESERVOIR OF PARTICLES.
WHICH *WOULD* BE KEPT ACROSS THE ROOM, WOULDN'T IT?
DRAT! WELL DONE, HANK.
EASY, FELLA...
GOT NO CHOICE--

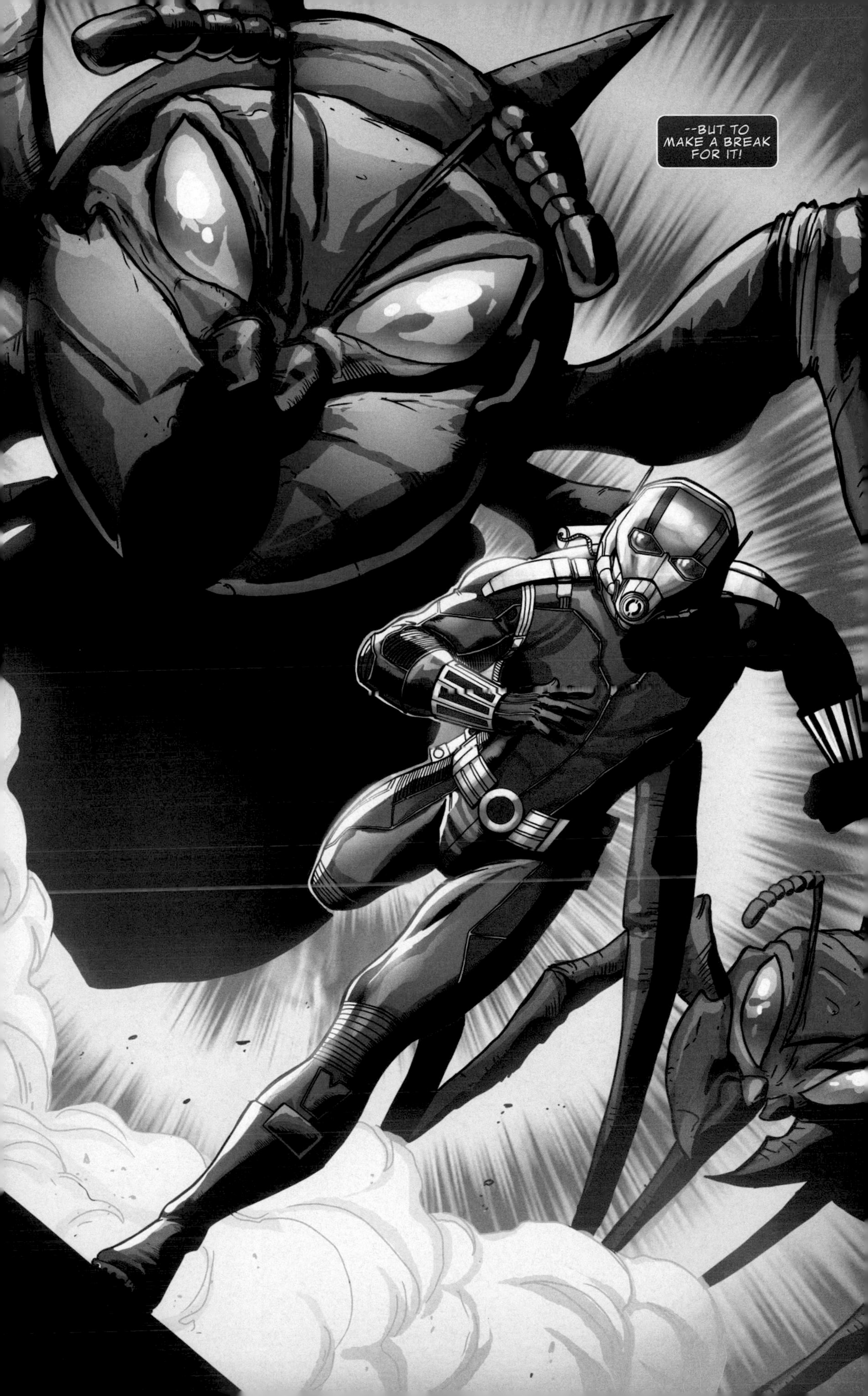
--BUT TO MAKE A BREAK FOR IT!

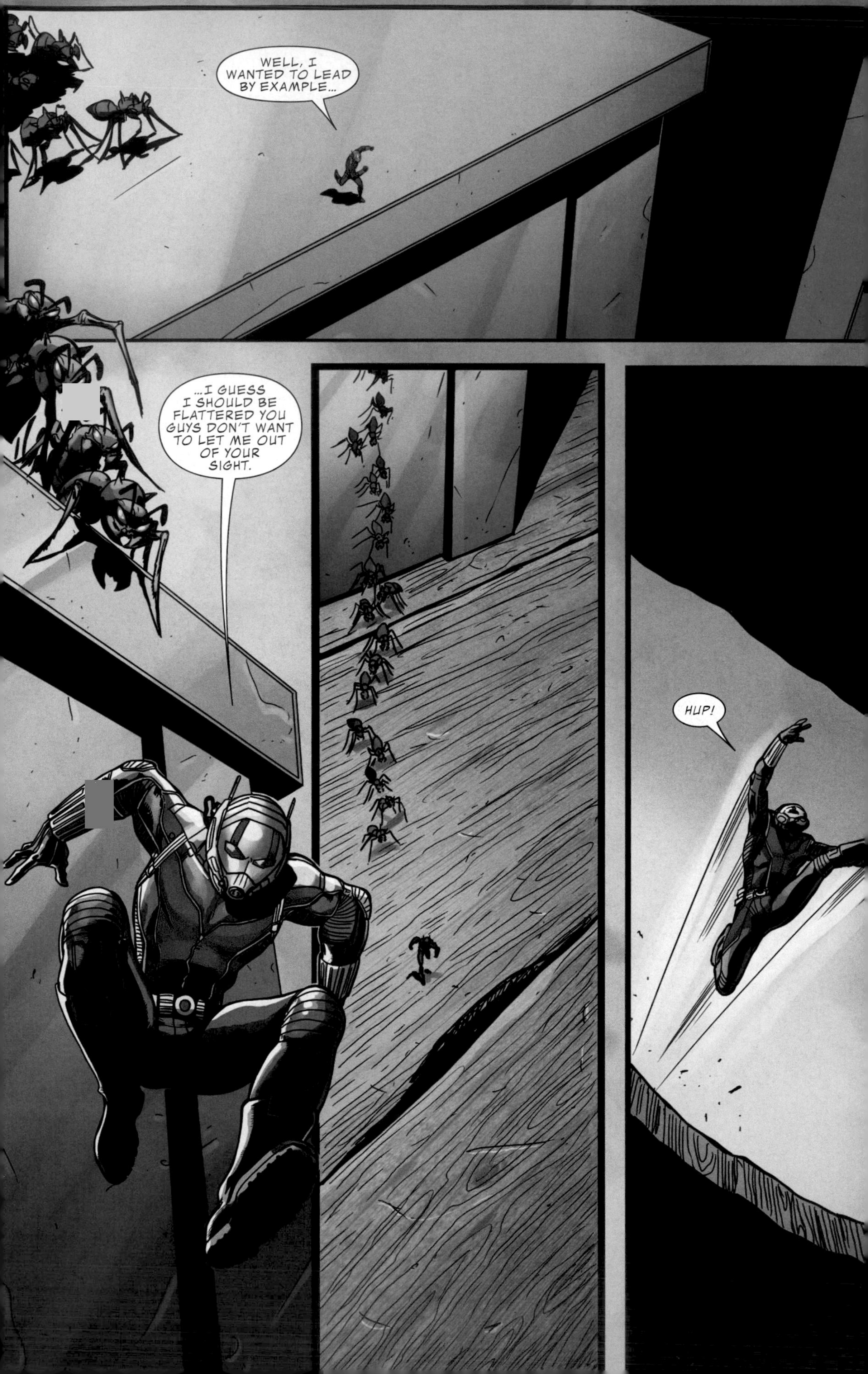
WELL, I WANTED TO LEAD BY EXAMPLE...
...I GUESS I SHOULD BE FLATTERED YOU GUYS DON'T WANT TO LET ME OUT OF YOUR SIGHT.
HUP!

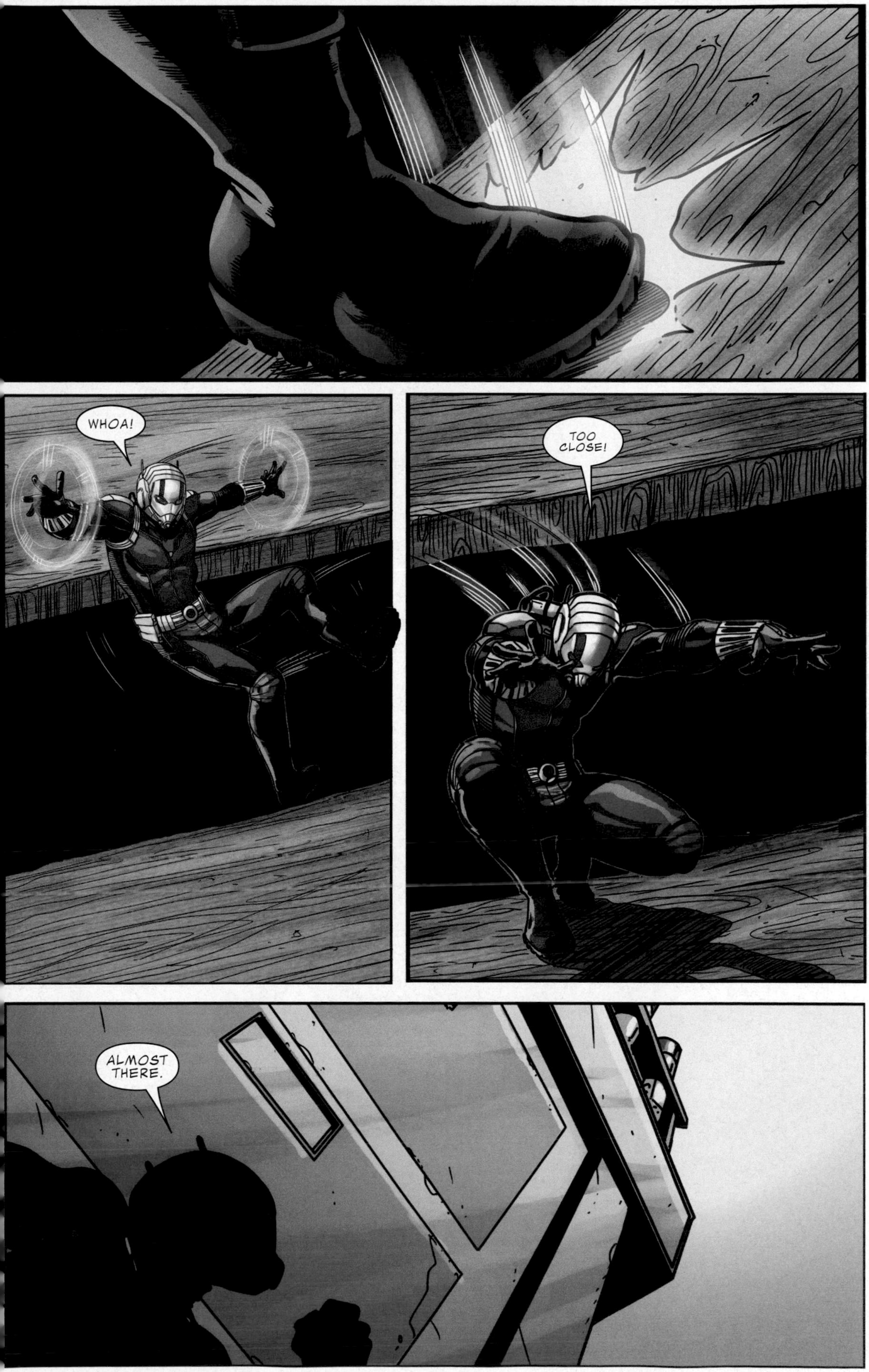
WHOA!
TOO CLOSE!
ALMOST THERE.

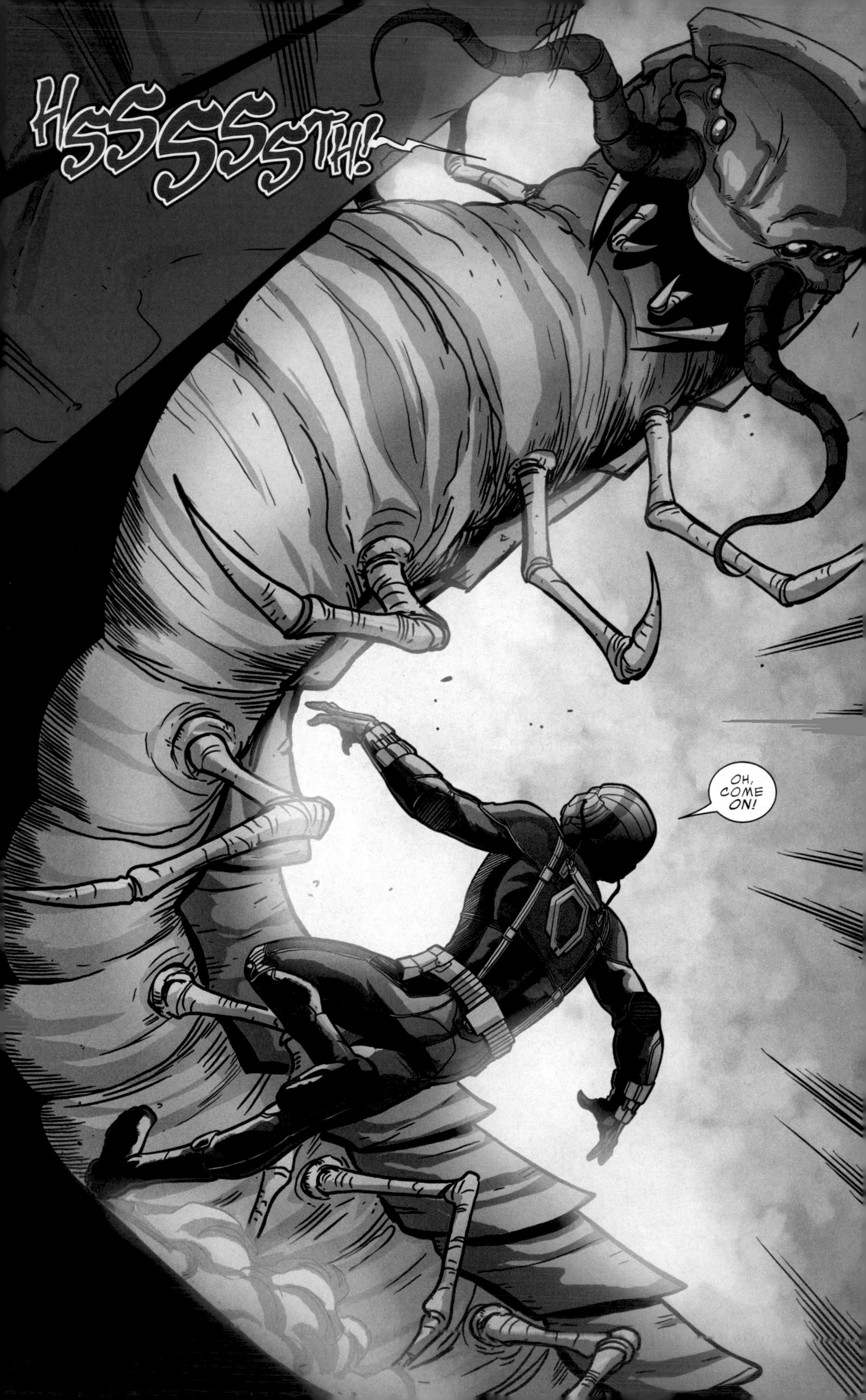
HSSSSSTH!
OH, COME ON!

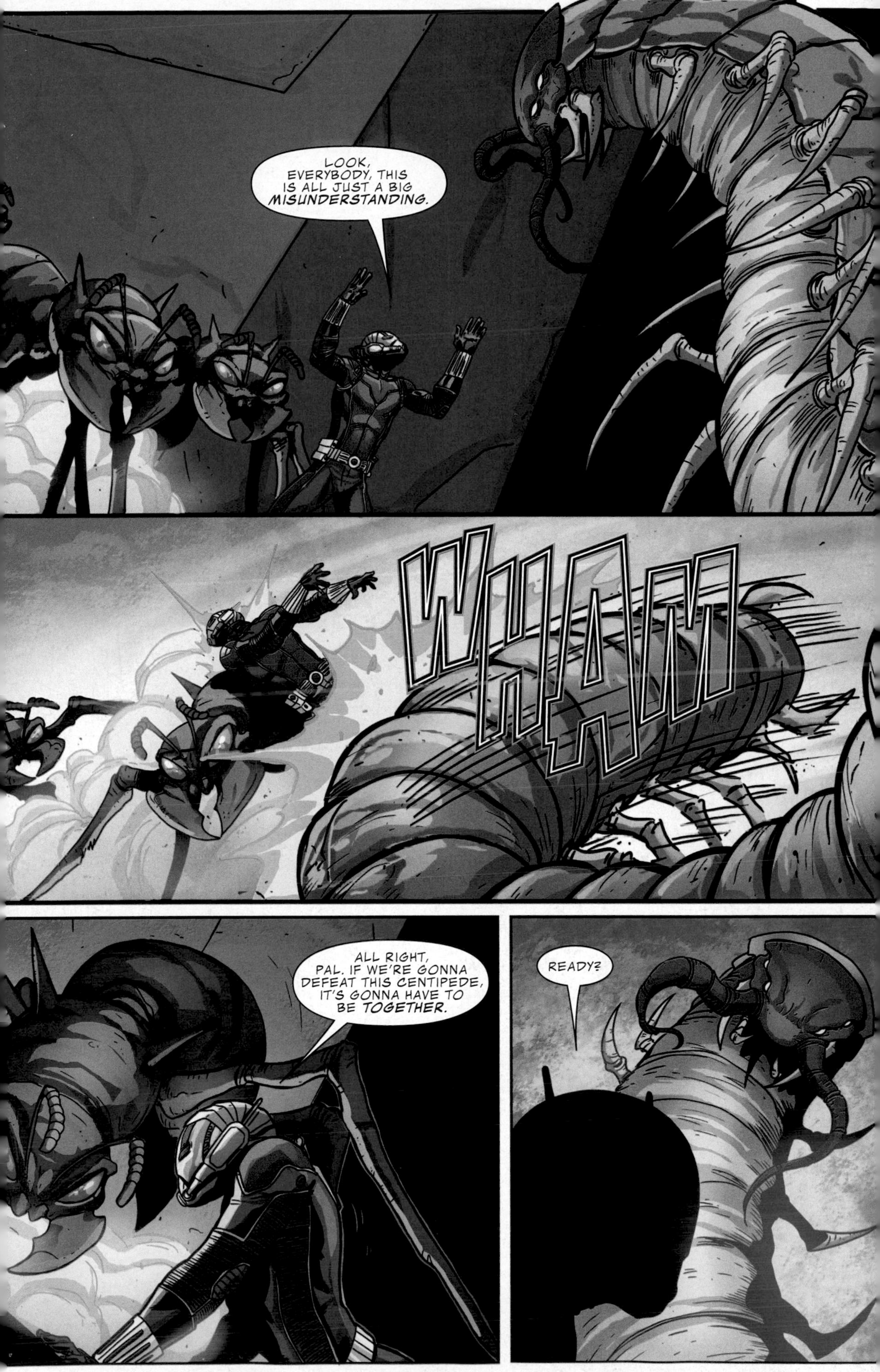
LOOK, EVERYBODY, THIS IS ALL JUST A BIG *MISUNDERSTANDING*.
WHAM
ALL RIGHT, PAL. IF WE'RE GONNA DEFEAT THIS CENTIPEDE, IT'S GONNA HAVE TO BE *TOGETHER*.
READY?

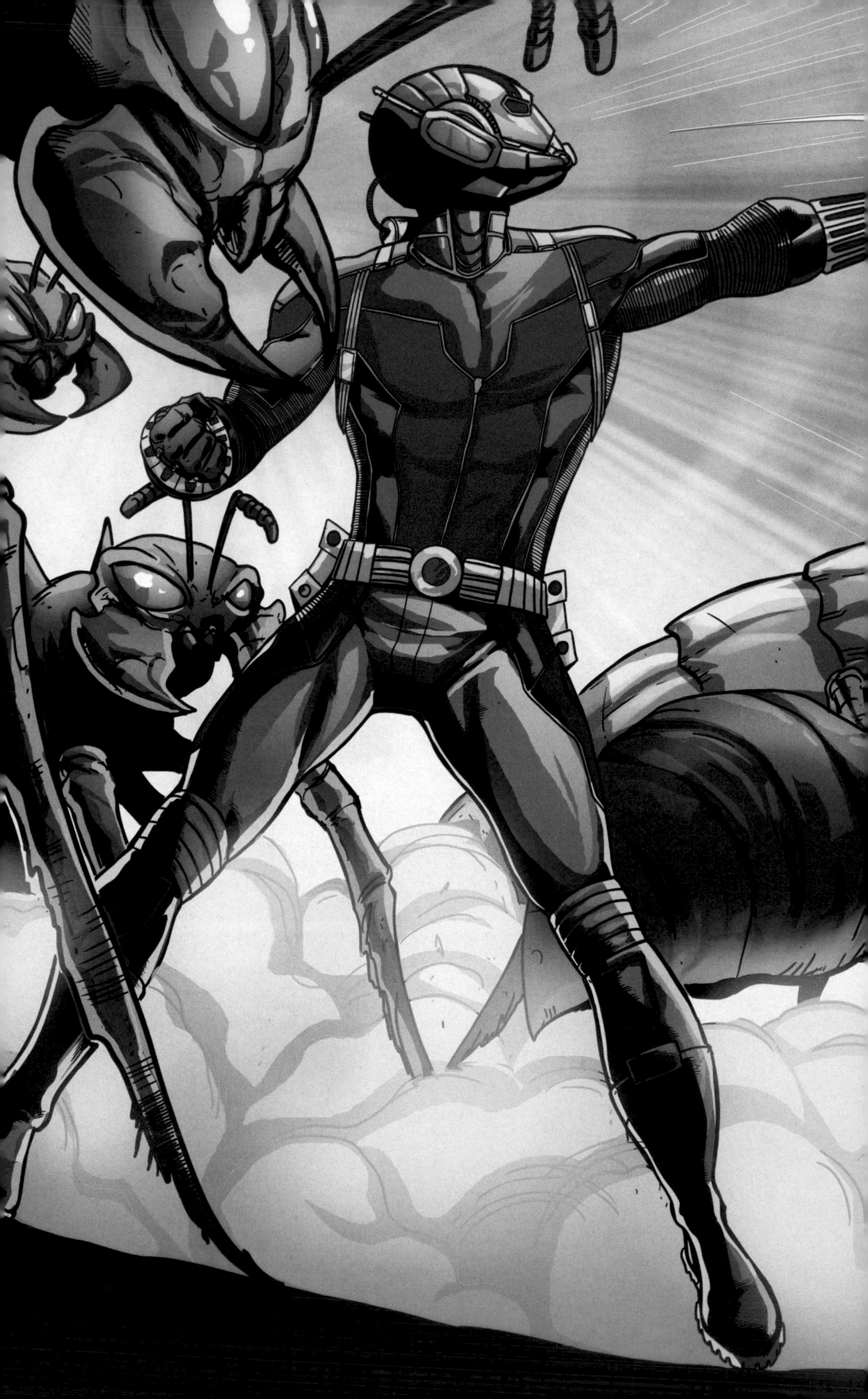

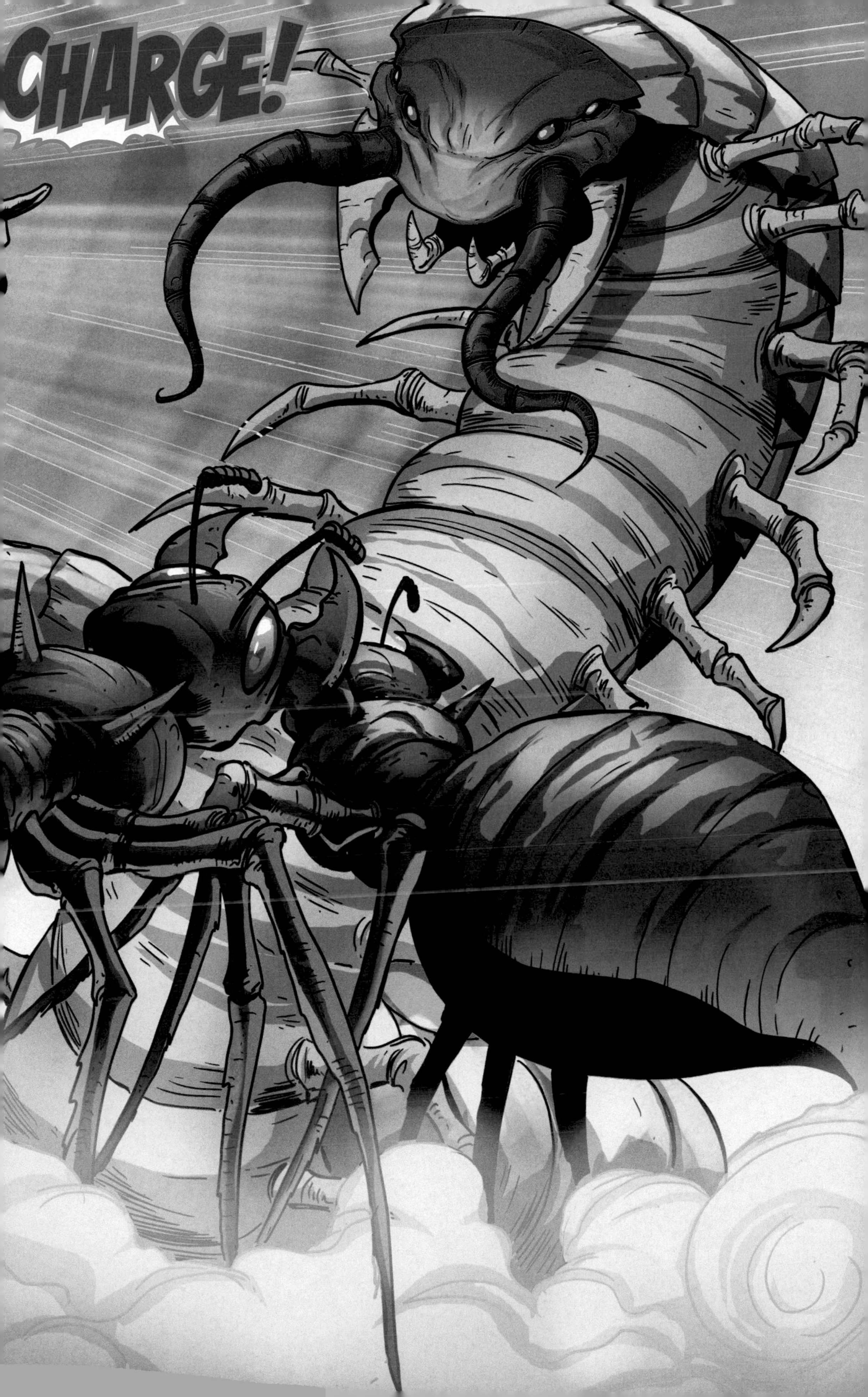
CHARGE!

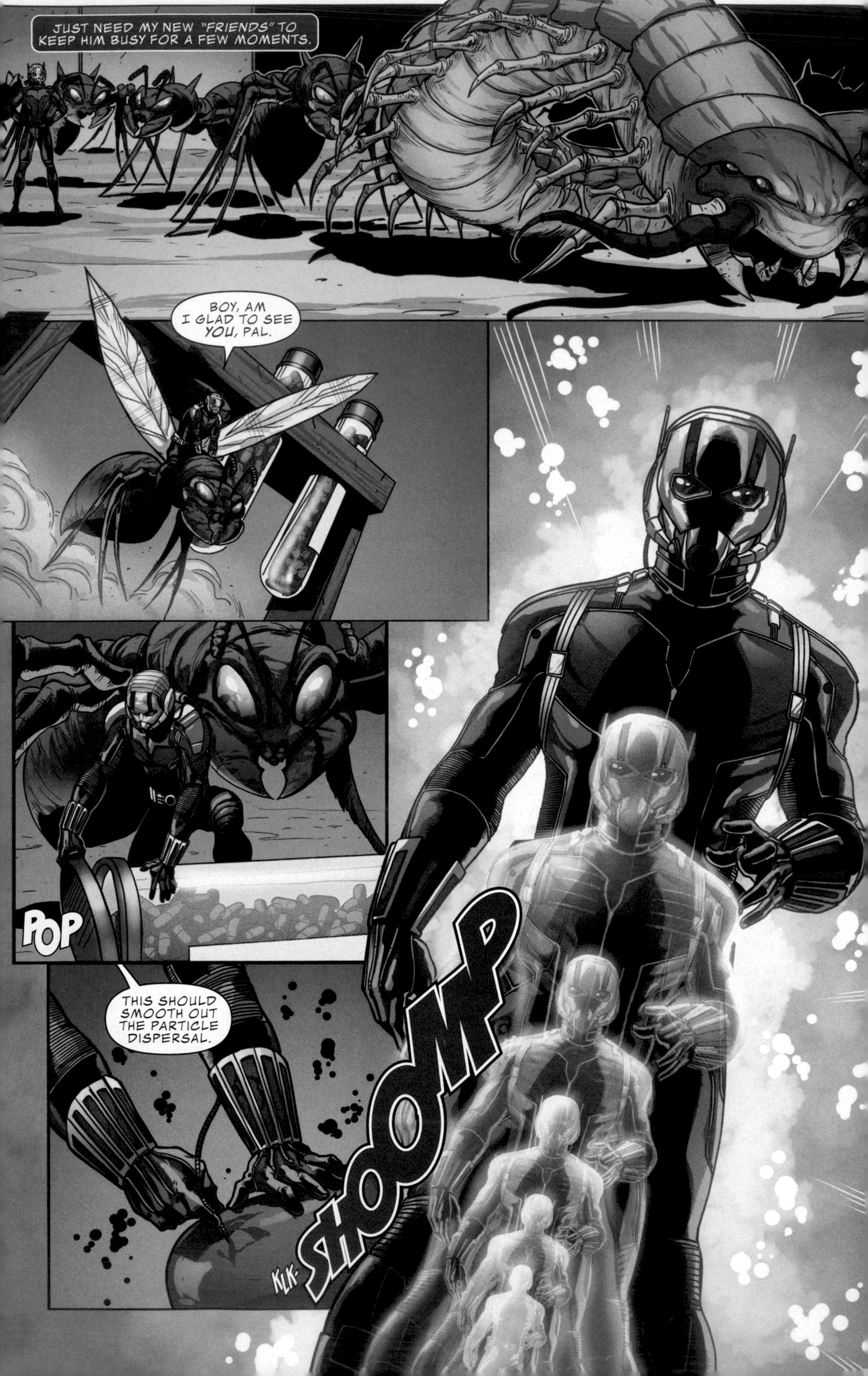
JUST NEED MY NEW "FRIENDS" TO KEEP HIM BUSY FOR A FEW MOMENTS.
BOY, AM I GLAD TO SEE YOU, PAL.
POP
THIS SHOULD SMOOTH OUT THE PARTICLE DISPERSAL.
KLK-
SHOOMP

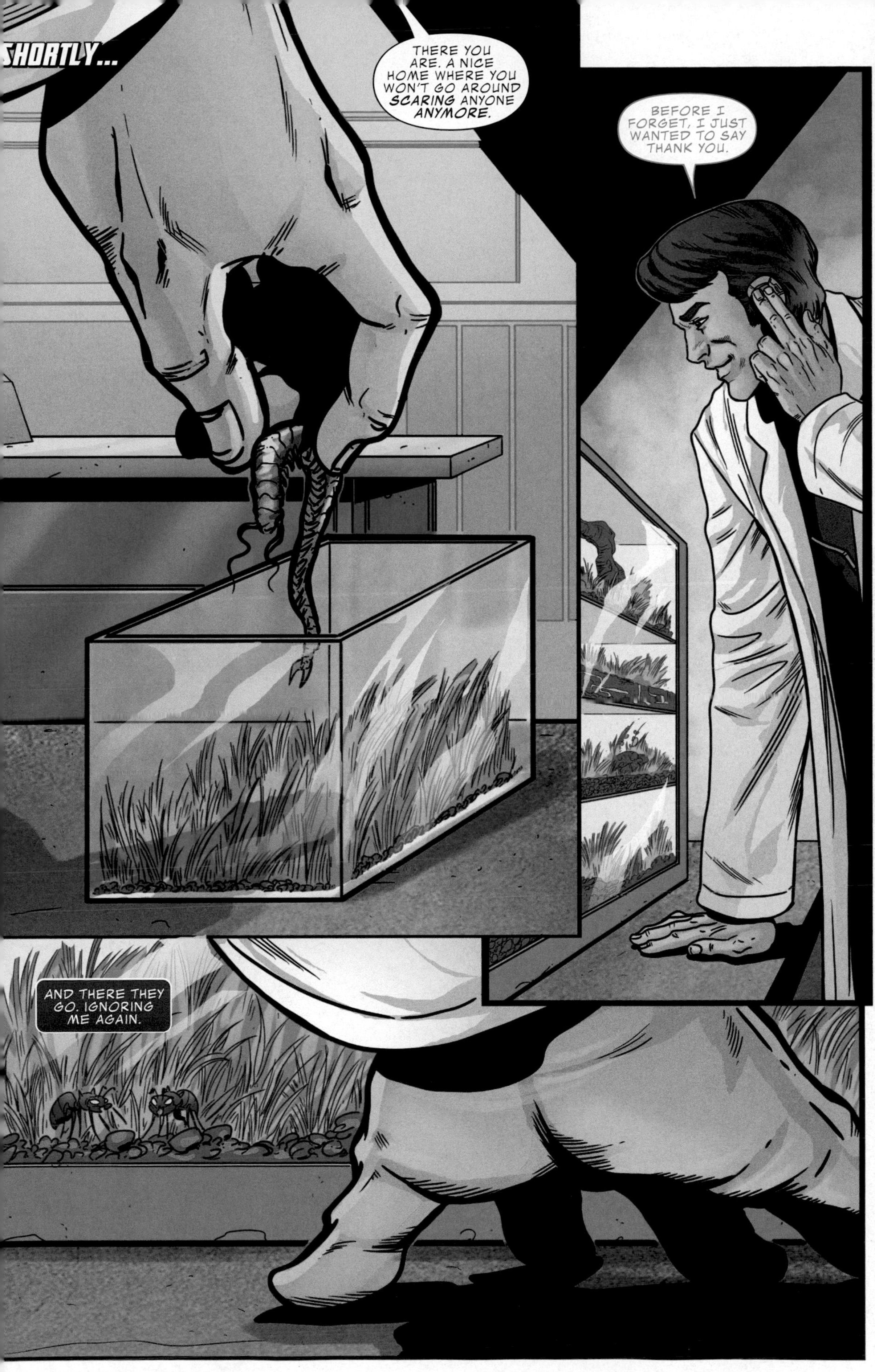
SHORTLY...
THERE YOU ARE. A NICE HOME WHERE YOU WON'T GO AROUND SCARING ANYONE ANYMORE.
BEFORE I FORGET, I JUST WANTED TO SAY THANK YOU.
AND THERE THEY GO. IGNORING ME AGAIN.

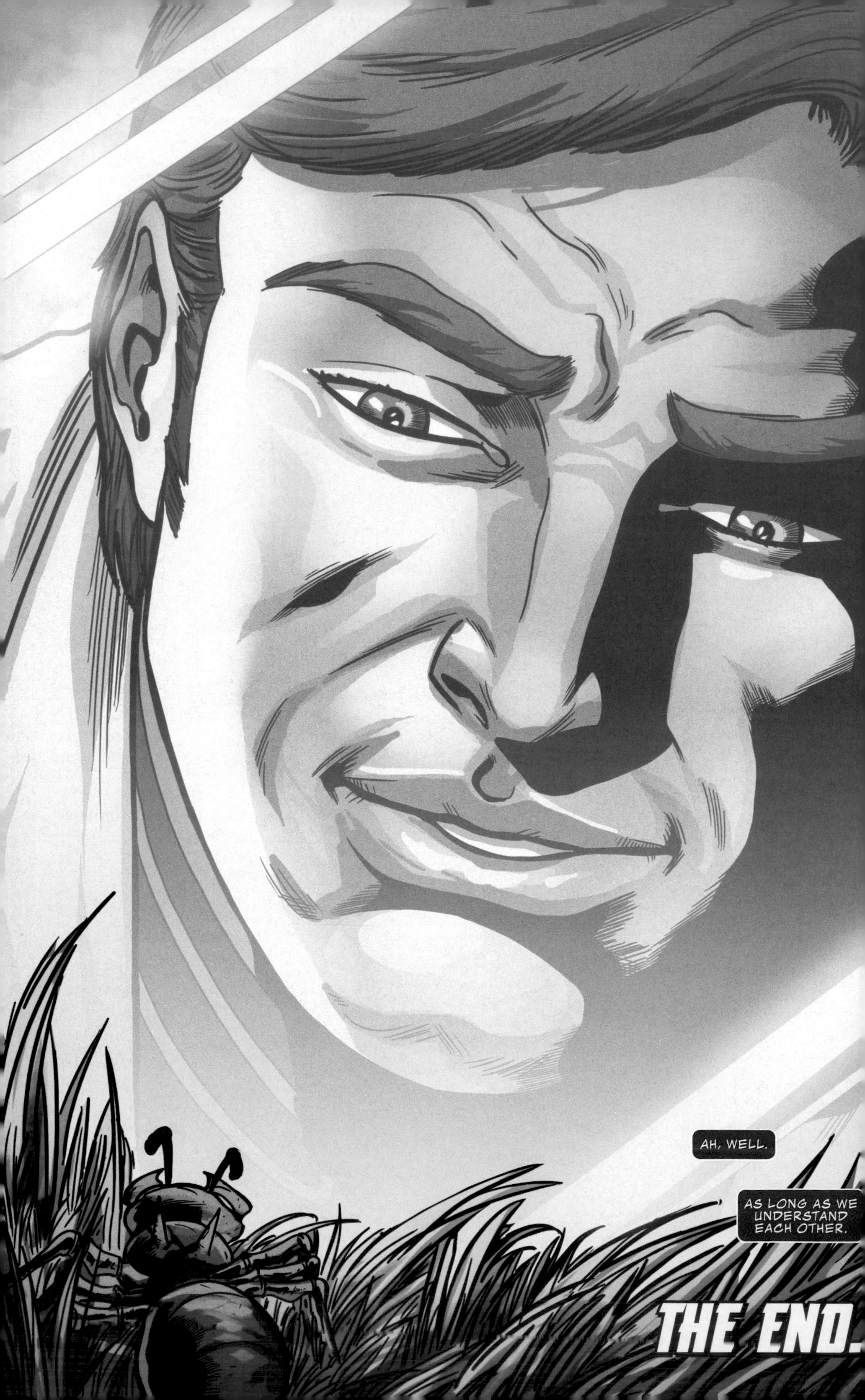
AH, WELL.
AS LONG AS WE UNDERSTAND EACH OTHER.
THE END.

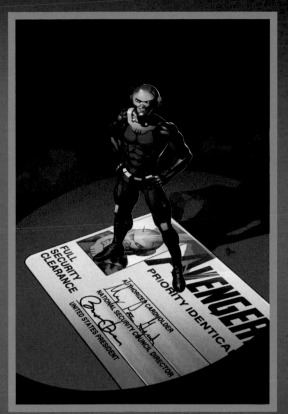

FULL
SECURITY
CLEARANCE
AUTHORIZED CARDHOLDER
NATIONAL SECURITY COUNCIL DIRECTOR
UNITED STATES PRESIDENT

ANT-MAN: LARGER THAN LIFE #1 VARIANT
BY MIKE DEODATO JR. & FRANK MARTIN

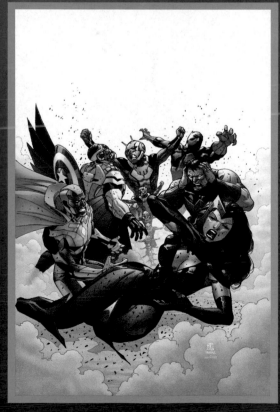

ANT-MAN: LARGER THAN LIFE #1 VARIANT
BY KHOI PHAM & JESUS ALBURTOV

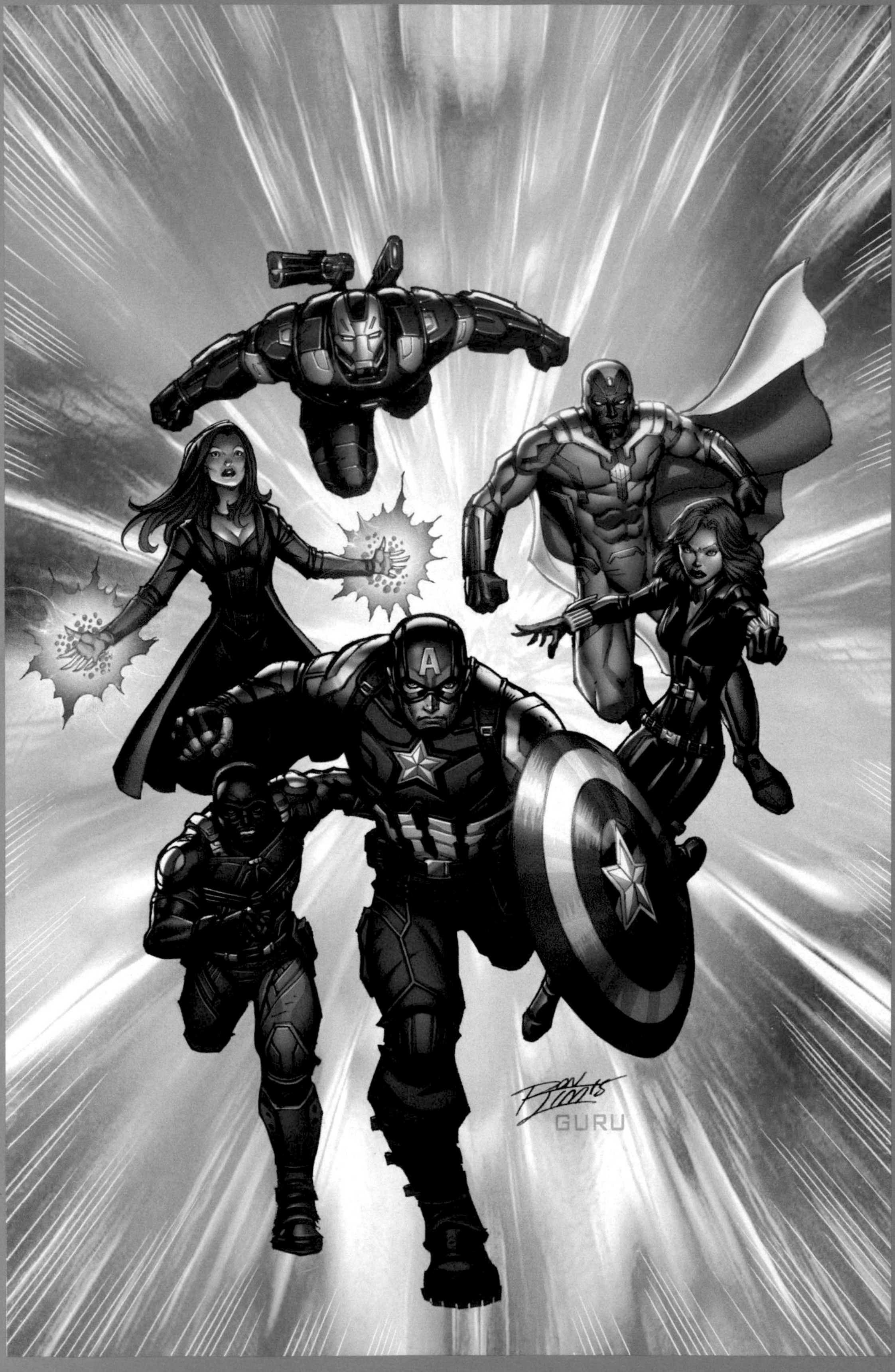
GURU

CAPTAIN AMERICA: ROAD TO WAR #1

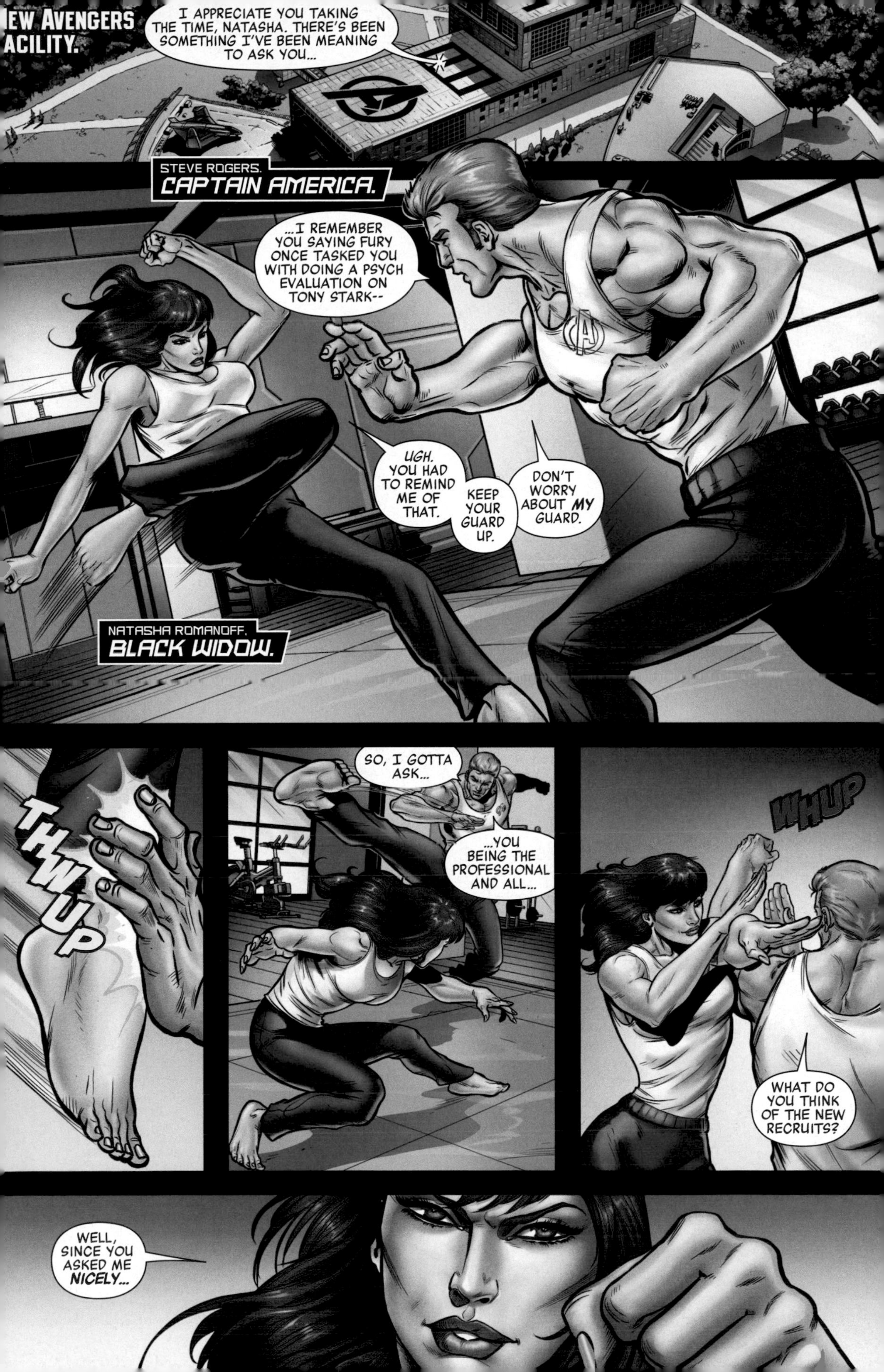
EW AVENGERS
ACILITY.
I APPRECIATE YOU TAKING THE TIME, NATASHA. THERE'S BEEN SOMETHING I'VE BEEN MEANING TO ASK YOU...
STEVE ROGERS. CAPTAIN AMERICA.
...I REMEMBER YOU SAYING FURY ONCE TASKED YOU WITH DOING A PSYCH EVALUATION ON TONY STARK--
UGH. YOU HAD TO REMIND ME OF THAT.
KEEP YOUR GUARD UP.
DON'T WORRY ABOUT MY GUARD.
NATASHA ROMANOFF. BLACK WIDOW.
THWUP
SO, I GOTTA ASK...
...YOU BEING THE PROFESSIONAL AND ALL...
WHUP
WHAT DO YOU THINK OF THE NEW RECRUITS?
WELL, SINCE YOU ASKED ME NICELY...

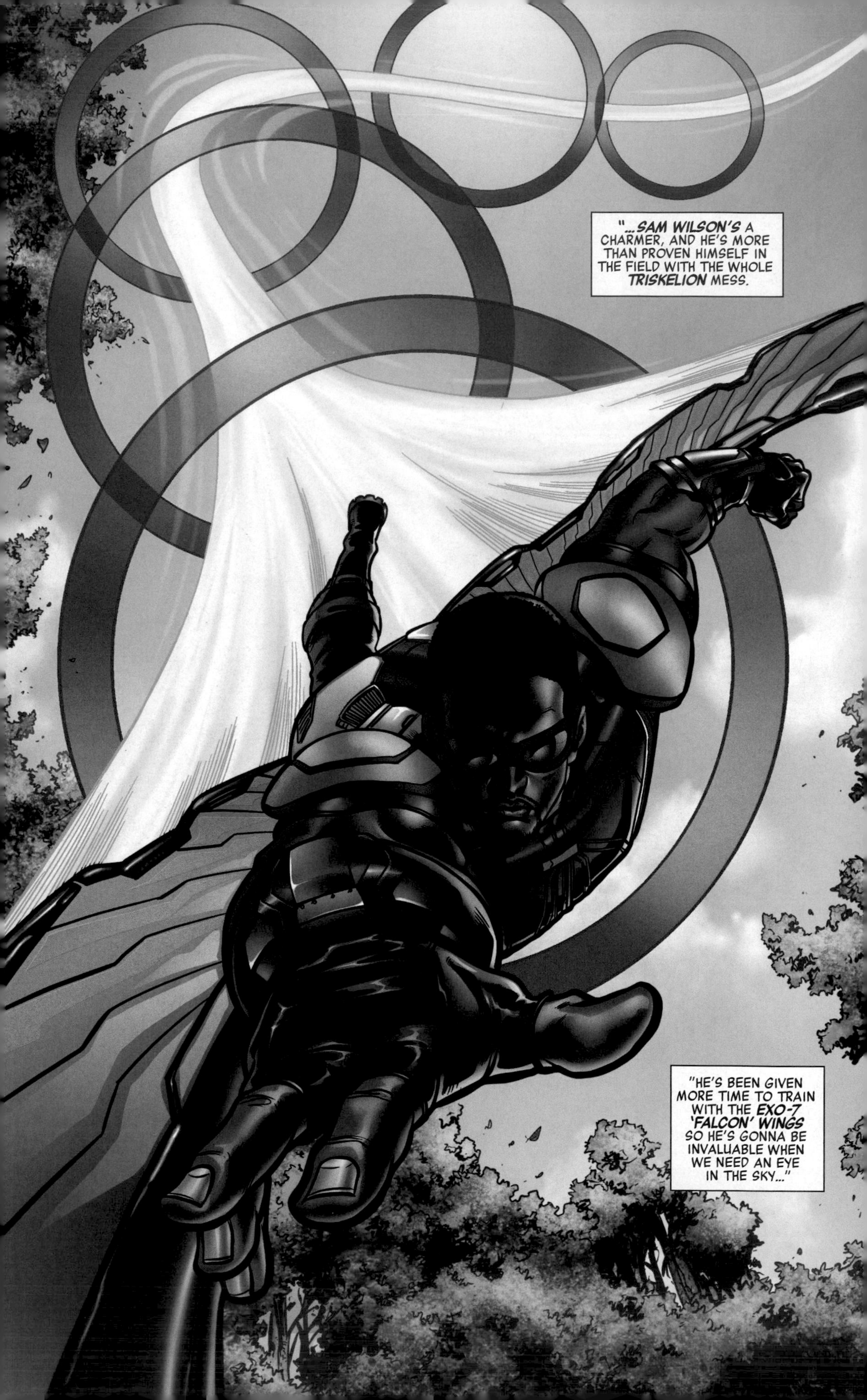
"...SAM WILSON'S A CHARMER, AND HE'S MORE THAN PROVEN HIMSELF IN THE FIELD WITH THE WHOLE TRISKELION MESS.
"HE'S BEEN GIVEN MORE TIME TO TRAIN WITH THE EXO-7 'FALCON' WINGS SO HE'S GONNA BE INVALUABLE WHEN WE NEED AN EYE IN THE SKY..."

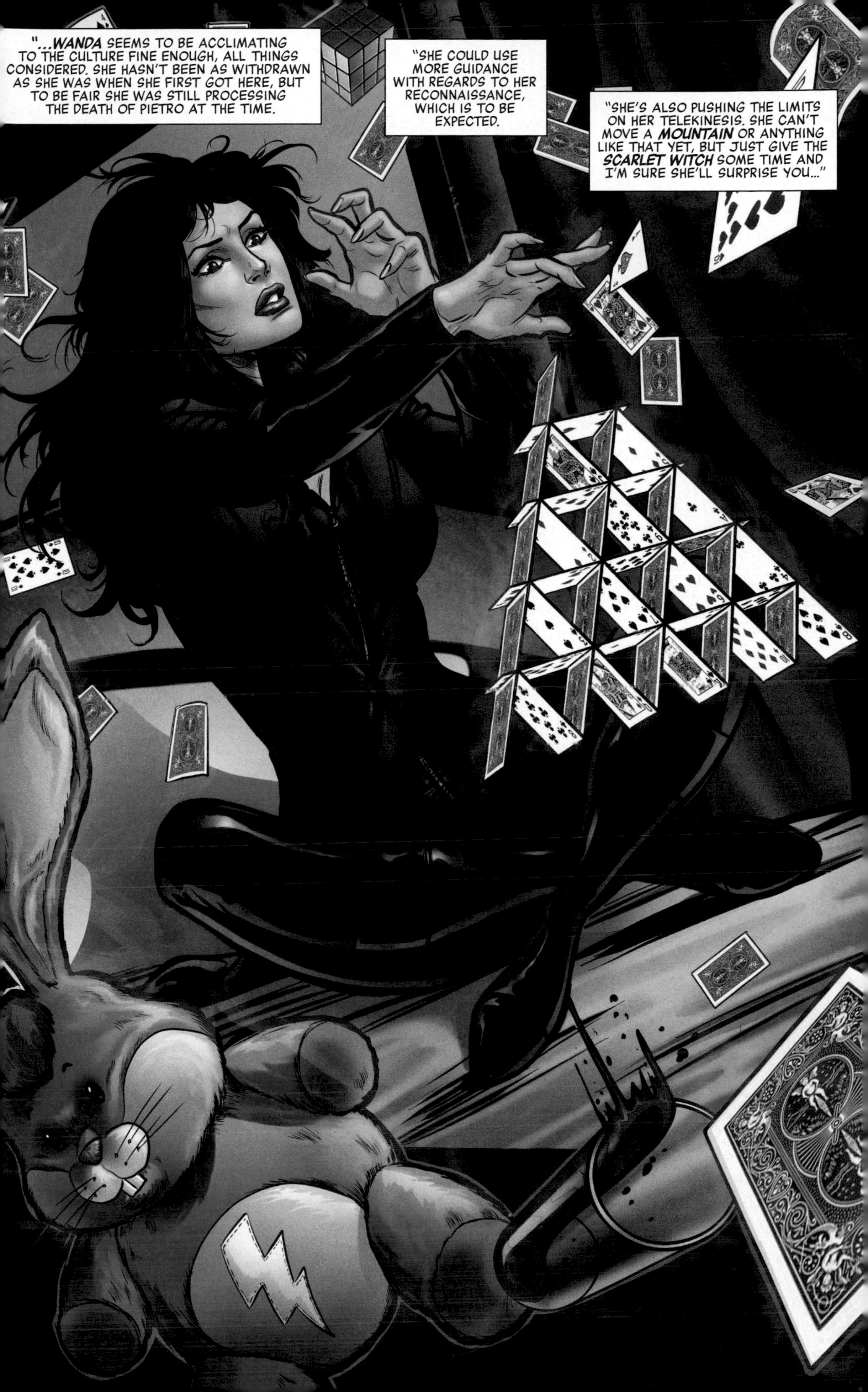
"...WANDA SEEMS TO BE ACCLIMATING TO THE CULTURE FINE ENOUGH, ALL THINGS CONSIDERED. SHE HASN'T BEEN AS WITHDRAWN AS SHE WAS WHEN SHE FIRST GOT HERE, BUT TO BE FAIR SHE WAS STILL PROCESSING THE DEATH OF PIETRO AT THE TIME.
"SHE COULD USE MORE GUIDANCE WITH REGARDS TO HER RECONNAISSANCE, WHICH IS TO BE EXPECTED.
"SHE'S ALSO PUSHING THE LIMITS ON HER TELEKINESIS. SHE CAN'T MOVE A MOUNTAIN OR ANYTHING LIKE THAT YET, BUT JUST GIVE THE SCARLET WITCH SOME TIME AND I'M SURE SHE'LL SURPRISE YOU..."

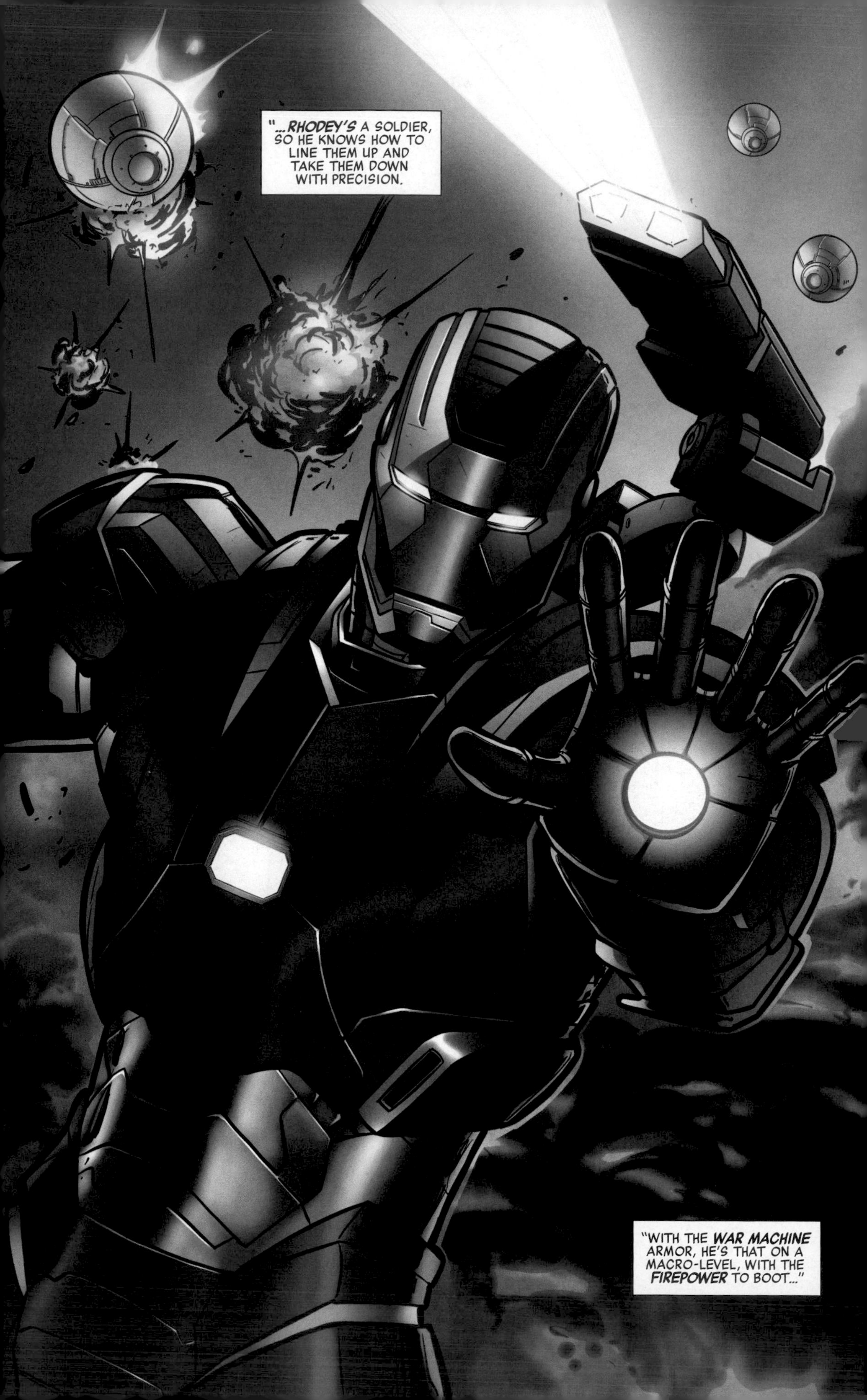
"...RHODEY'S A SOLDIER, SO HE KNOWS HOW TO LINE THEM UP AND TAKE THEM DOWN WITH PRECISION.
"WITH THE WAR MACHINE ARMOR, HE'S THAT ON A MACRO-LEVEL, WITH THE FIREPOWER TO BOOT..."

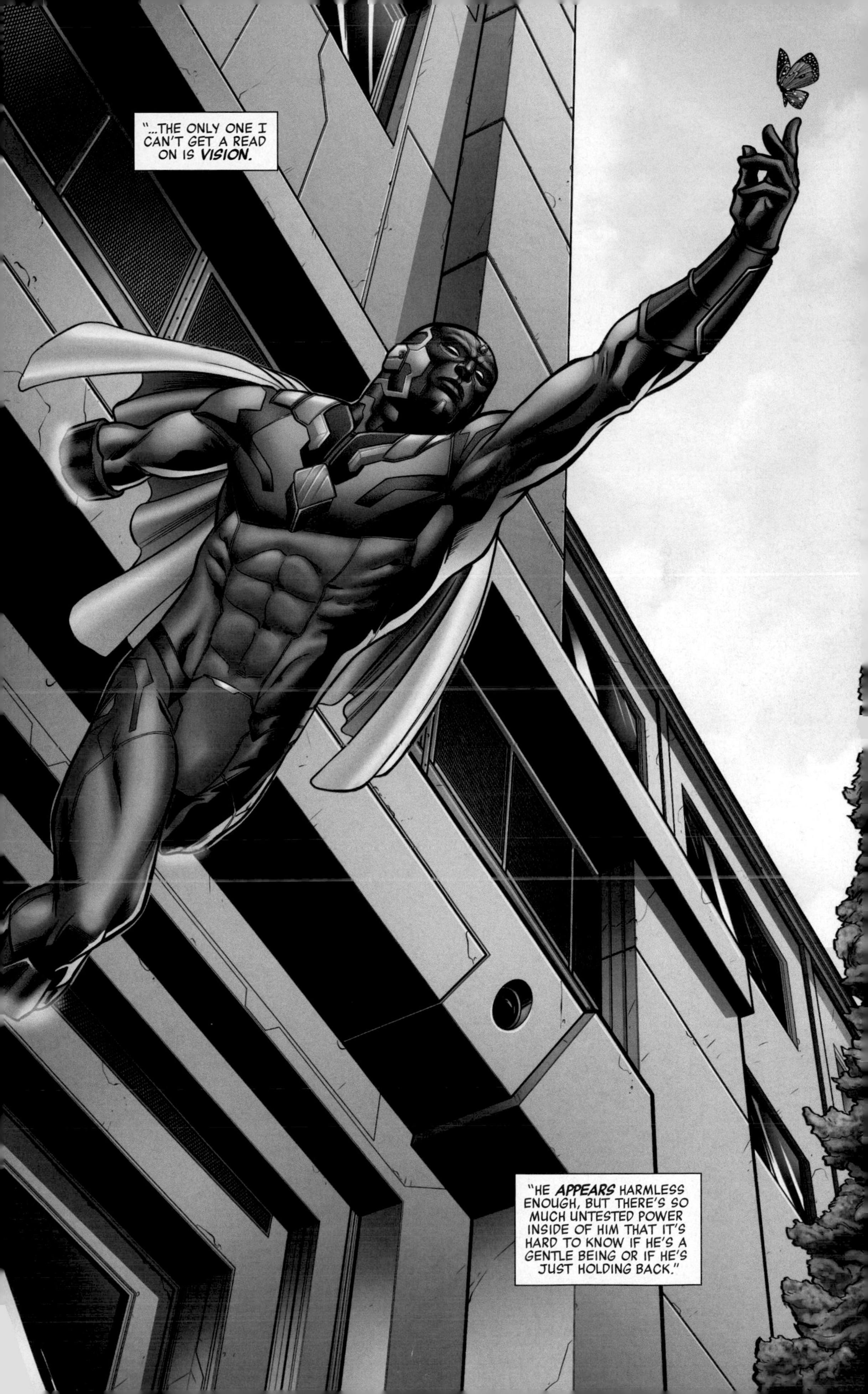
"...THE ONLY ONE I CAN'T GET A READ ON IS VISION.
"HE APPEARS HARMLESS ENOUGH, BUT THERE'S SO MUCH UNTESTED POWER INSIDE OF HIM THAT IT'S HARD TO KNOW IF HE'S A GENTLE BEING OR IF HE'S JUST HOLDING BACK."

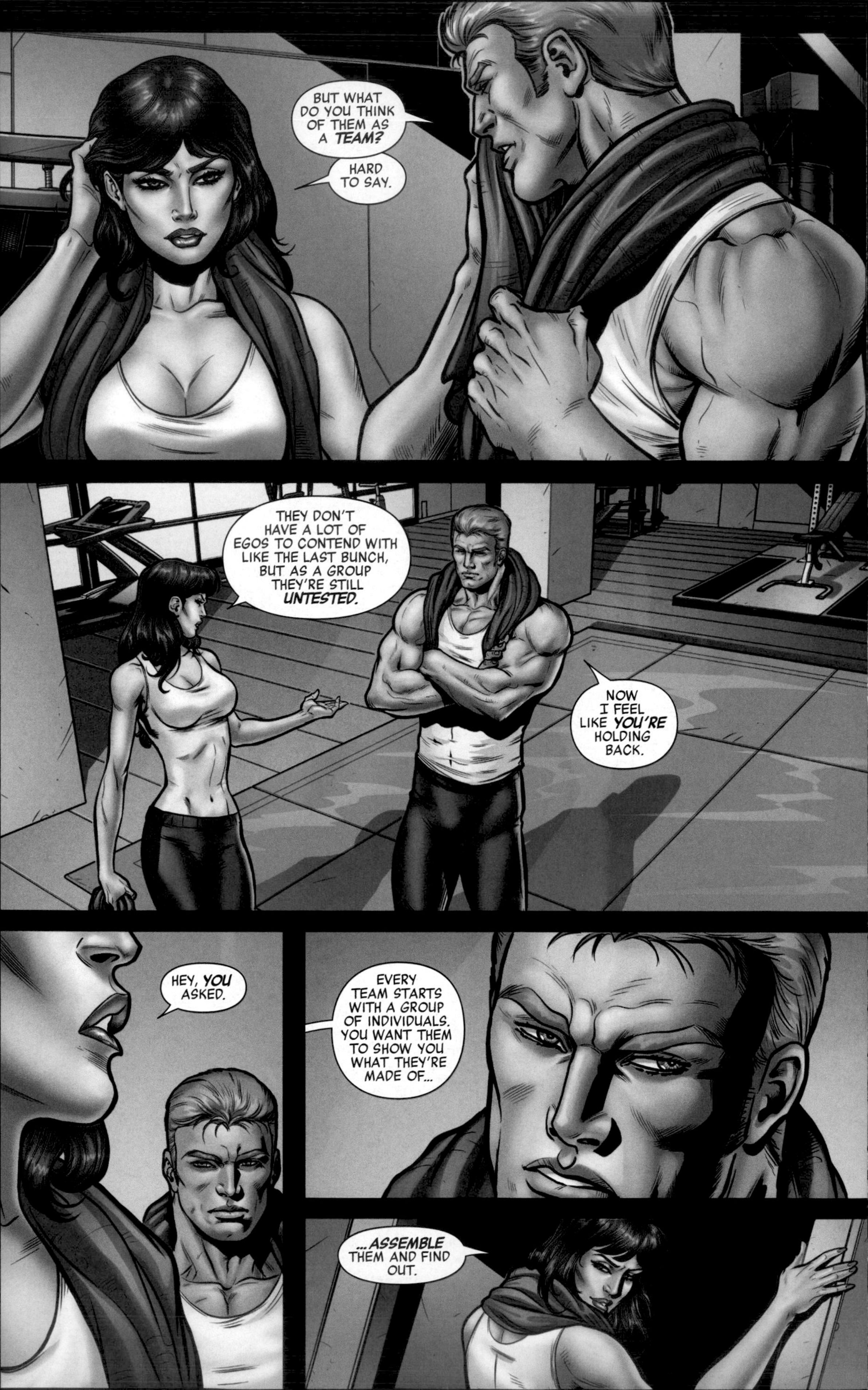
BUT WHAT DO YOU THINK OF THEM AS A TEAM?
HARD TO SAY.
THEY DON'T HAVE A LOT OF EGOS TO CONTEND WITH LIKE THE LAST BUNCH, BUT AS A GROUP THEY'RE STILL UNTESTED.
NOW I FEEL LIKE YOU'RE HOLDING BACK.
HEY, YOU ASKED.
EVERY TEAM STARTS WITH A GROUP OF INDIVIDUALS. YOU WANT THEM TO SHOW YOU WHAT THEY'RE MADE OF...
...ASSEMBLE THEM AND FIND OUT.

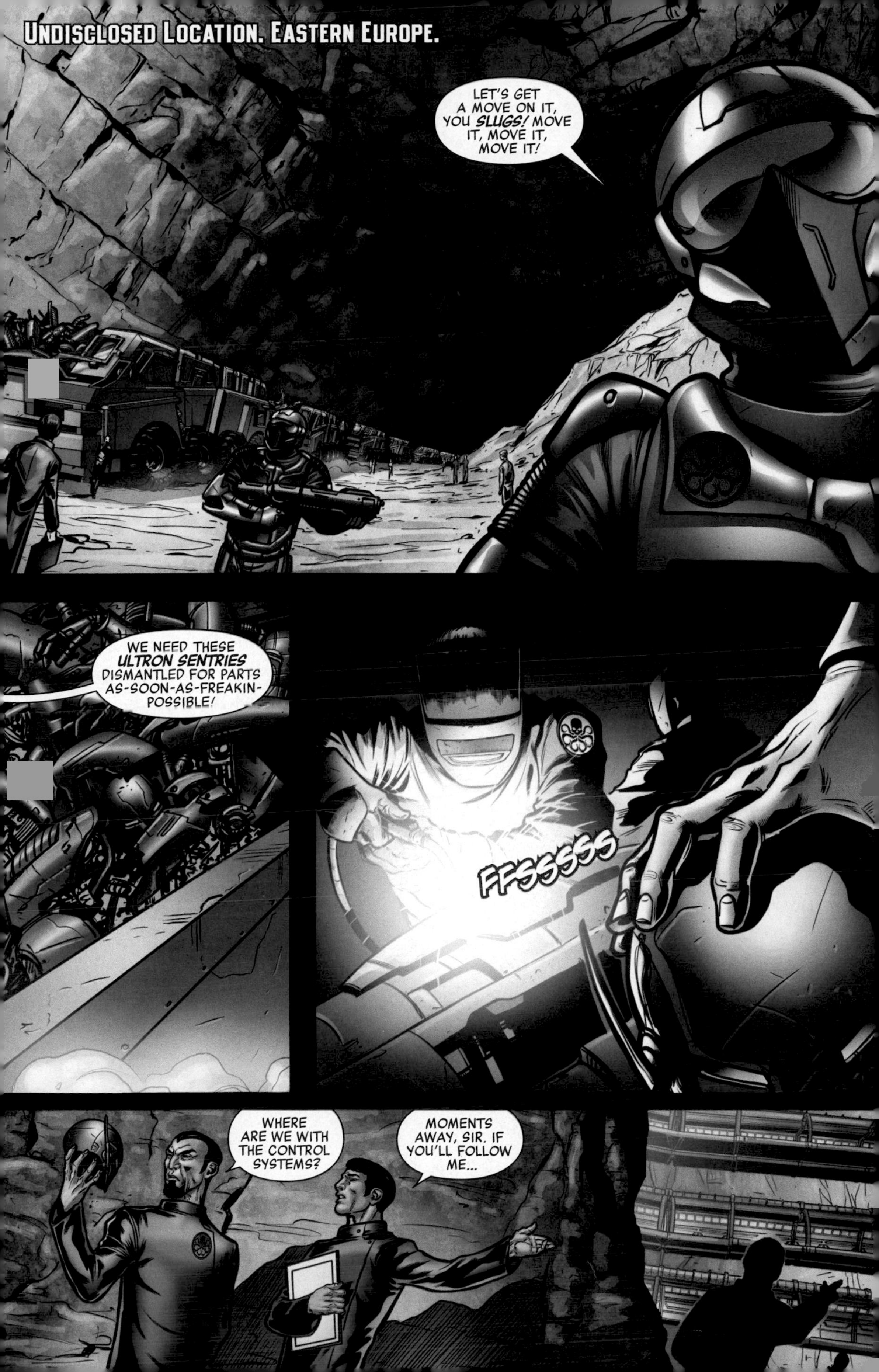
UNDISCLOSED LOCATION. EASTERN EUROPE.
LET'S GET A MOVE ON IT, YOU SLUGS! MOVE IT, MOVE IT, MOVE IT!
WE NEED THESE ULTRON SENTRIES DISMANTLED FOR PARTS AS-SOON-AS-FREAKIN-POSSIBLE!
FFSSSSS
WHERE ARE WE WITH THE CONTROL SYSTEMS?
MOMENTS AWAY, SIR. IF YOU'LL FOLLOW ME...

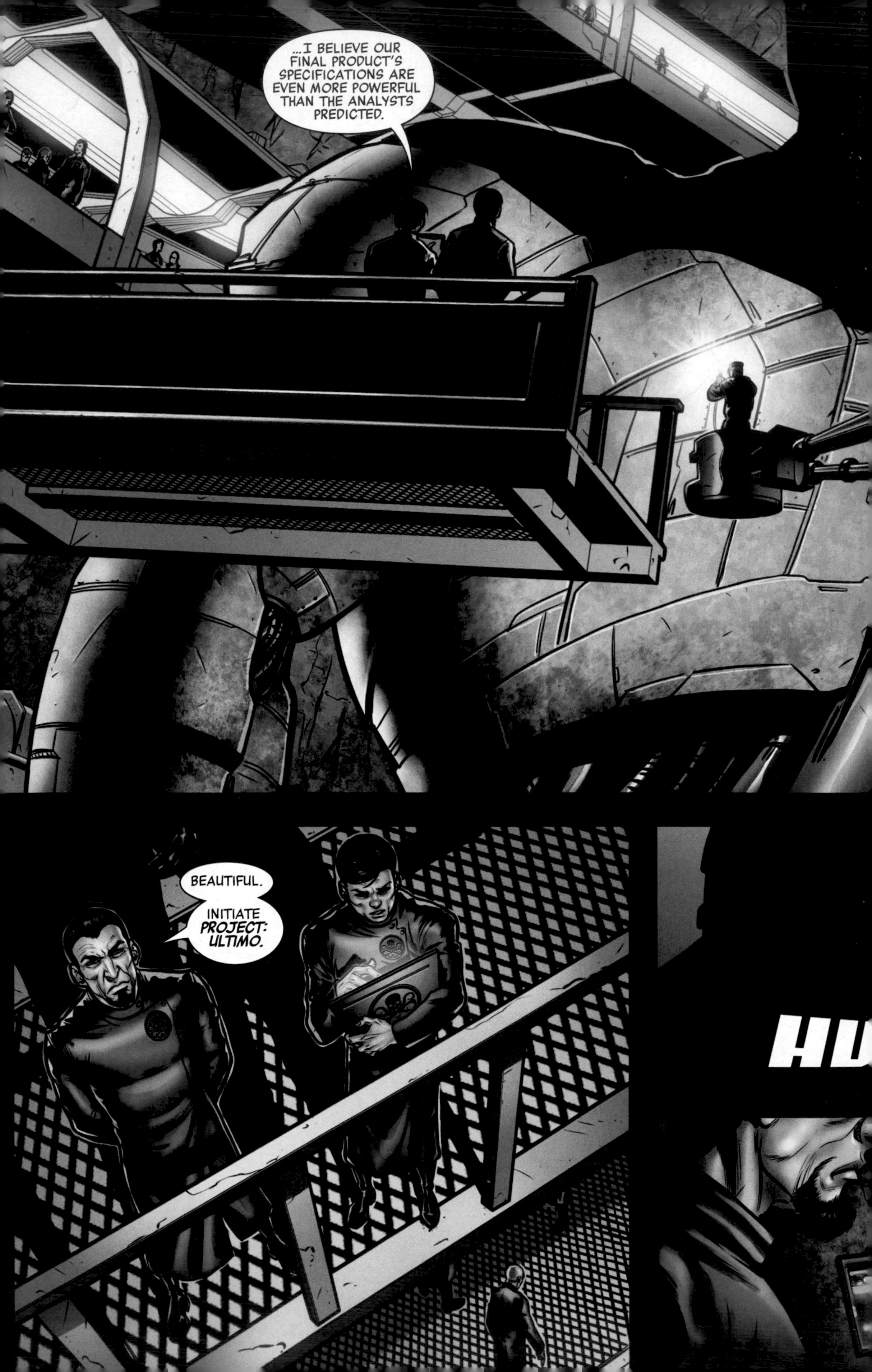
...I BELIEVE OUR FINAL PRODUCT'S SPECIFICATIONS ARE EVEN MORE POWERFUL THAN THE ANALYSTS PREDICTED.
BEAUTIFUL.
INITIATE PROJECT: ULTIMO.

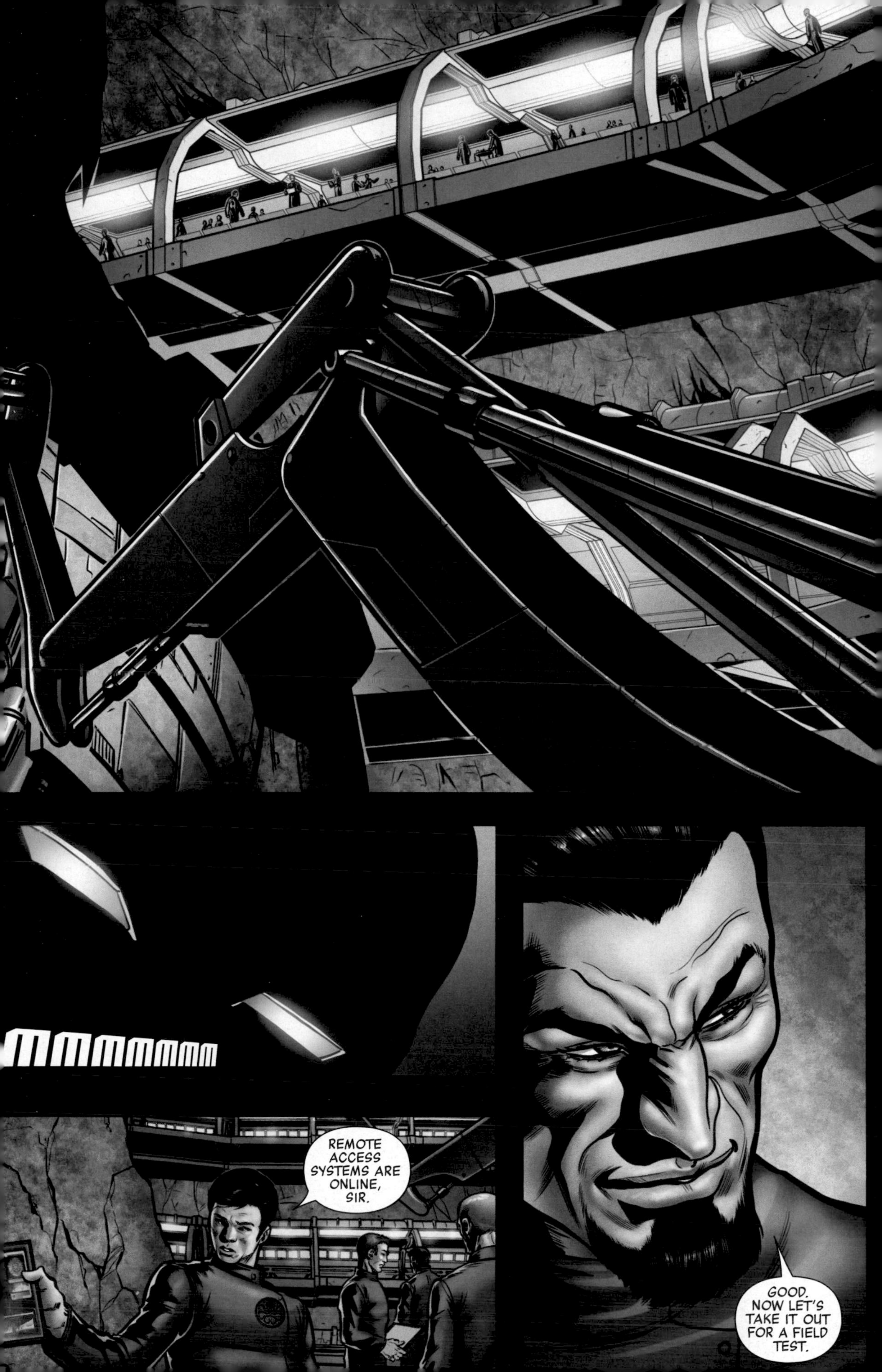
MMMMMMMMM
REMOTE ACCESS SYSTEMS ARE ONLINE, SIR.
GOOD. NOW LET'S TAKE IT OUT FOR A FIELD TEST.

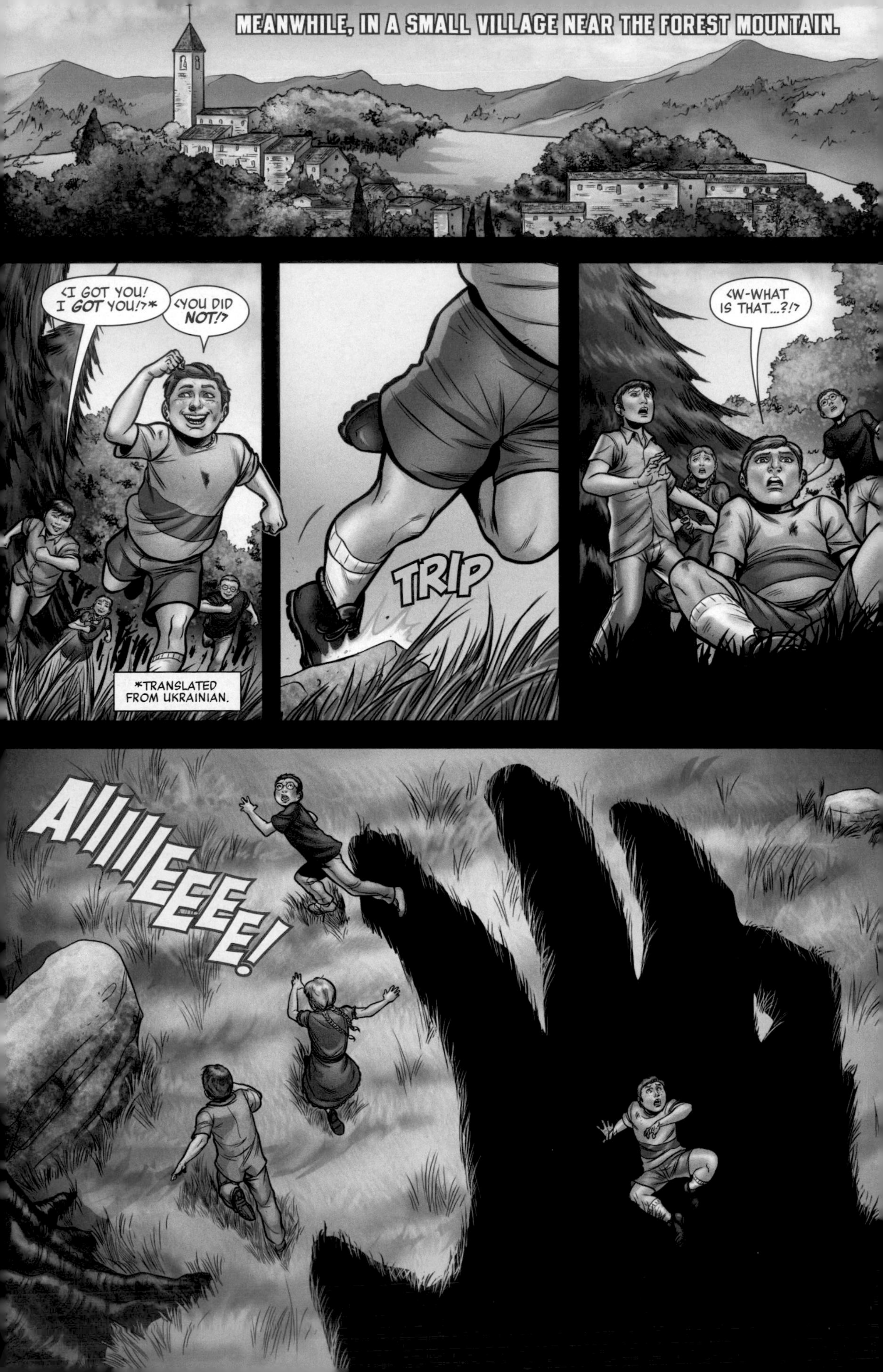
MEANWHILE, IN A SMALL VILLAGE NEAR THE FOREST MOUNTAIN.
<I GOT YOU! I GOT YOU!>*
<YOU DID NOT!>
*TRANSLATED FROM UKRAINIAN.
TRIP
<W-WHAT IS THAT...?!>
AIIIIEEEEE!

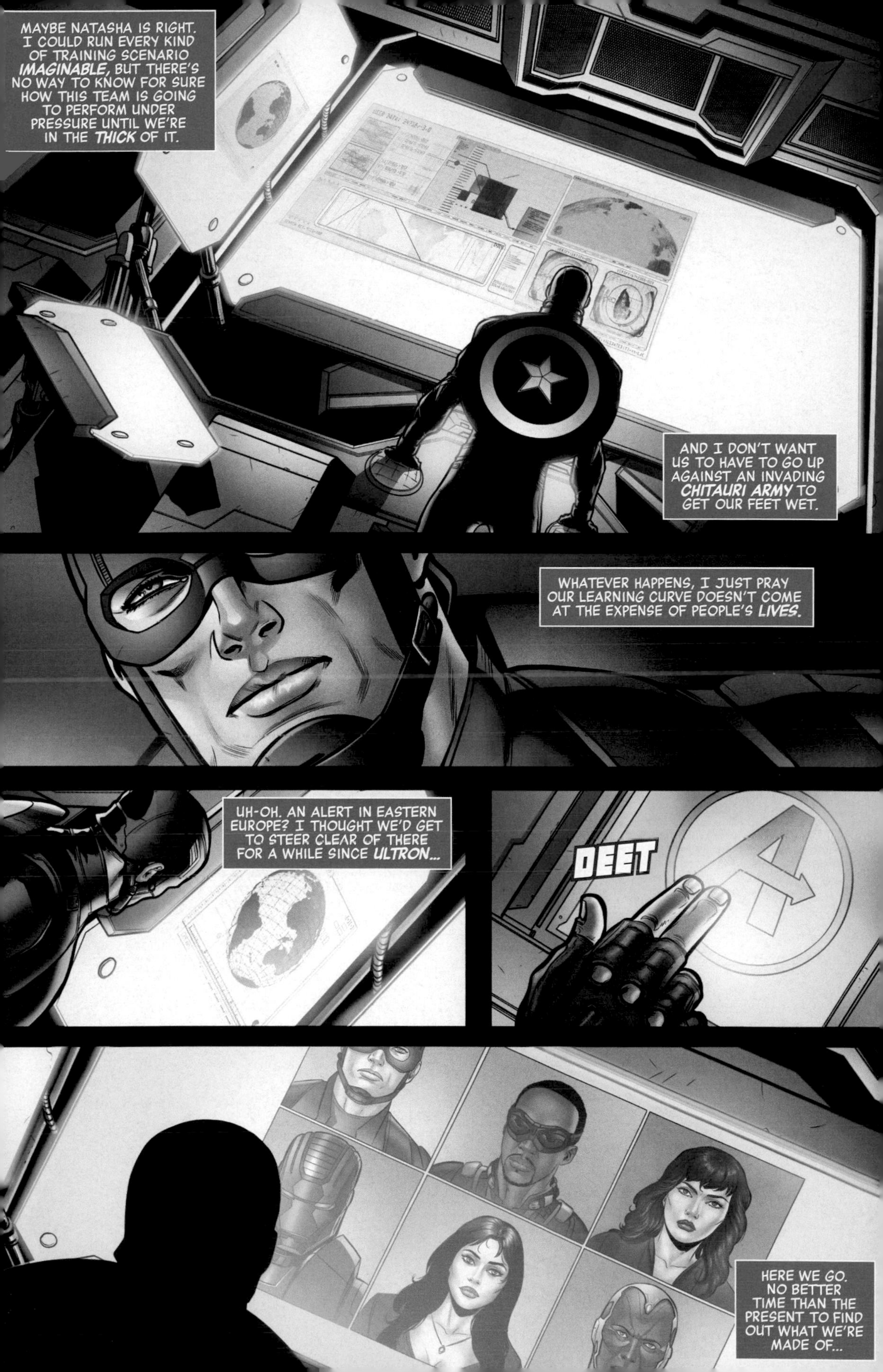

MAYBE NATASHA IS RIGHT. I COULD RUN EVERY KIND OF TRAINING SCENARIO IMAGINABLE, BUT THERE'S NO WAY TO KNOW FOR SURE HOW THIS TEAM IS GOING TO PERFORM UNDER PRESSURE UNTIL WE'RE IN THE THICK OF IT.
AND I DON'T WANT US TO HAVE TO GO UP AGAINST AN INVADING CHITAURI ARMY TO GET OUR FEET WET.
WHATEVER HAPPENS, I JUST PRAY OUR LEARNING CURVE DOESN'T COME AT THE EXPENSE OF PEOPLE'S LIVES.
UH-OH. AN ALERT IN EASTERN EUROPE? I THOUGHT WE'D GET TO STEER CLEAR OF THERE FOR A WHILE SINCE ULTRON...
DEET
HERE WE GO. NO BETTER TIME THAN THE PRESENT TO FIND OUT WHAT WE'RE MADE OF...

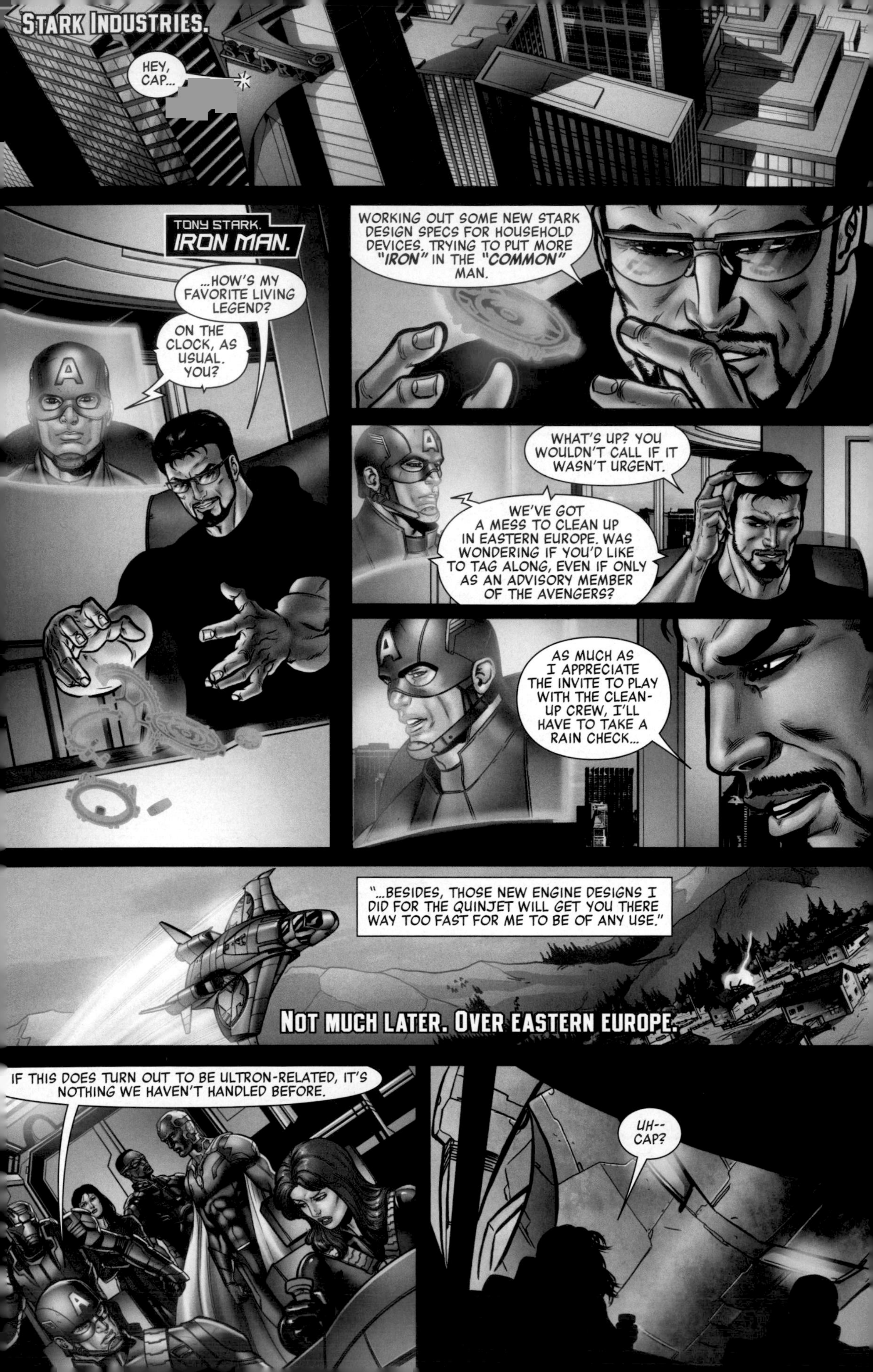

STARK INDUSTRIES.
HEY, CAP...
TONY STARK. IRON MAN.
...HOW'S MY FAVORITE LIVING LEGEND?
ON THE CLOCK, AS USUAL. YOU?
WORKING OUT SOME NEW STARK DESIGN SPECS FOR HOUSEHOLD DEVICES. TRYING TO PUT MORE "IRON" IN THE "COMMON" MAN.
WHAT'S UP? YOU WOULDN'T CALL IF IT WASN'T URGENT.
WE'VE GOT A MESS TO CLEAN UP IN EASTERN EUROPE. WAS WONDERING IF YOU'D LIKE TO TAG ALONG, EVEN IF ONLY AS AN ADVISORY MEMBER OF THE AVENGERS?
AS MUCH AS I APPRECIATE THE INVITE TO PLAY WITH THE CLEAN-UP CREW, I'LL HAVE TO TAKE A RAIN CHECK...
"...BESIDES, THOSE NEW ENGINE DESIGNS I DID FOR THE QUINJET WILL GET YOU THERE WAY TOO FAST FOR ME TO BE OF ANY USE."
NOT MUCH LATER. OVER EASTERN EUROPE.
IF THIS DOES TURN OUT TO BE ULTRON-RELATED, IT'S NOTHING WE HAVEN'T HANDLED BEFORE.
UH-- CAP?

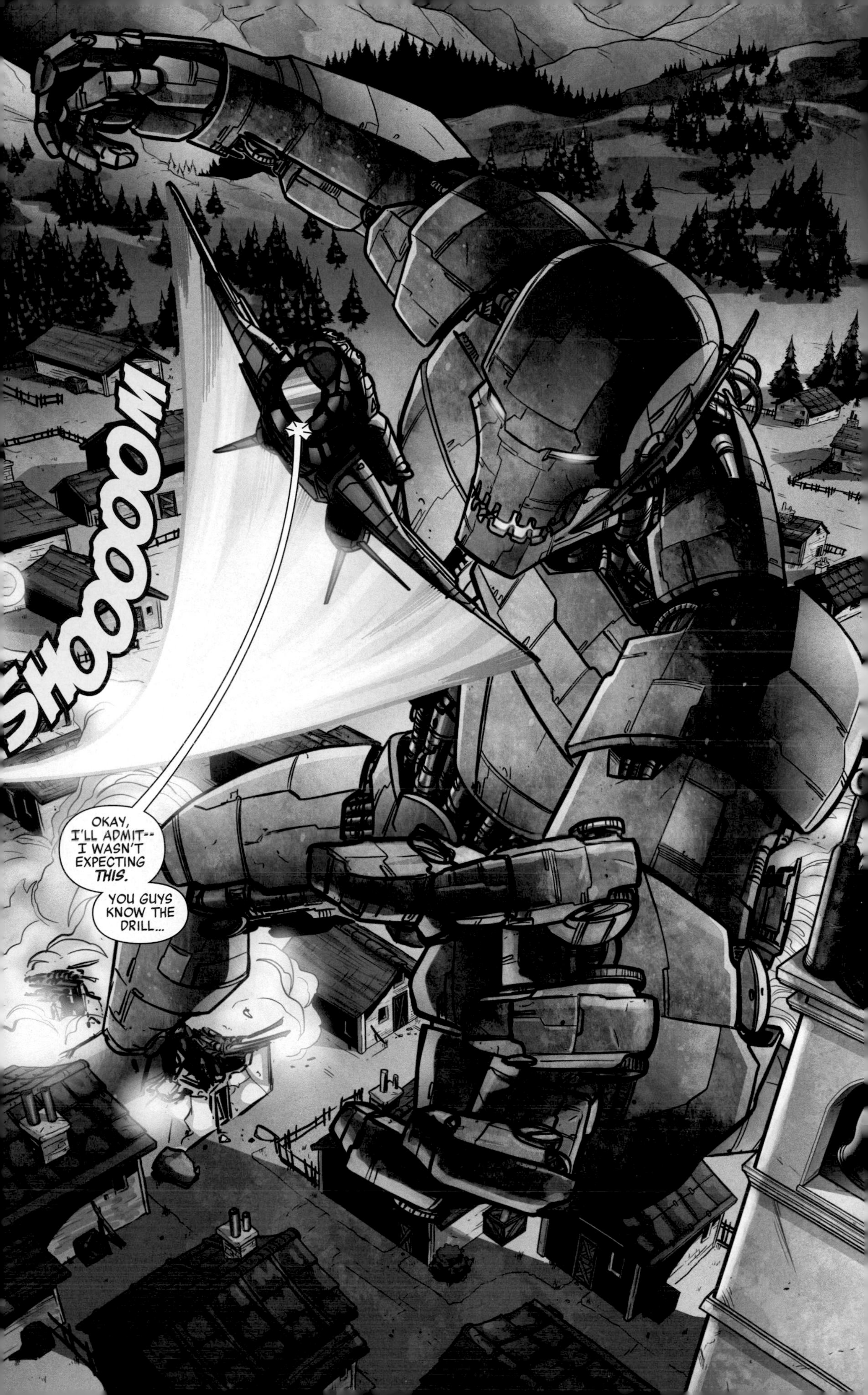
SHOOOOM
OKAY, I'LL ADMIT-- I WASN'T EXPECTING THIS.
YOU GUYS KNOW THE DRILL...

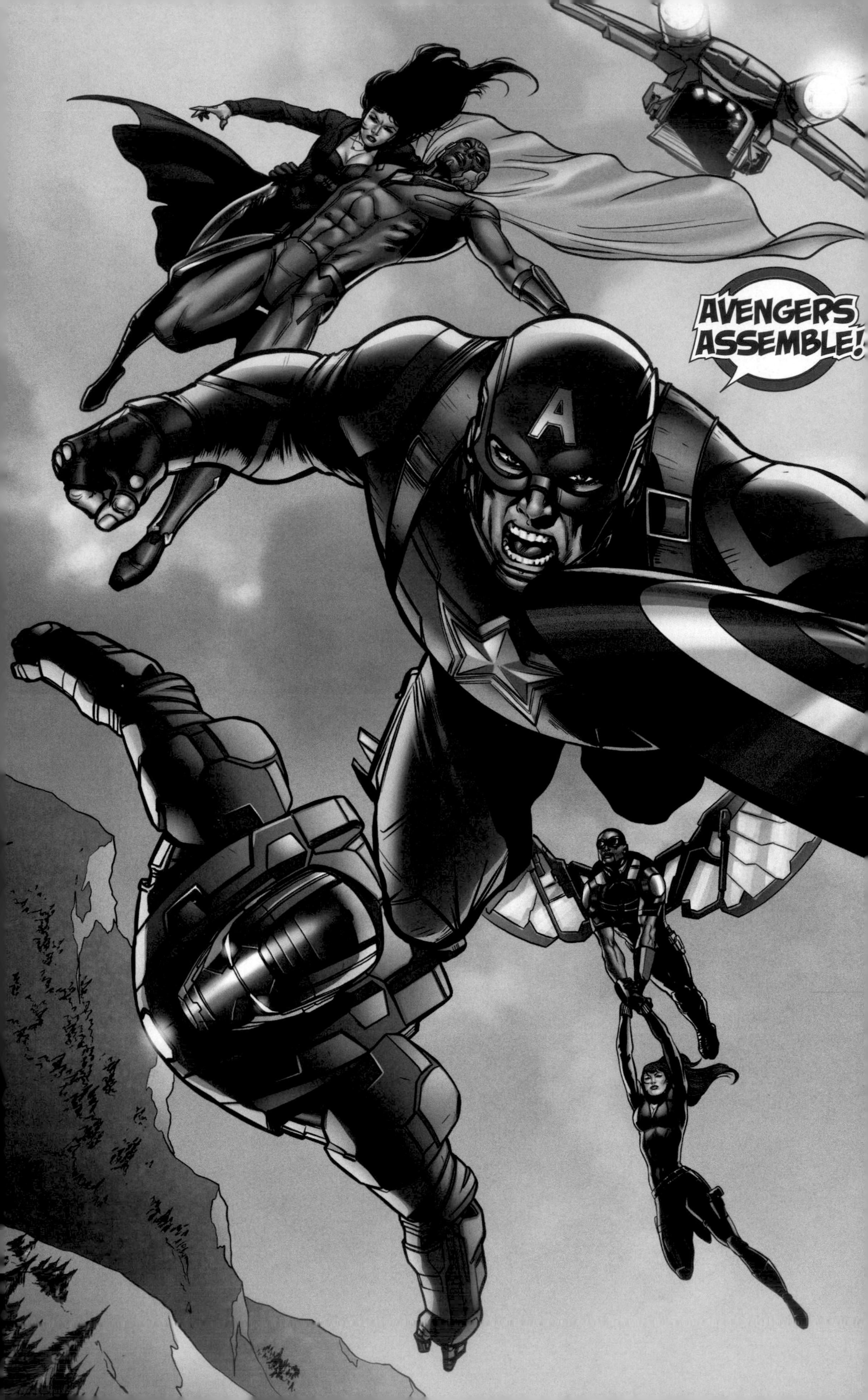
AVENGERS ASSEMBLE!

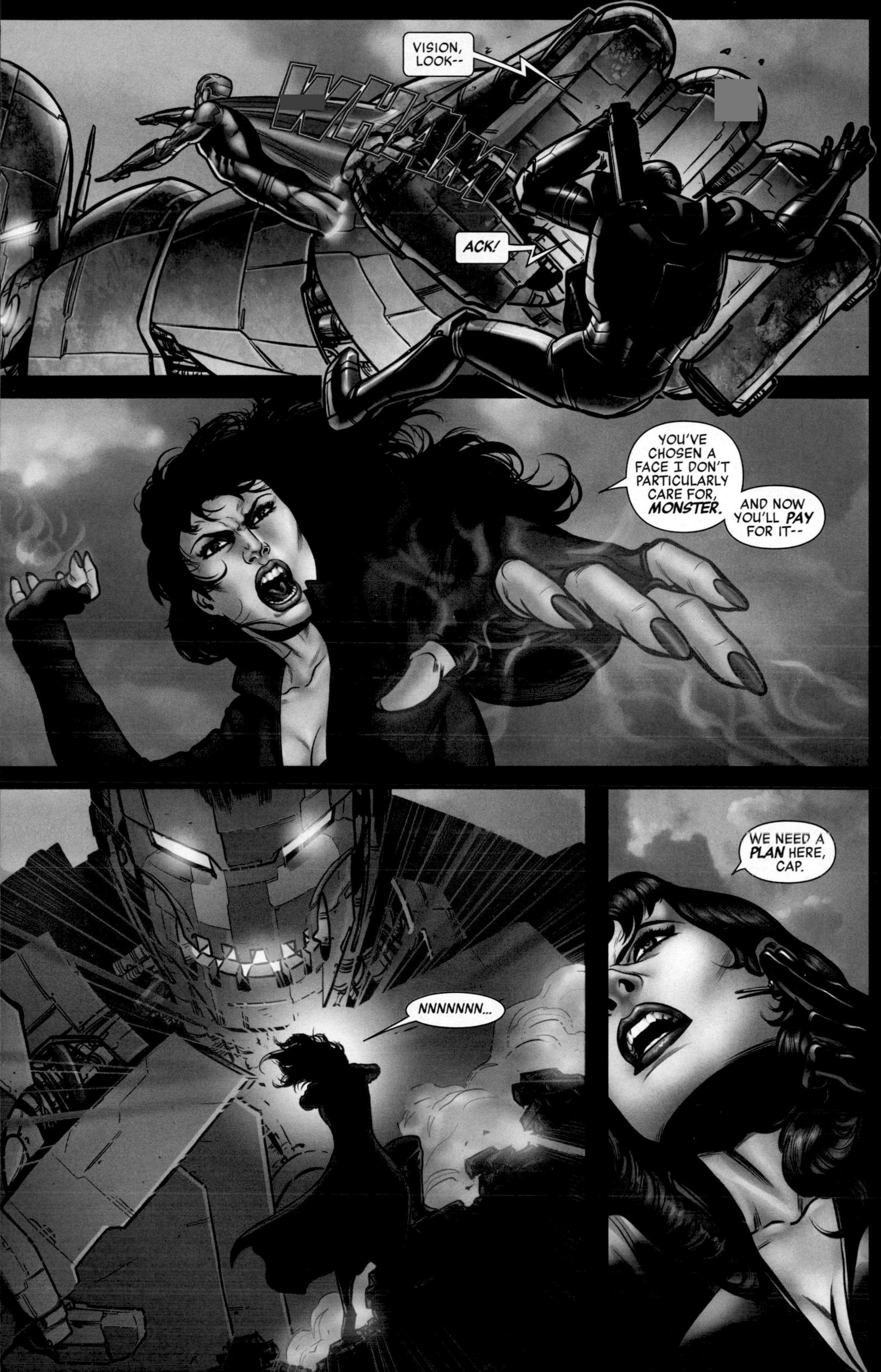
VISION, LOOK--
WHAM
ACK!
YOU'VE CHOSEN A FACE I DON'T PARTICULARLY CARE FOR, **MONSTER.**
AND NOW YOU'LL **PAY** FOR IT--
NNNNNNN...
WE NEED A **PLAN** HERE, CAP.

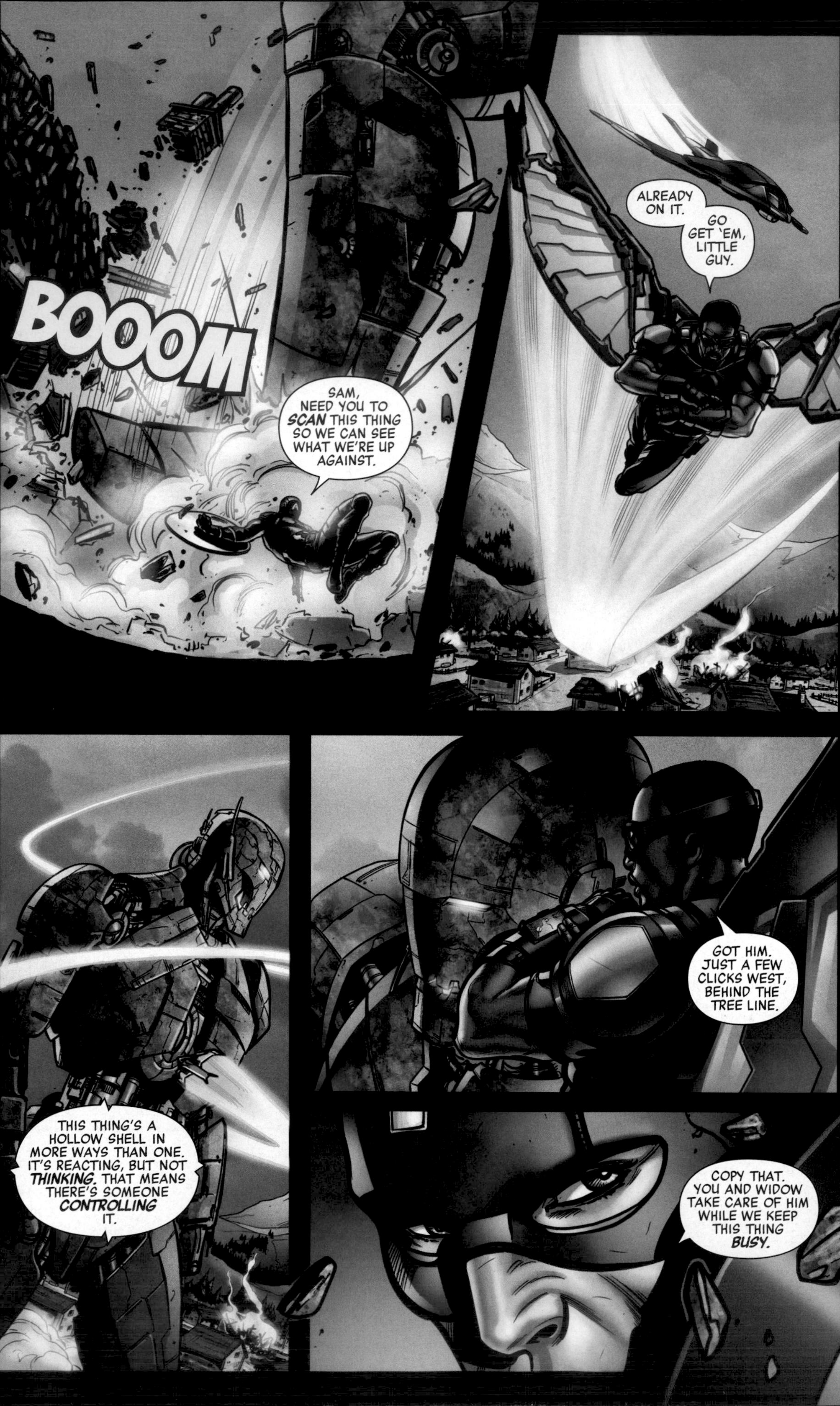
BOOOM
SAM, NEED YOU TO SCAN THIS THING SO WE CAN SEE WHAT WE'RE UP AGAINST.
ALREADY ON IT.
GO GET 'EM, LITTLE GUY.
THIS THING'S A HOLLOW SHELL IN MORE WAYS THAN ONE. IT'S REACTING, BUT NOT THINKING. THAT MEANS THERE'S SOMEONE CONTROLLING IT.
GOT HIM. JUST A FEW CLICKS WEST, BEHIND THE TREE LINE.
COPY THAT. YOU AND WIDOW TAKE CARE OF HIM WHILE WE KEEP THIS THING BUSY.

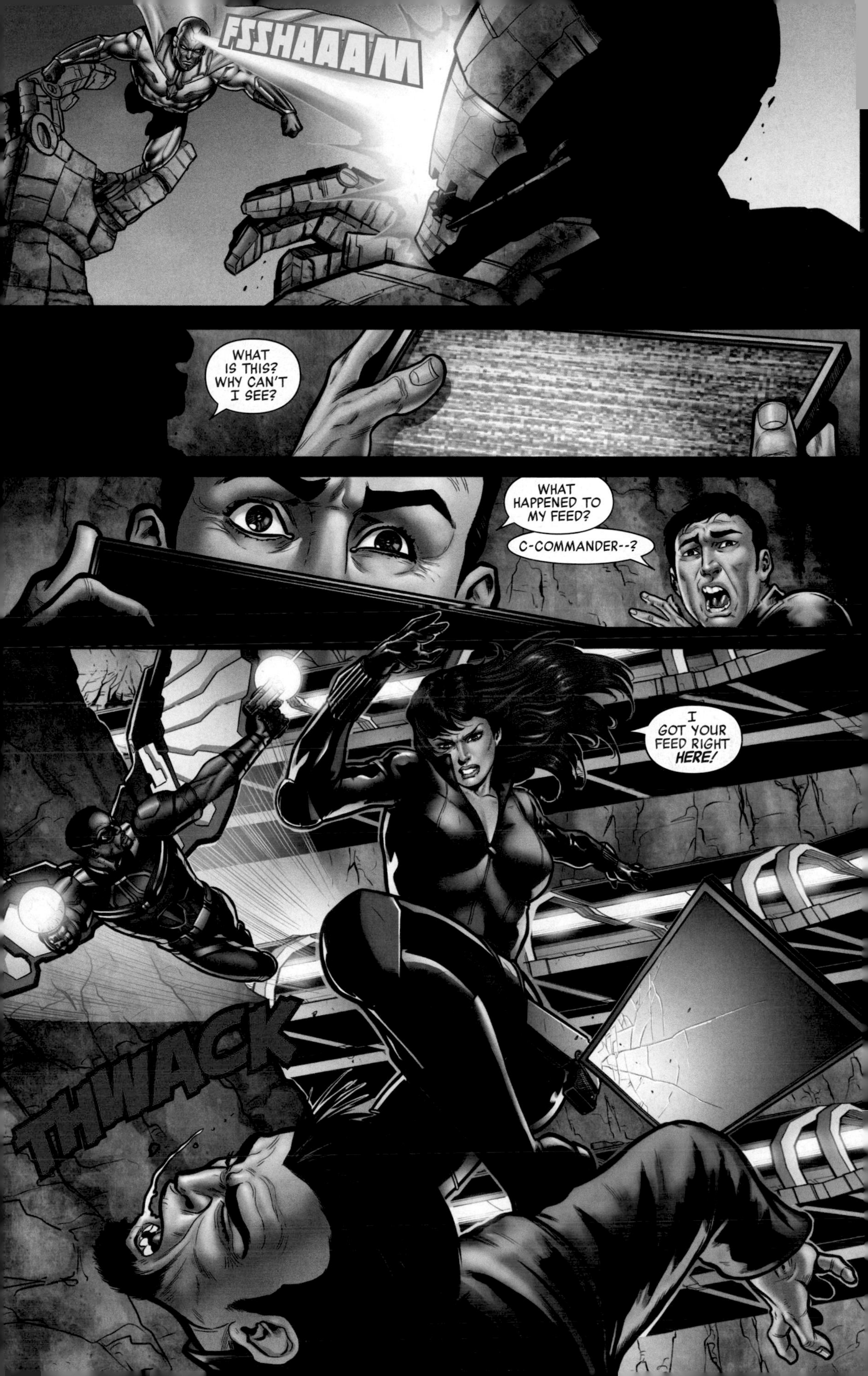
FSSHAAAM
WHAT IS THIS? WHY CAN'T I SEE?
WHAT HAPPENED TO MY FEED?
C-COMMANDER--?
I GOT YOUR FEED RIGHT HERE!
THWACK

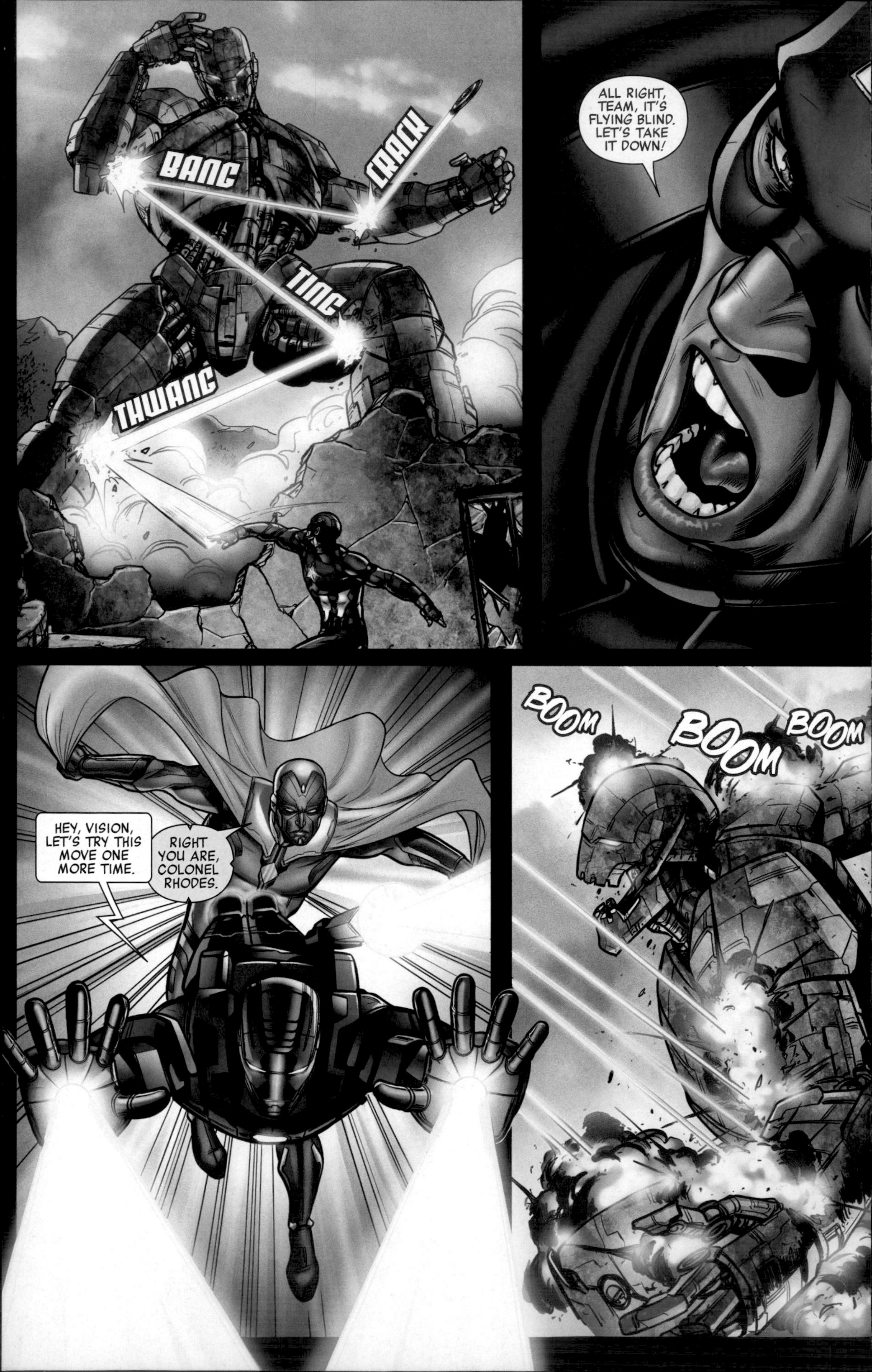
BANG
CRACK
TING
THWANG
ALL RIGHT, TEAM, IT'S FLYING BLIND. LET'S TAKE IT DOWN!
HEY, VISION, LET'S TRY THIS MOVE ONE MORE TIME.
RIGHT YOU ARE, COLONEL RHODES.
BOOM
BOOM
BOOM

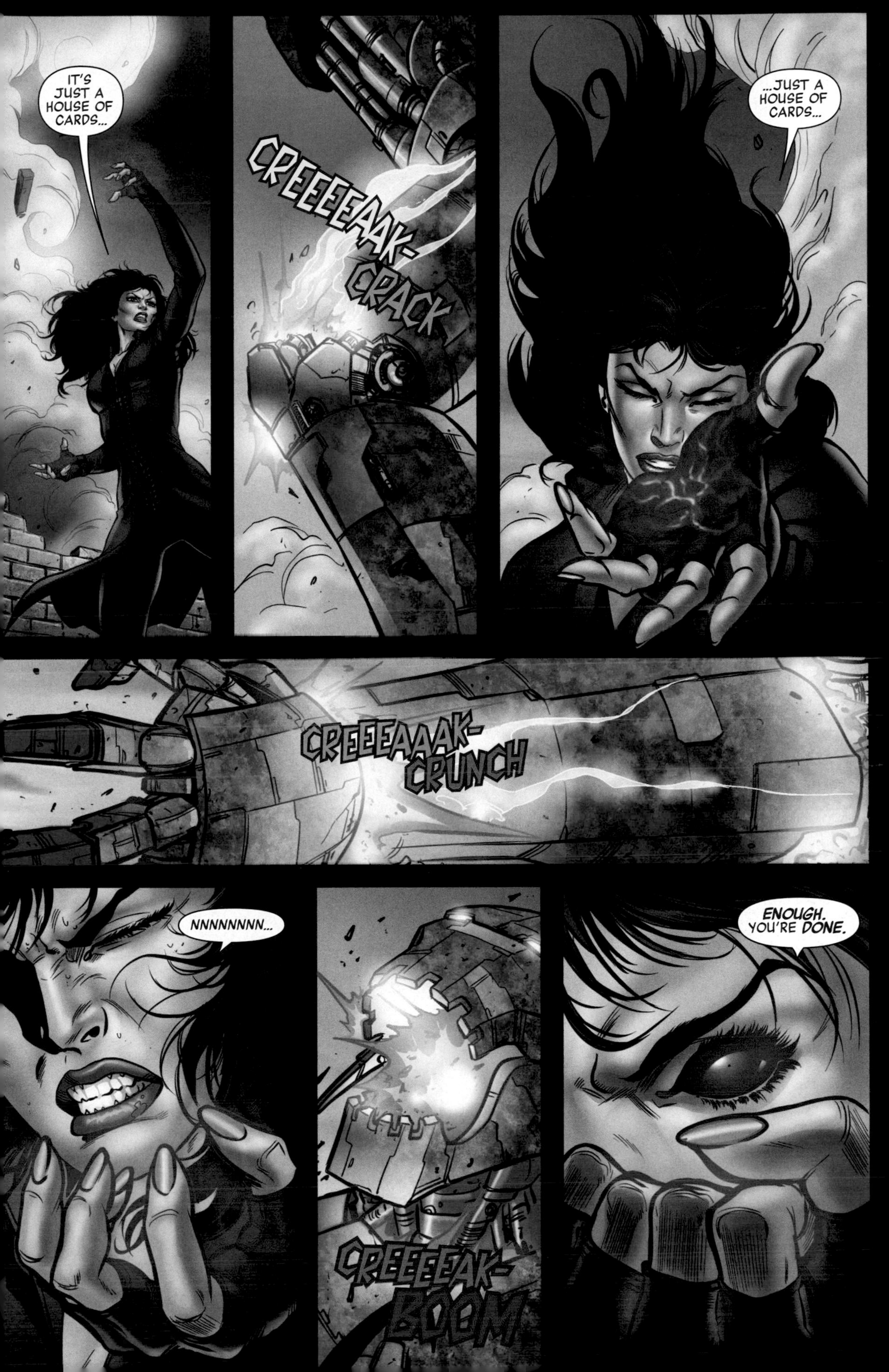
IT'S JUST A HOUSE OF CARDS...
CREEEEAAK-CRACK
...JUST A HOUSE OF CARDS...
CREEEAAAK-CRUNCH
NNNNNNNN...
CREEEEAK-BOOM
ENOUGH. YOU'RE DONE.

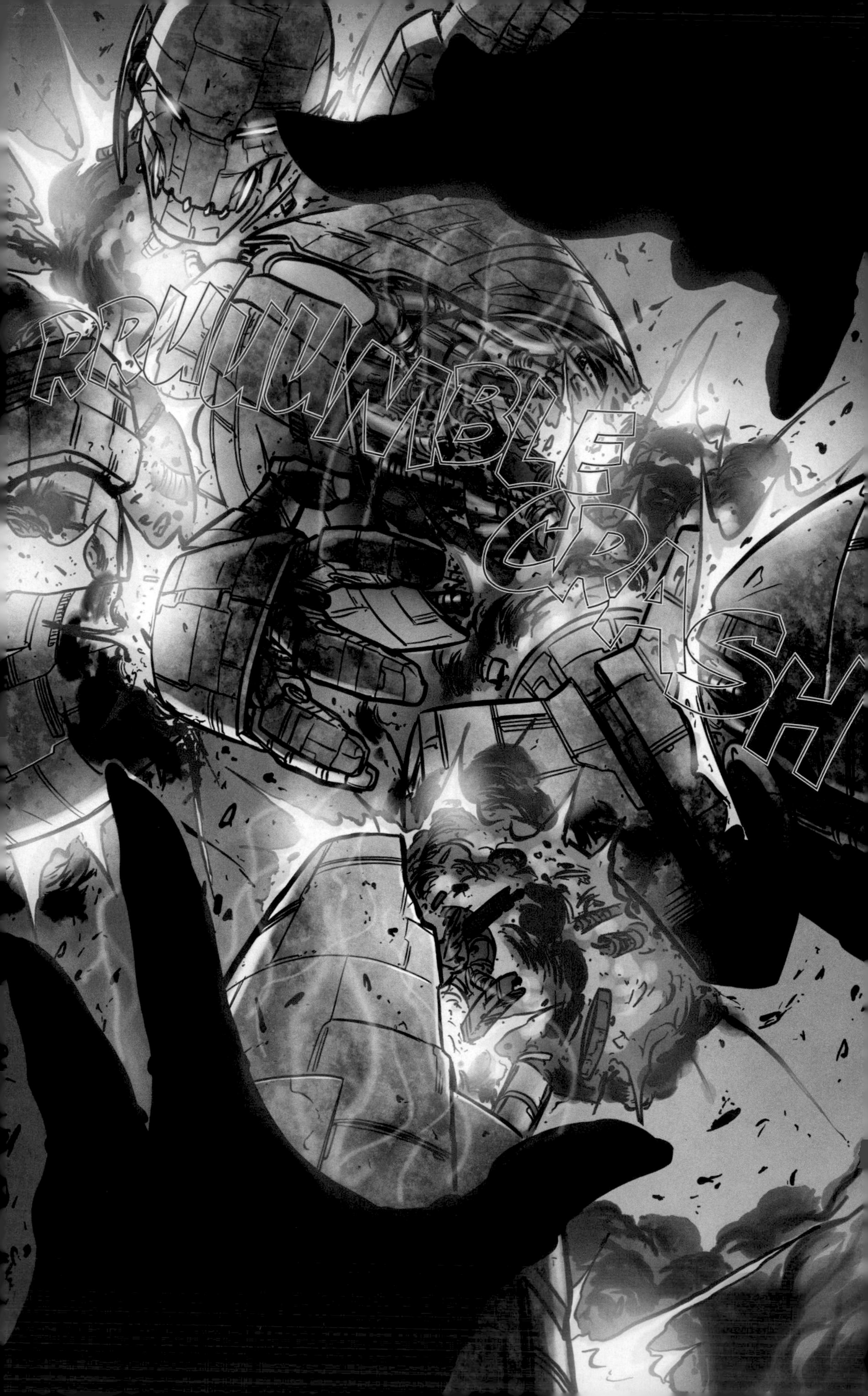
RRUUUMBLE
CRASH

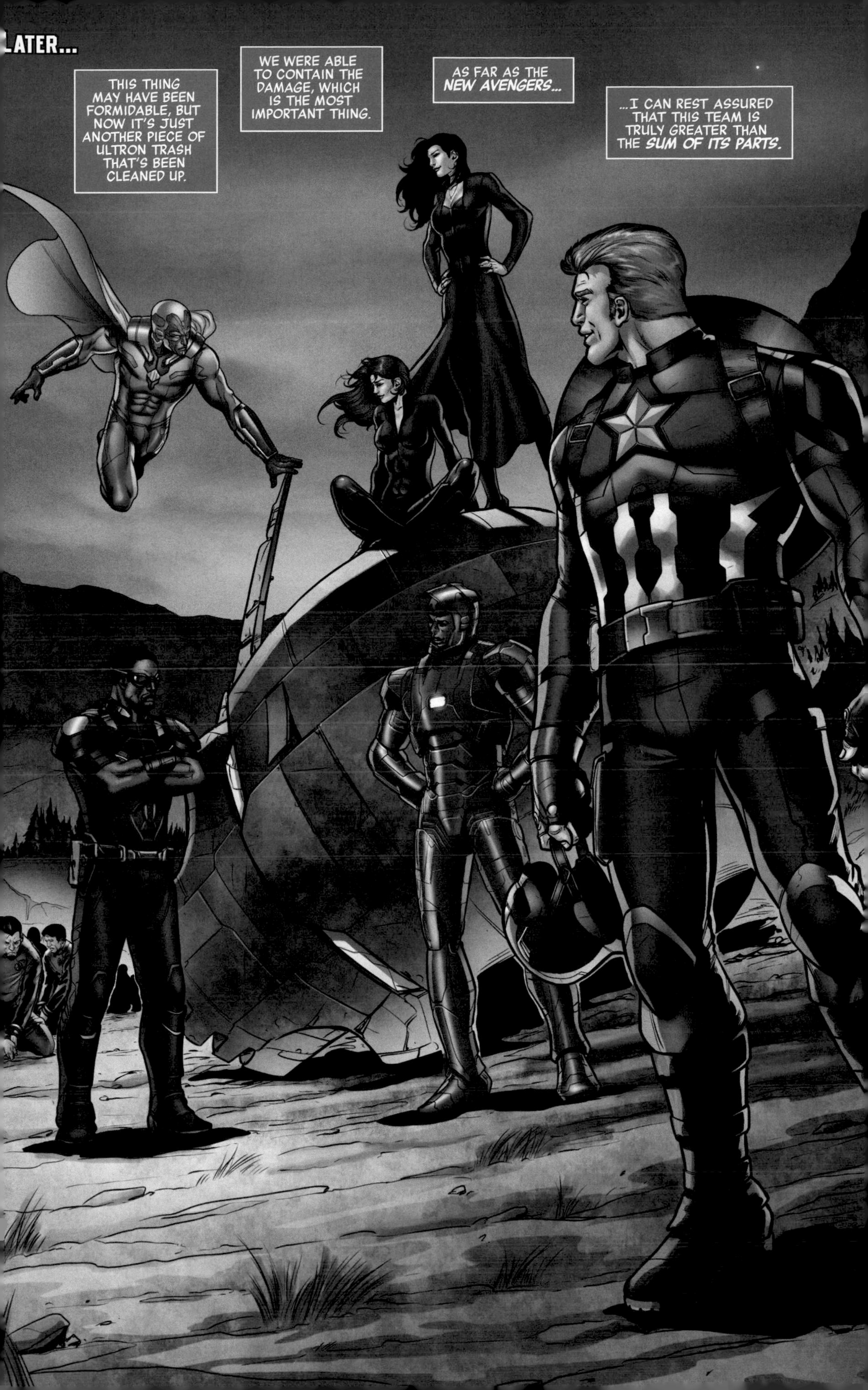
LATER...
THIS THING MAY HAVE BEEN FORMIDABLE, BUT NOW IT'S JUST ANOTHER PIECE OF ULTRON TRASH THAT'S BEEN CLEANED UP.
WE WERE ABLE TO CONTAIN THE DAMAGE, WHICH IS THE MOST IMPORTANT THING.
AS FAR AS THE *NEW AVENGERS*...
...I CAN REST ASSURED THAT THIS TEAM IS TRULY GREATER THAN THE *SUM OF ITS PARTS*.

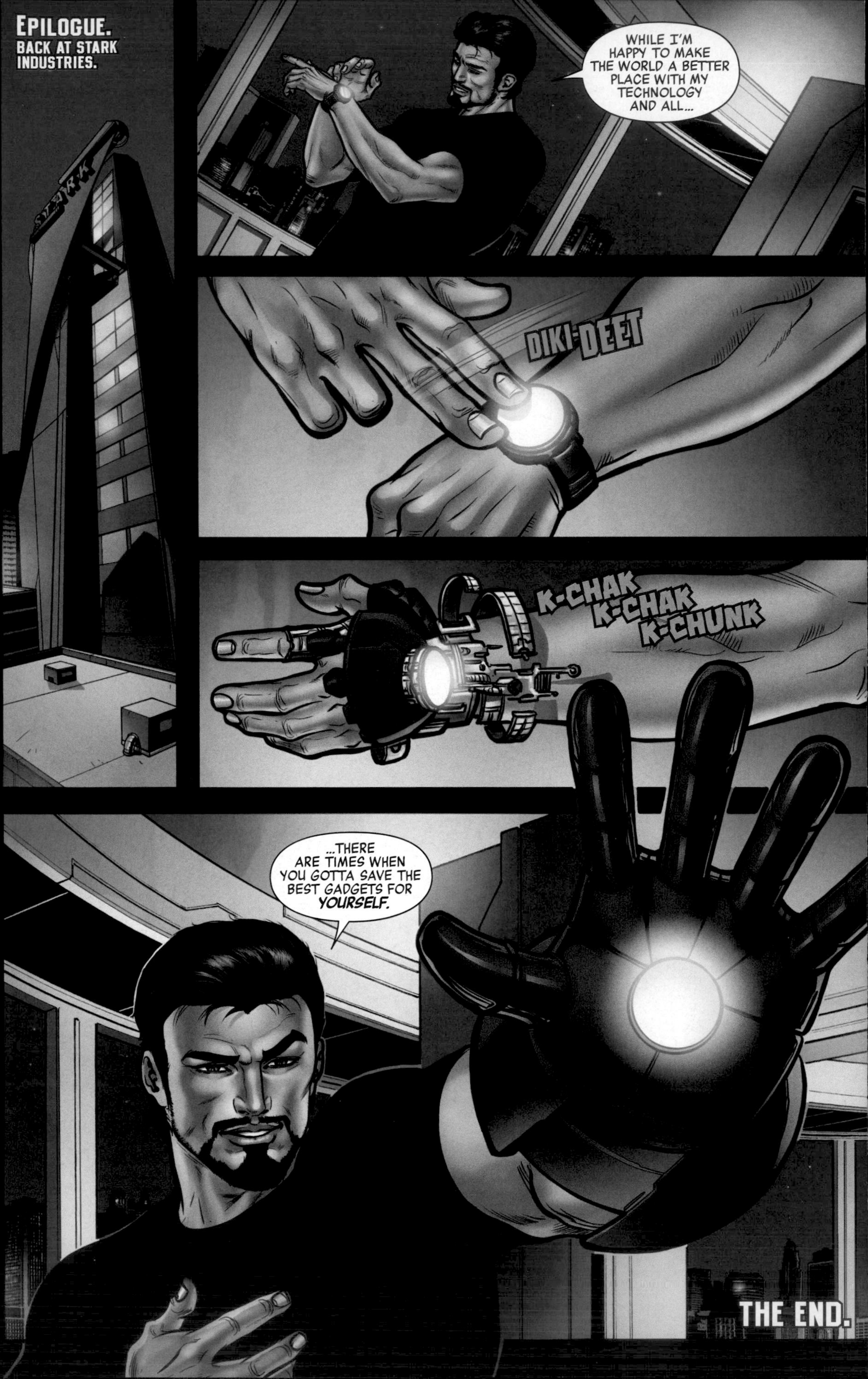
EPILOGUE.
BACK AT STARK INDUSTRIES.
STARK
WHILE I'M HAPPY TO MAKE THE WORLD A BETTER PLACE WITH MY TECHNOLOGY AND ALL...
DIKI-DEET
K-CHAK
K-CHAK
K-CHUNK
...THERE ARE TIMES WHEN YOU GOTTA SAVE THE BEST GADGETS FOR YOURSELF.
THE END.

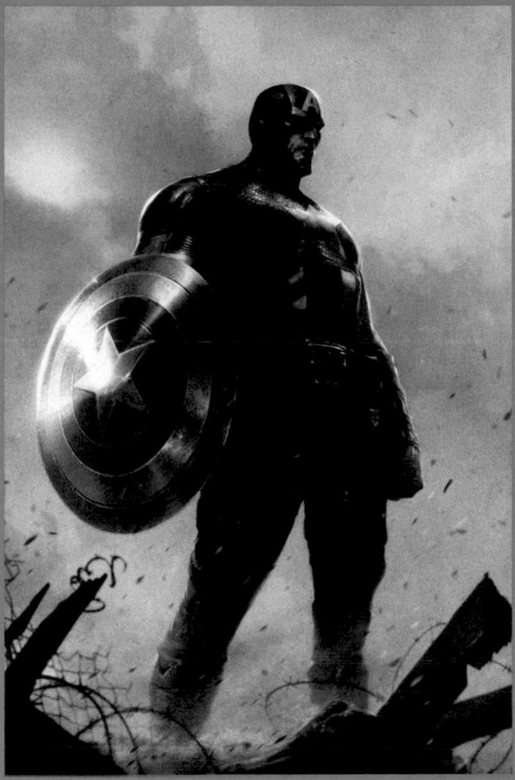

CAPTAIN AMERICA: ROAD TO WAR #1
VARIANT BY **FRANCESCO MATTINA**

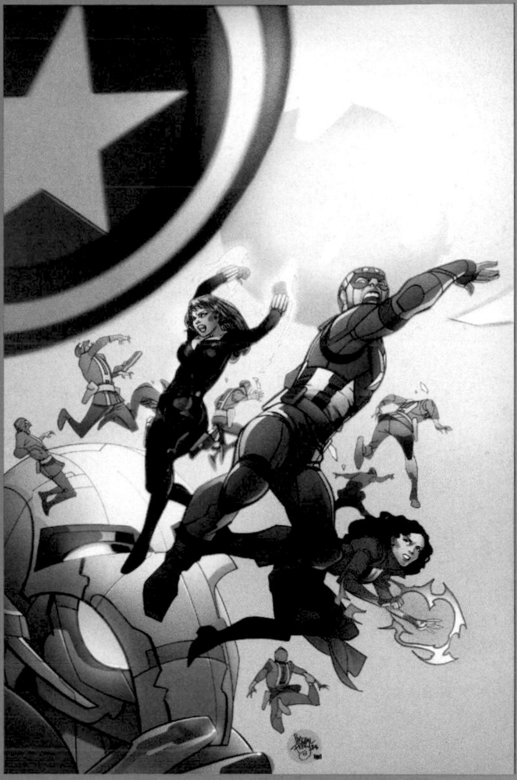

CAPTAIN AMERICA: ROAD TO WAR #1
VARIANT BY **PASQUAL FERRY & FRANK D'ARMATA**

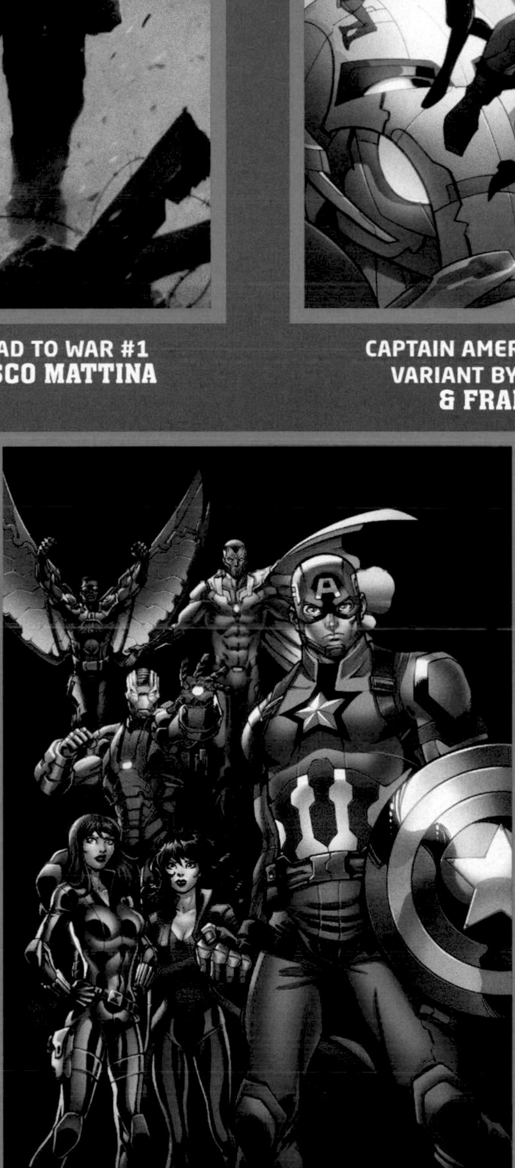

CAPTAIN AMERICA: ROAD TO WAR #1
VARIANT BY **TODD NAUCK & RACHELLE ROSENBERG**

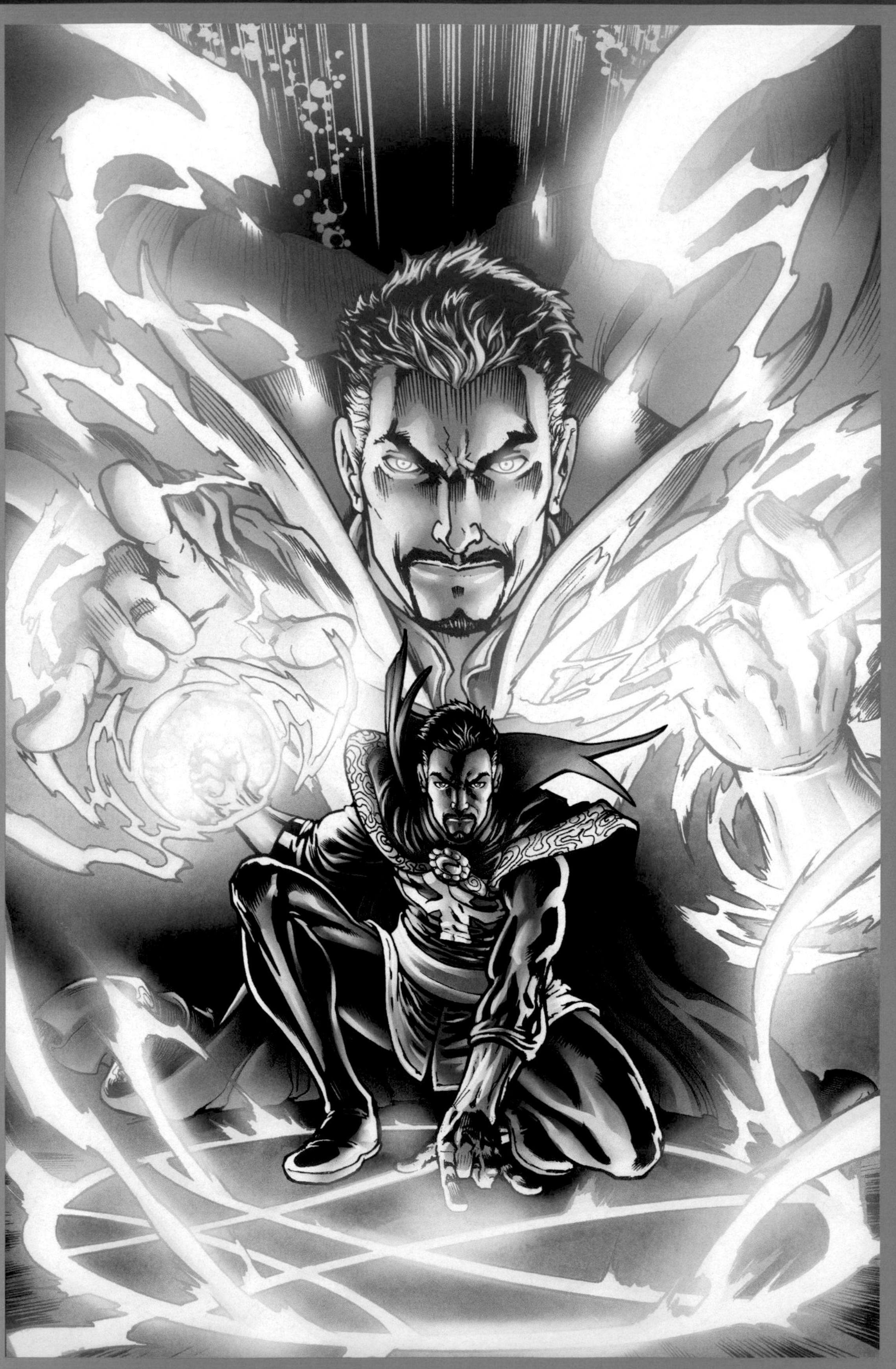

DOCTOR STRANGE: MYSTIC APPRENTICE #1

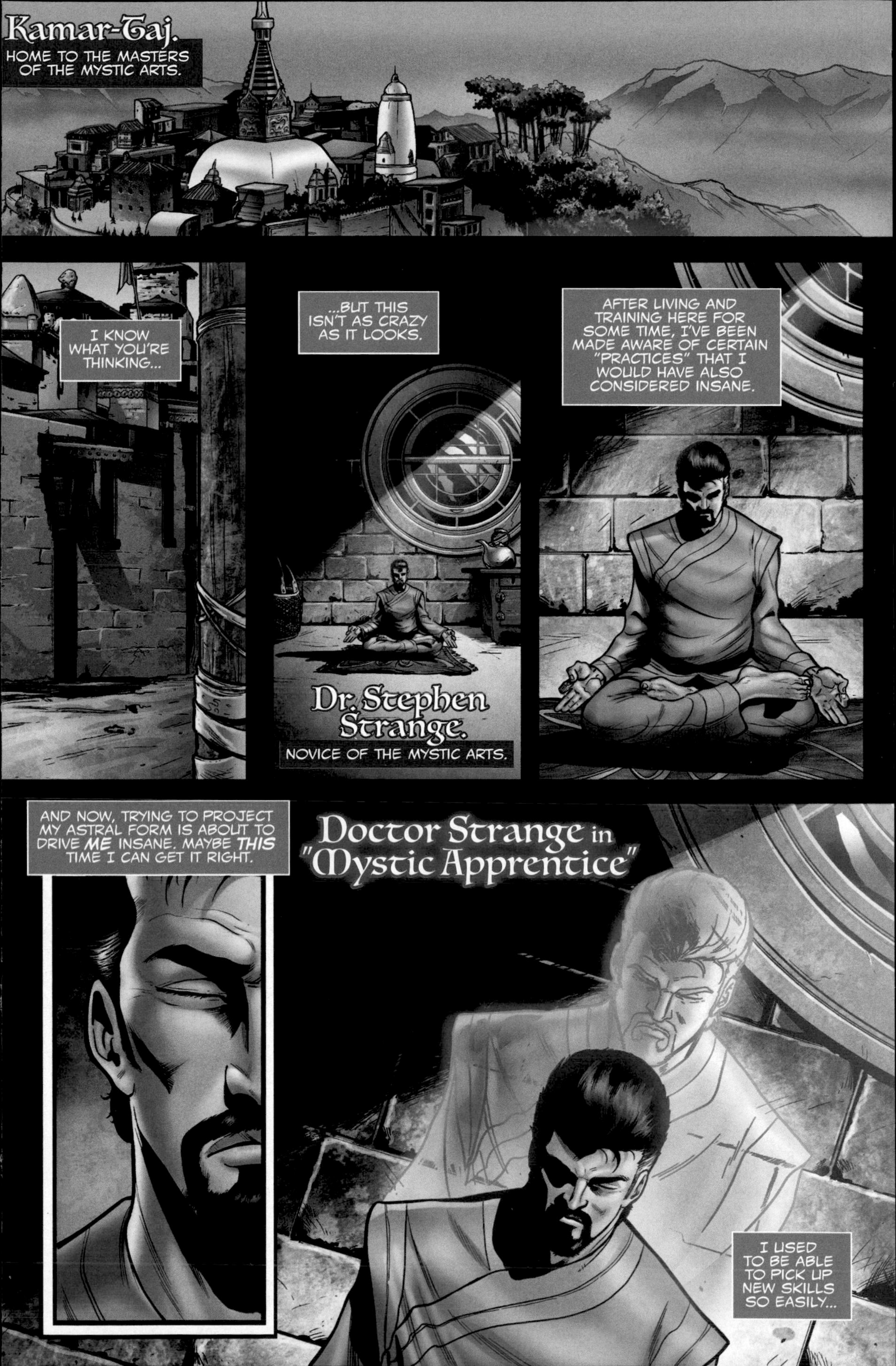
Kamar-Taj.
HOME TO THE MASTERS OF THE MYSTIC ARTS.
I KNOW WHAT YOU'RE THINKING...
...BUT THIS ISN'T AS CRAZY AS IT LOOKS.
Dr. Stephen Strange.
NOVICE OF THE MYSTIC ARTS.
AFTER LIVING AND TRAINING HERE FOR SOME TIME, I'VE BEEN MADE AWARE OF CERTAIN "PRACTICES" THAT I WOULD HAVE ALSO CONSIDERED INSANE.
AND NOW, TRYING TO PROJECT MY ASTRAL FORM IS ABOUT TO DRIVE ME INSANE. MAYBE THIS TIME I CAN GET IT RIGHT.
Doctor Strange in "Mystic Apprentice"
I USED TO BE ABLE TO PICK UP NEW SKILLS SO EASILY...

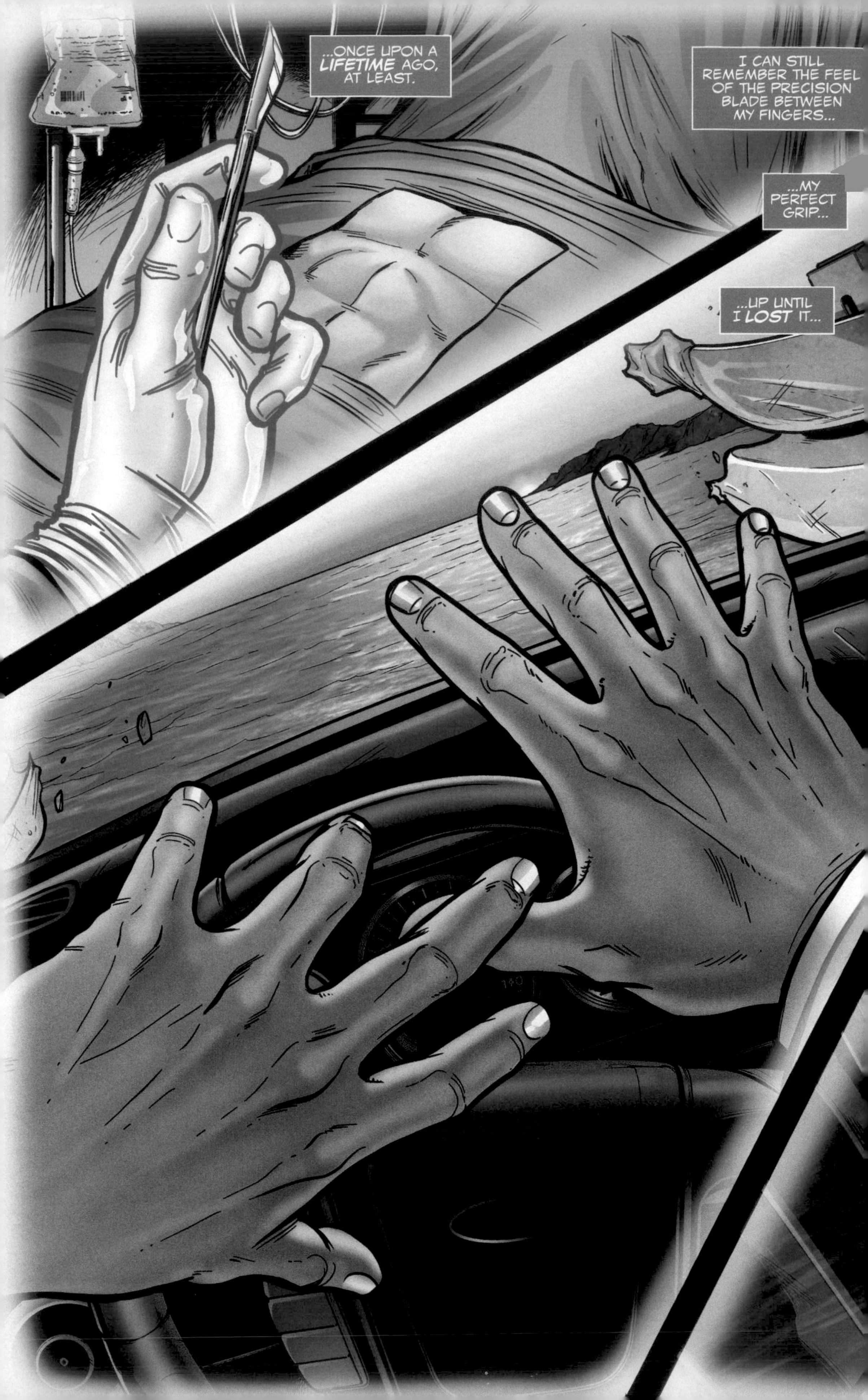
...ONCE UPON A LIFETIME AGO, AT LEAST.
I CAN STILL REMEMBER THE FEEL OF THE PRECISION BLADE BETWEEN MY FINGERS...
...MY PERFECT GRIP...
...UP UNTIL I LOST IT...

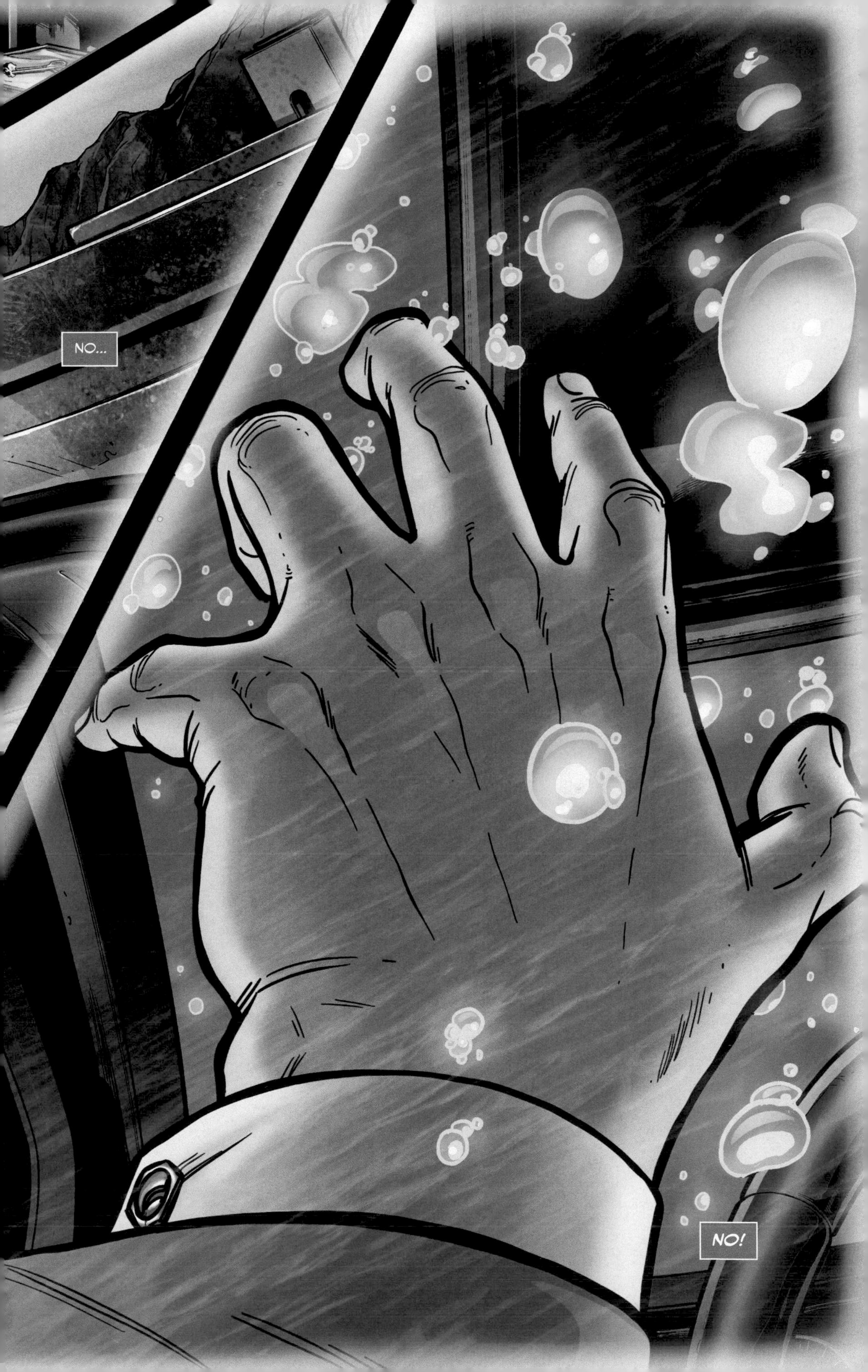
NO...
NO!

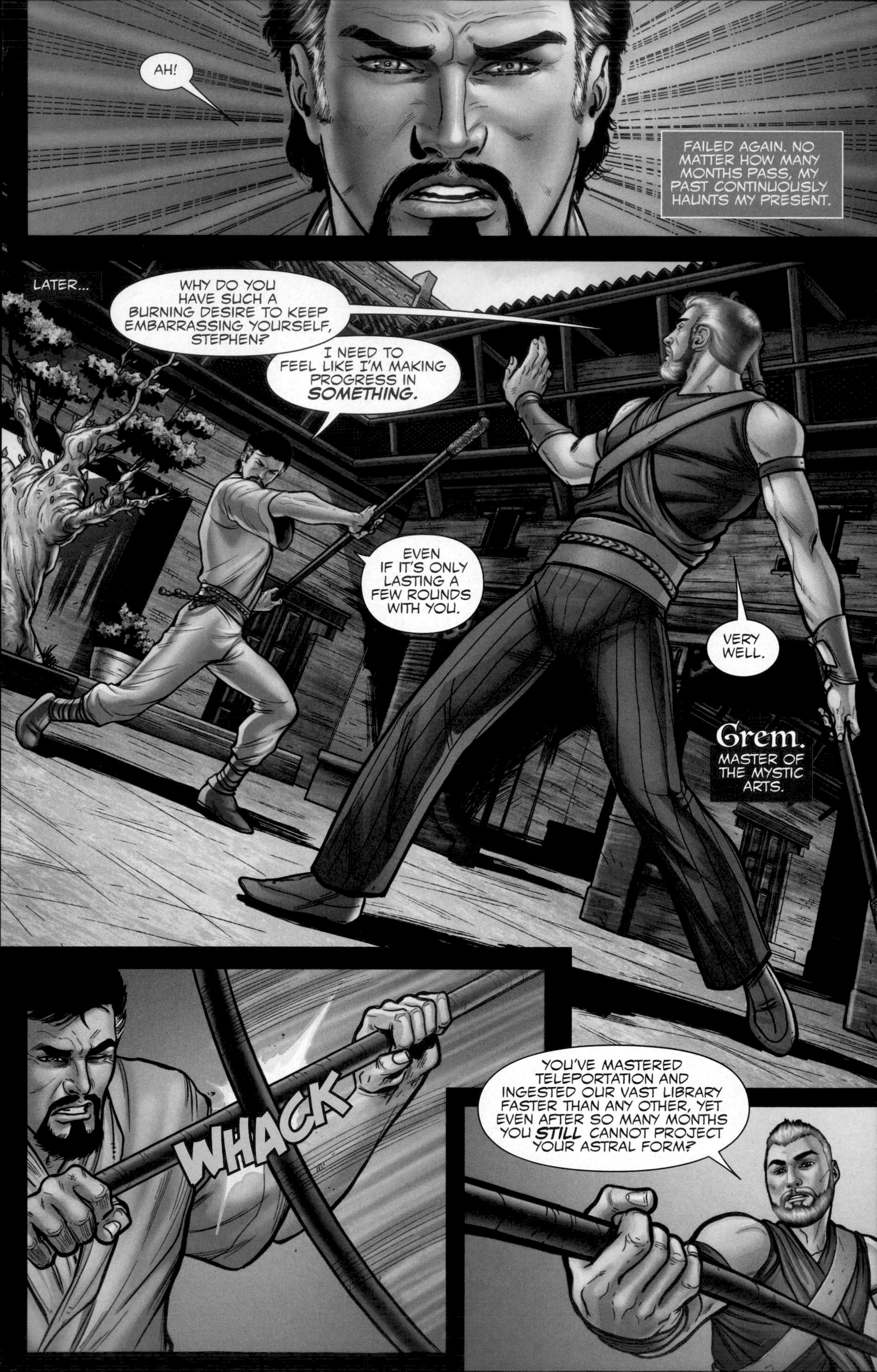
AH!
FAILED AGAIN. NO MATTER HOW MANY MONTHS PASS, MY PAST CONTINUOUSLY HAUNTS MY PRESENT.
LATER...
WHY DO YOU HAVE SUCH A BURNING DESIRE TO KEEP EMBARRASSING YOURSELF, STEPHEN?
I NEED TO FEEL LIKE I'M MAKING PROGRESS IN SOMETHING.
EVEN IF IT'S ONLY LASTING A FEW ROUNDS WITH YOU.
VERY WELL.
Grem.
MASTER OF THE MYSTIC ARTS.
WHACK
YOU'VE MASTERED TELEPORTATION AND INGESTED OUR VAST LIBRARY FASTER THAN ANY OTHER, YET EVEN AFTER SO MANY MONTHS YOU STILL CANNOT PROJECT YOUR ASTRAL FORM?

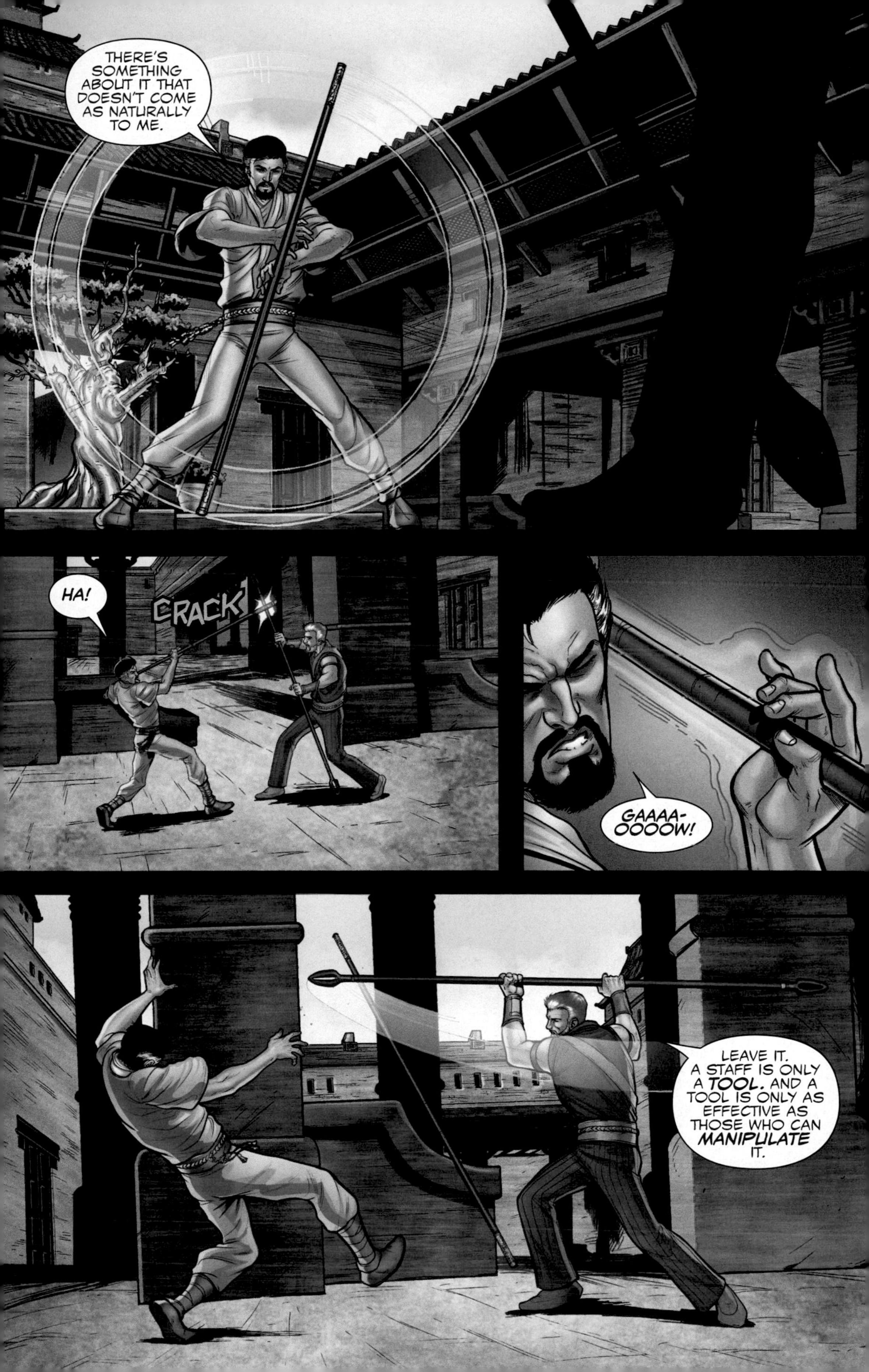
THERE'S SOMETHING ABOUT IT THAT DOESN'T COME AS NATURALLY TO ME.
HA!
CRACK
GAAAA-OOOOW!
LEAVE IT. A STAFF IS ONLY A TOOL. AND A TOOL IS ONLY AS EFFECTIVE AS THOSE WHO CAN MANIPULATE IT.

IF YOU RELY ON IT TOO HEAVILY--YOU FORGET ITS ORIGINAL PURPOSE, TAKE IT FOR GRANTED--AND THAT TOOL WILL *FAIL* YOU.

AS YOUR REAR END CAN ATTEST.

SO, ALL I GOT OUT OF THAT IS YOU THINK I'M A *TOOL.*

YOUR *MIND* IS THE TOOL. YOU NEED ONLY LET IT DO ITS WORK FOR YOU TO SUCCEED.

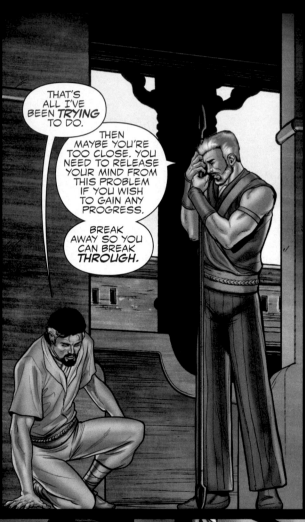

THAT'S ALL I'VE BEEN *TRYING* TO DO.

THEN MAYBE YOU'RE TOO CLOSE. YOU NEED TO RELEASE YOUR MIND FROM THIS PROBLEM IF YOU WISH TO GAIN ANY PROGRESS.

BREAK AWAY SO YOU CAN BREAK *THROUGH.*

EASY FOR YOU TO SAY.

THANKS FOR THE SPARRING LESSON.

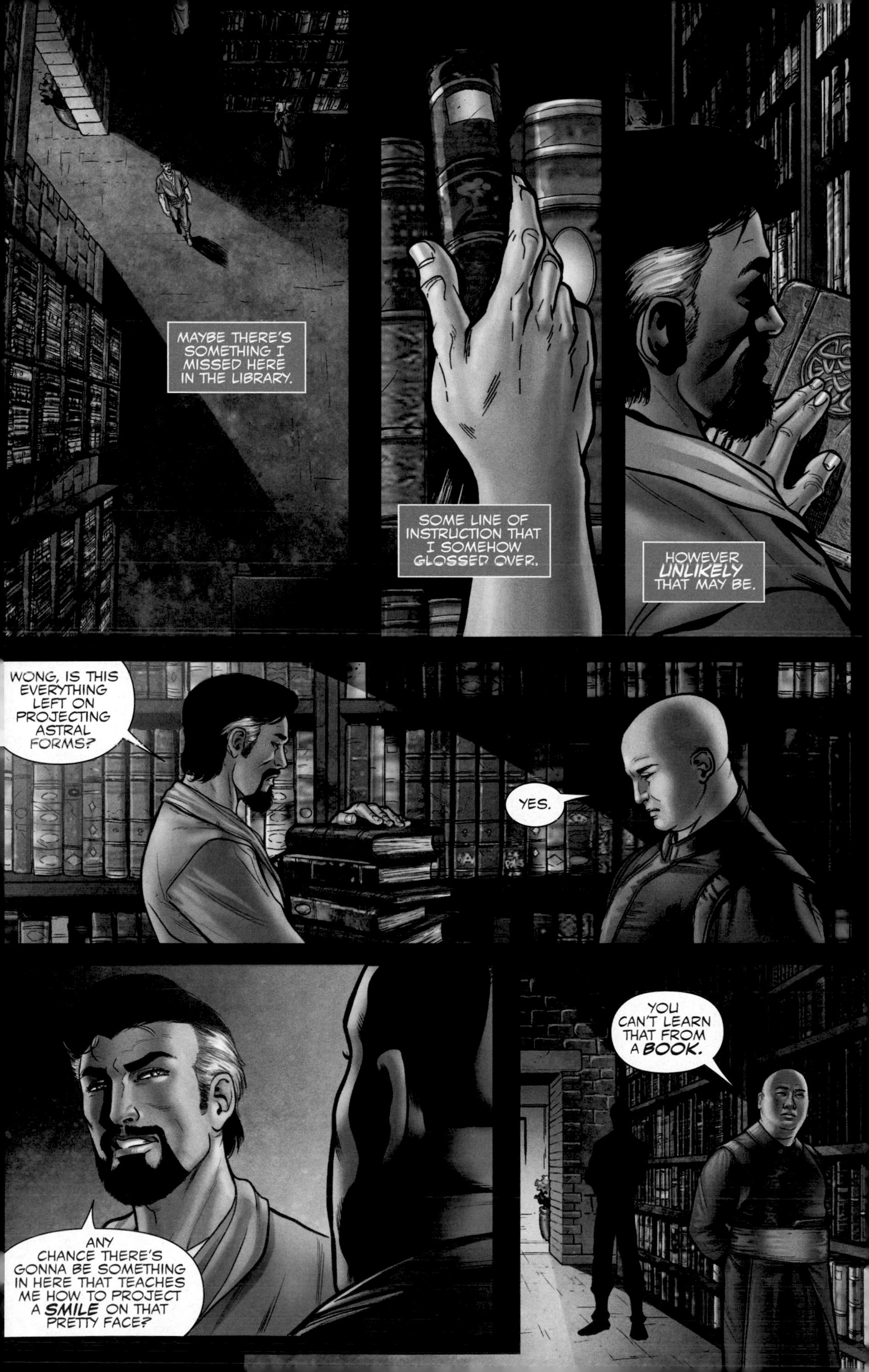
MAYBE THERE'S SOMETHING I MISSED HERE IN THE LIBRARY.
SOME LINE OF INSTRUCTION THAT I SOMEHOW GLOSSED OVER.
HOWEVER UNLIKELY THAT MAY BE.
WONG, IS THIS EVERYTHING LEFT ON PROJECTING ASTRAL FORMS?
YES.
ANY CHANCE THERE'S GONNA BE SOMETHING IN HERE THAT TEACHES ME HOW TO PROJECT A SMILE ON THAT PRETTY FACE?
YOU CAN'T LEARN THAT FROM A BOOK.

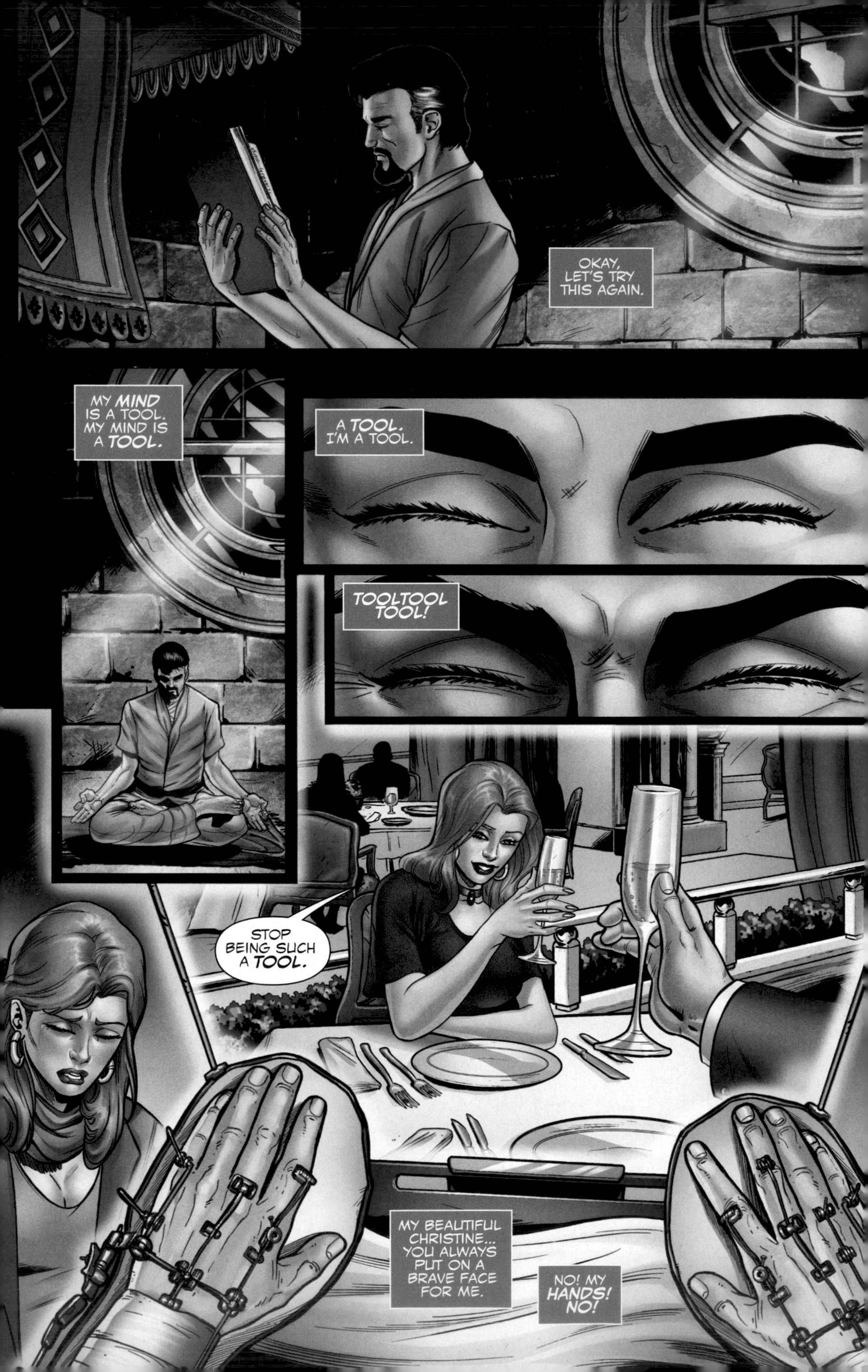
OKAY, LET'S TRY THIS AGAIN.
MY MIND IS A TOOL. MY MIND IS A TOOL.
A TOOL. I'M A TOOL.
TOOLTOOL TOOL!
STOP BEING SUCH A TOOL.
MY BEAUTIFUL CHRISTINE... YOU ALWAYS PUT ON A BRAVE FACE FOR ME.
NO! MY HANDS! NO!

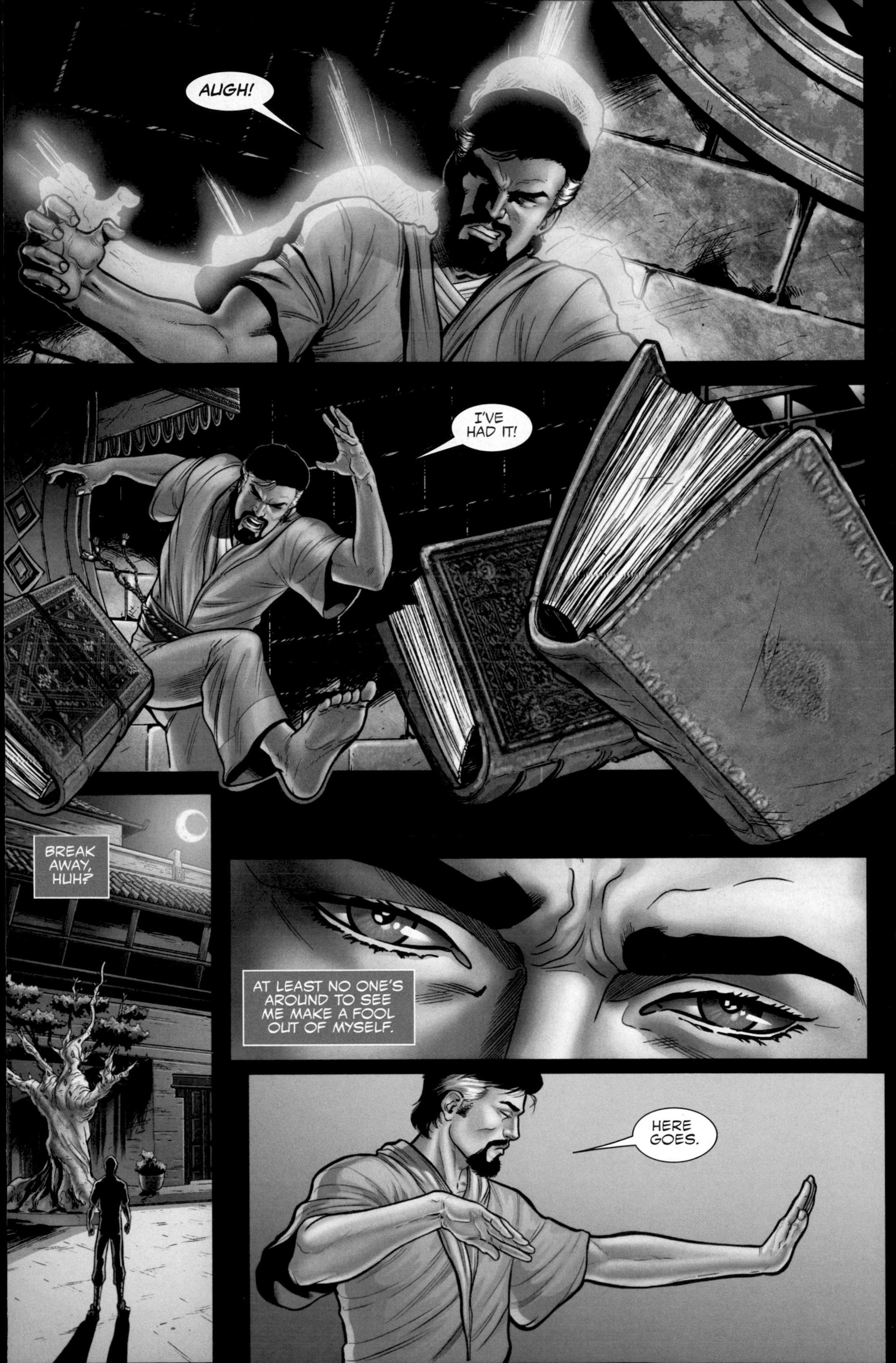
AUGH!
I'VE HAD IT!
BREAK AWAY, HUH?
AT LEAST NO ONE'S AROUND TO SEE ME MAKE A FOOL OUT OF MYSELF.
HERE GOES.

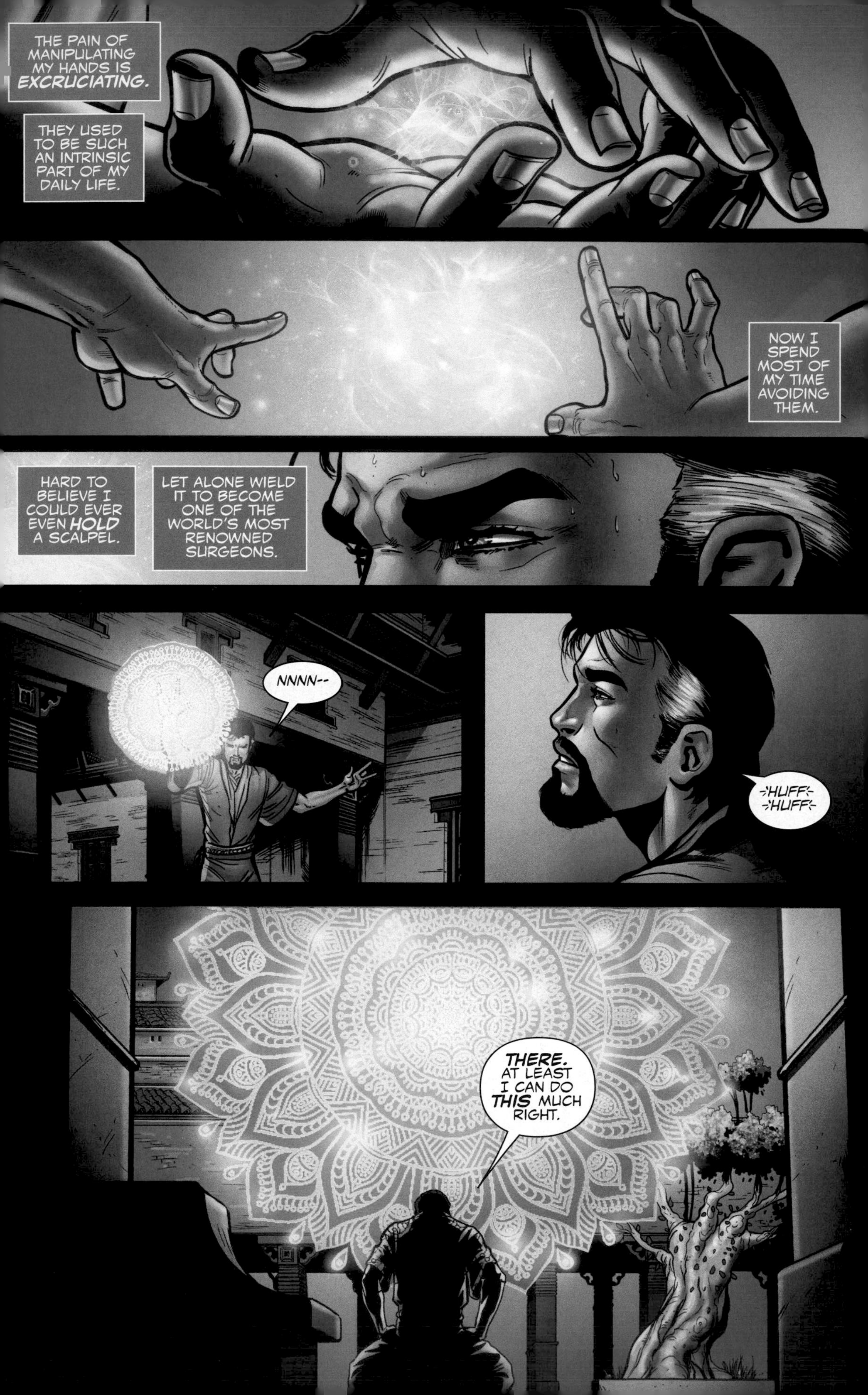
THE PAIN OF MANIPULATING MY HANDS IS EXCRUCIATING.
THEY USED TO BE SUCH AN INTRINSIC PART OF MY DAILY LIFE.
NOW I SPEND MOST OF MY TIME AVOIDING THEM.
HARD TO BELIEVE I COULD EVER EVEN HOLD A SCALPEL.
LET ALONE WIELD IT TO BECOME ONE OF THE WORLD'S MOST RENOWNED SURGEONS.
NNNN--
HUFF HUFF
THERE. AT LEAST I CAN DO THIS MUCH RIGHT.

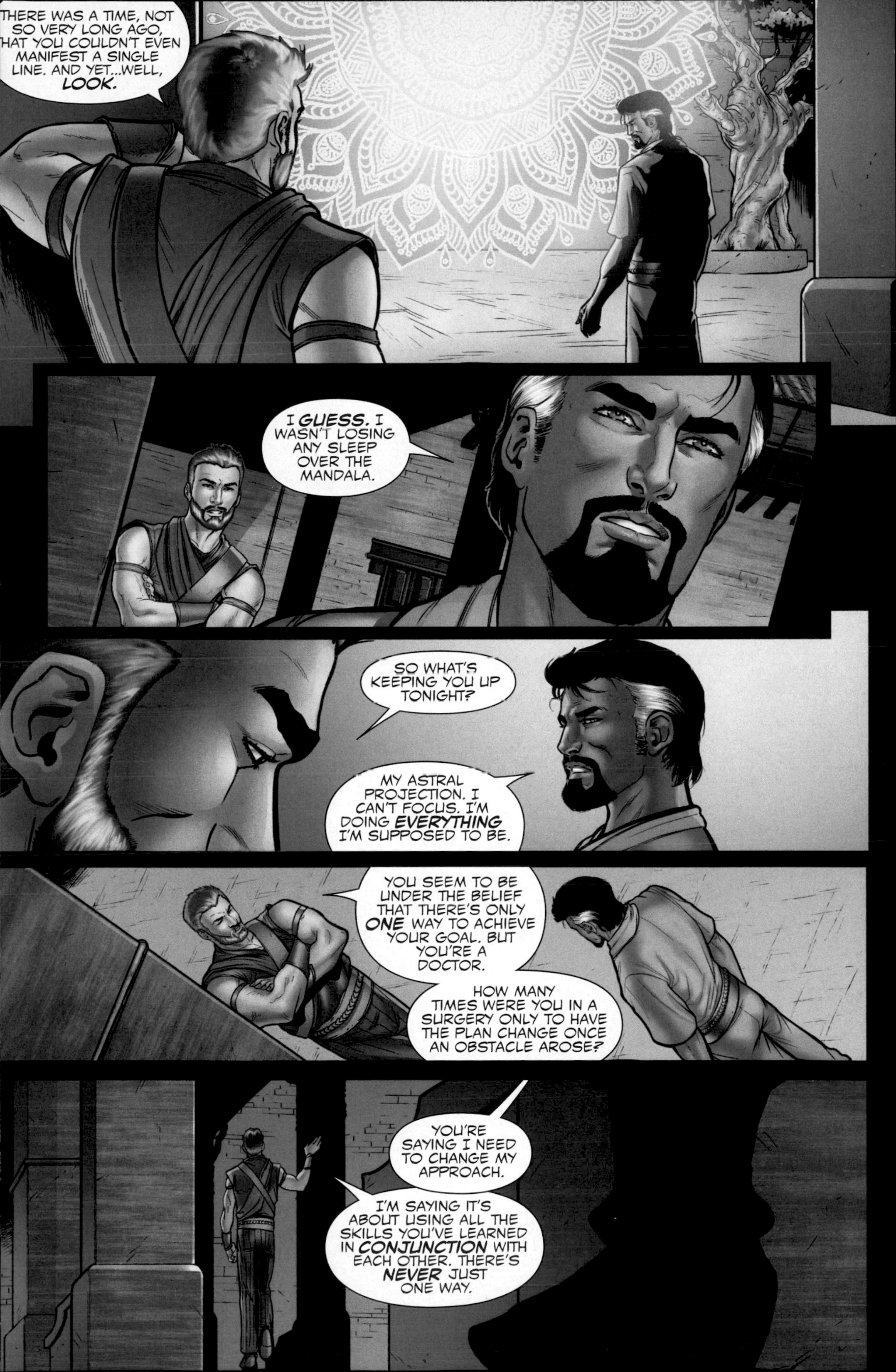
THERE WAS A TIME, NOT SO VERY LONG AGO, THAT YOU COULDN'T EVEN MANIFEST A SINGLE LINE. AND YET...WELL, LOOK.
I GUESS. I WASN'T LOSING ANY SLEEP OVER THE MANDALA.
SO WHAT'S KEEPING YOU UP TONIGHT?
MY ASTRAL PROJECTION. I CAN'T FOCUS. I'M DOING EVERYTHING I'M SUPPOSED TO BE.
YOU SEEM TO BE UNDER THE BELIEF THAT THERE'S ONLY ONE WAY TO ACHIEVE YOUR GOAL. BUT YOU'RE A DOCTOR.
HOW MANY TIMES WERE YOU IN A SURGERY ONLY TO HAVE THE PLAN CHANGE ONCE AN OBSTACLE AROSE?
YOU'RE SAYING I NEED TO CHANGE MY APPROACH.
I'M SAYING IT'S ABOUT USING ALL THE SKILLS YOU'VE LEARNED IN CONJUNCTION WITH EACH OTHER. THERE'S NEVER JUST ONE WAY.

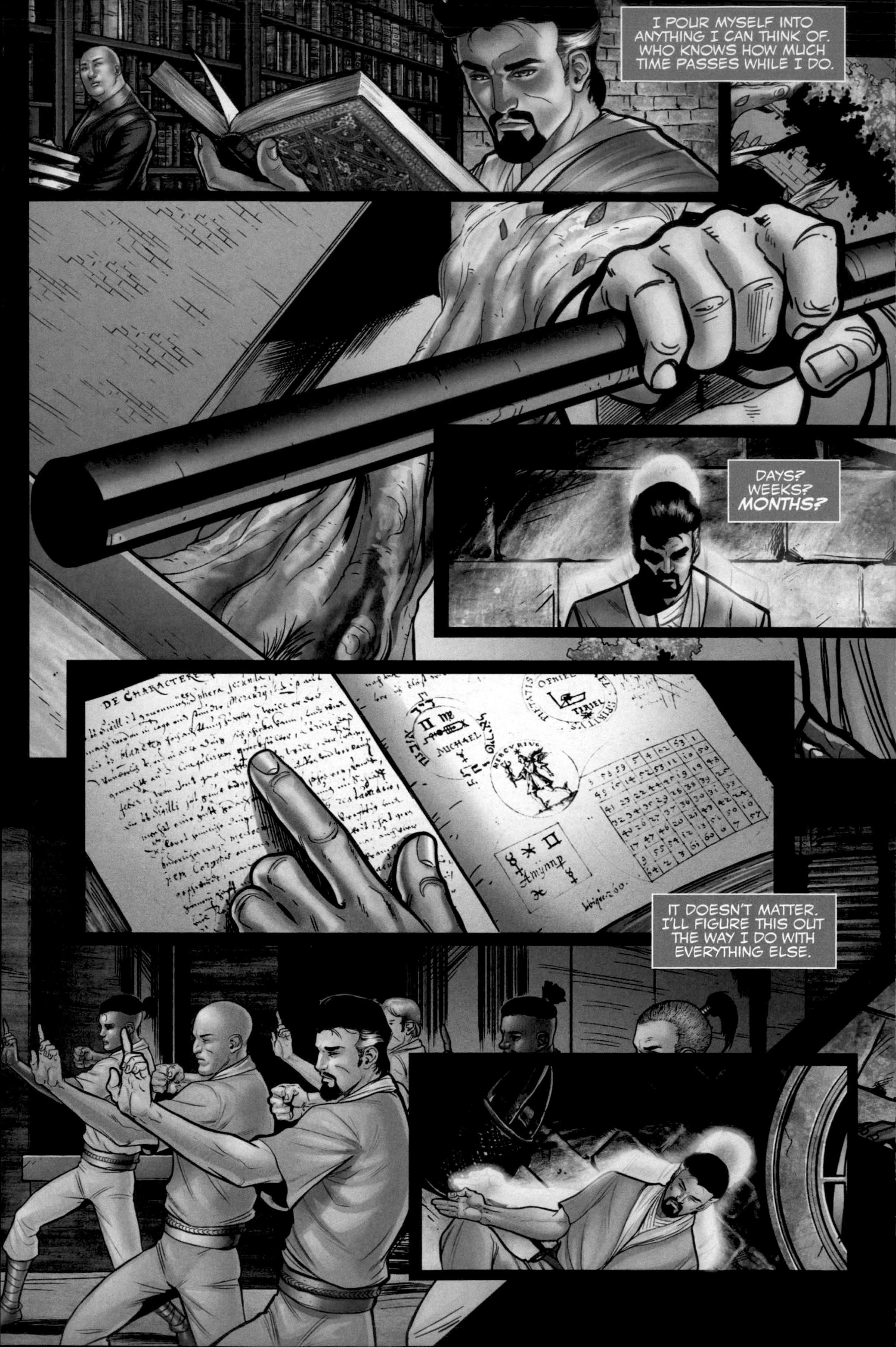
I POUR MYSELF INTO ANYTHING I CAN THINK OF. WHO KNOWS HOW MUCH TIME PASSES WHILE I DO.
DAYS? WEEKS? *MONTHS?*
IT DOESN'T MATTER. I'LL FIGURE THIS OUT THE WAY I DO WITH EVERYTHING ELSE.

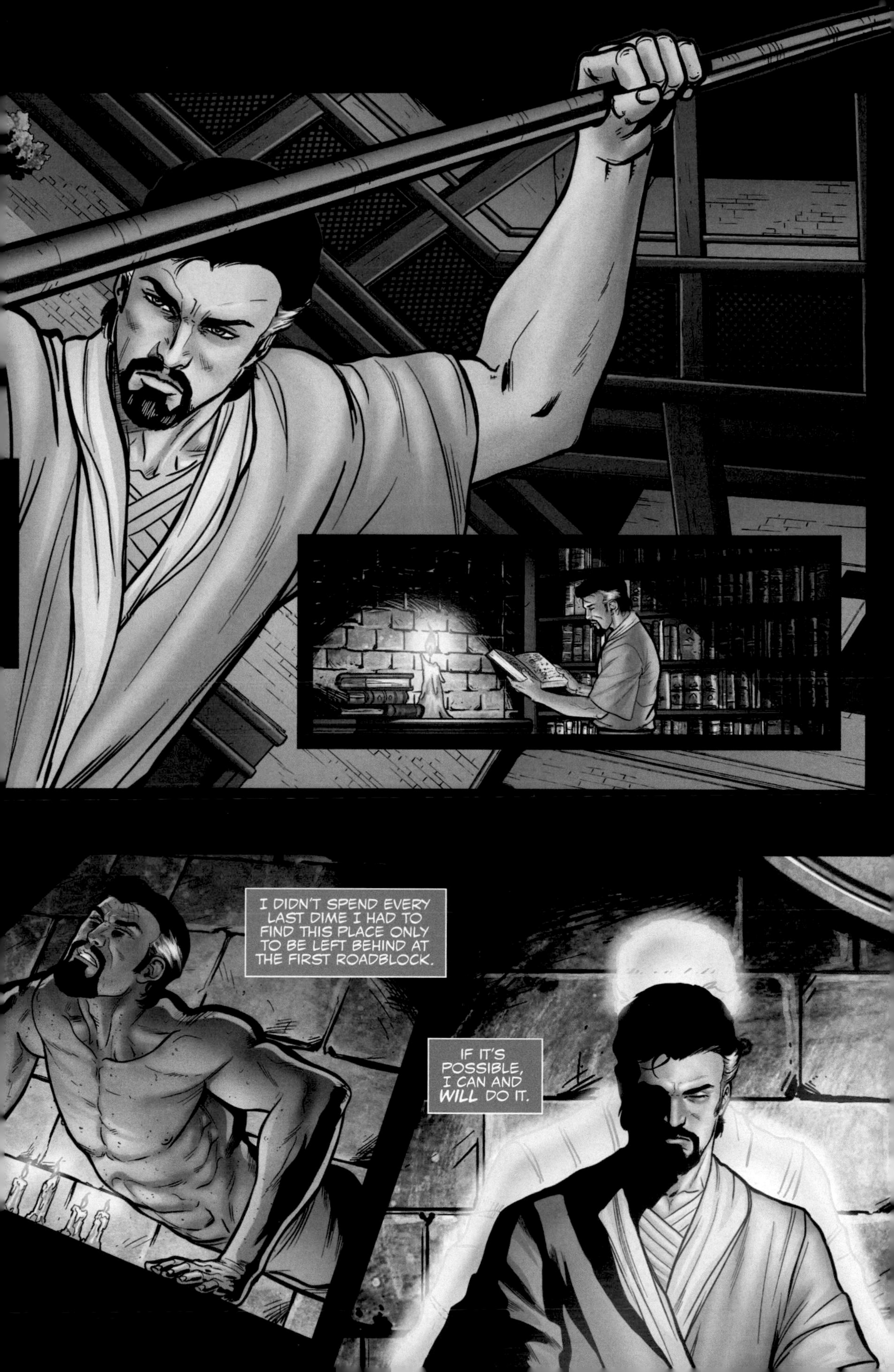
I DIDN'T SPEND EVERY LAST DIME I HAD TO FIND THIS PLACE ONLY TO BE LEFT BEHIND AT THE FIRST ROADBLOCK.
IF IT'S POSSIBLE, I CAN AND *WILL* DO IT.

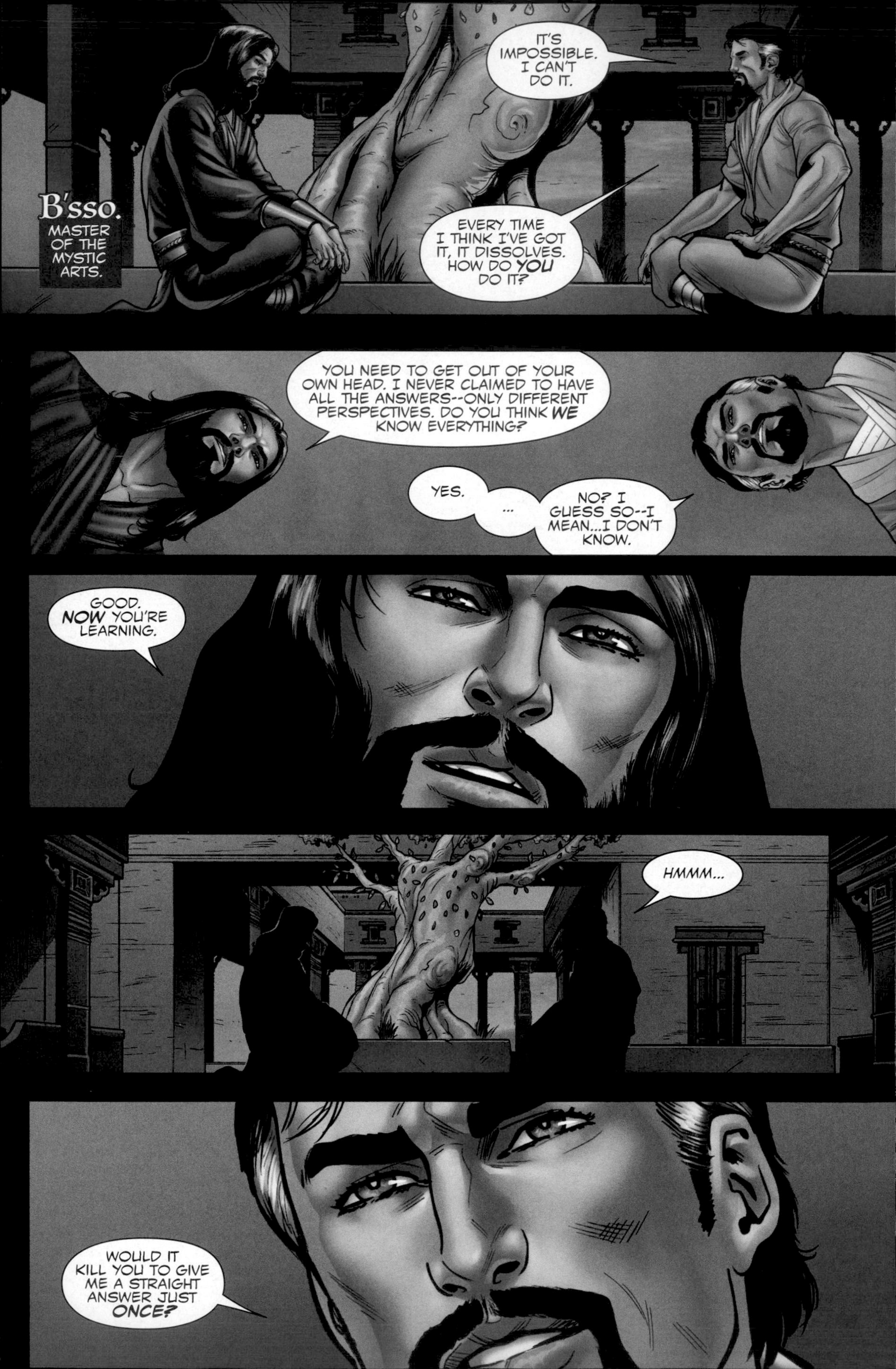
B'sso.
MASTER OF THE MYSTIC ARTS.
IT'S IMPOSSIBLE. I CAN'T DO IT.
EVERY TIME I THINK I'VE GOT IT, IT DISSOLVES. HOW DO YOU DO IT?
YOU NEED TO GET OUT OF YOUR OWN HEAD. I NEVER CLAIMED TO HAVE ALL THE ANSWERS--ONLY DIFFERENT PERSPECTIVES. DO YOU THINK WE KNOW EVERYTHING?
YES.
...
NO? I GUESS SO--I MEAN...I DON'T KNOW.
GOOD. NOW YOU'RE LEARNING.
HMMM...
WOULD IT KILL YOU TO GIVE ME A STRAIGHT ANSWER JUST ONCE?

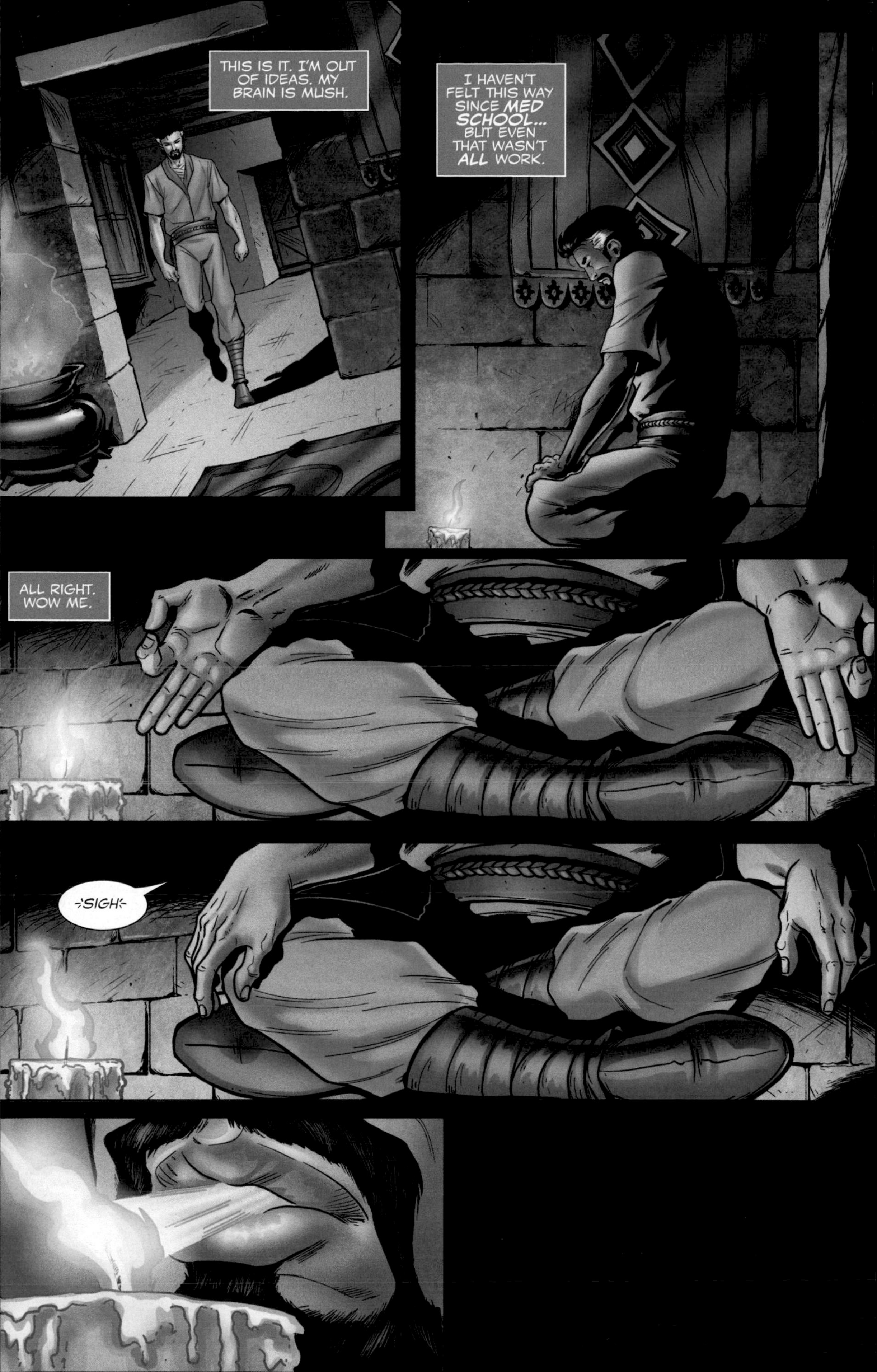
THIS IS IT. I'M OUT OF IDEAS. MY BRAIN IS MUSH.
I HAVEN'T FELT THIS WAY SINCE MED SCHOOL... BUT EVEN THAT WASN'T ALL WORK.
ALL RIGHT. WOW ME.
-SIGH-

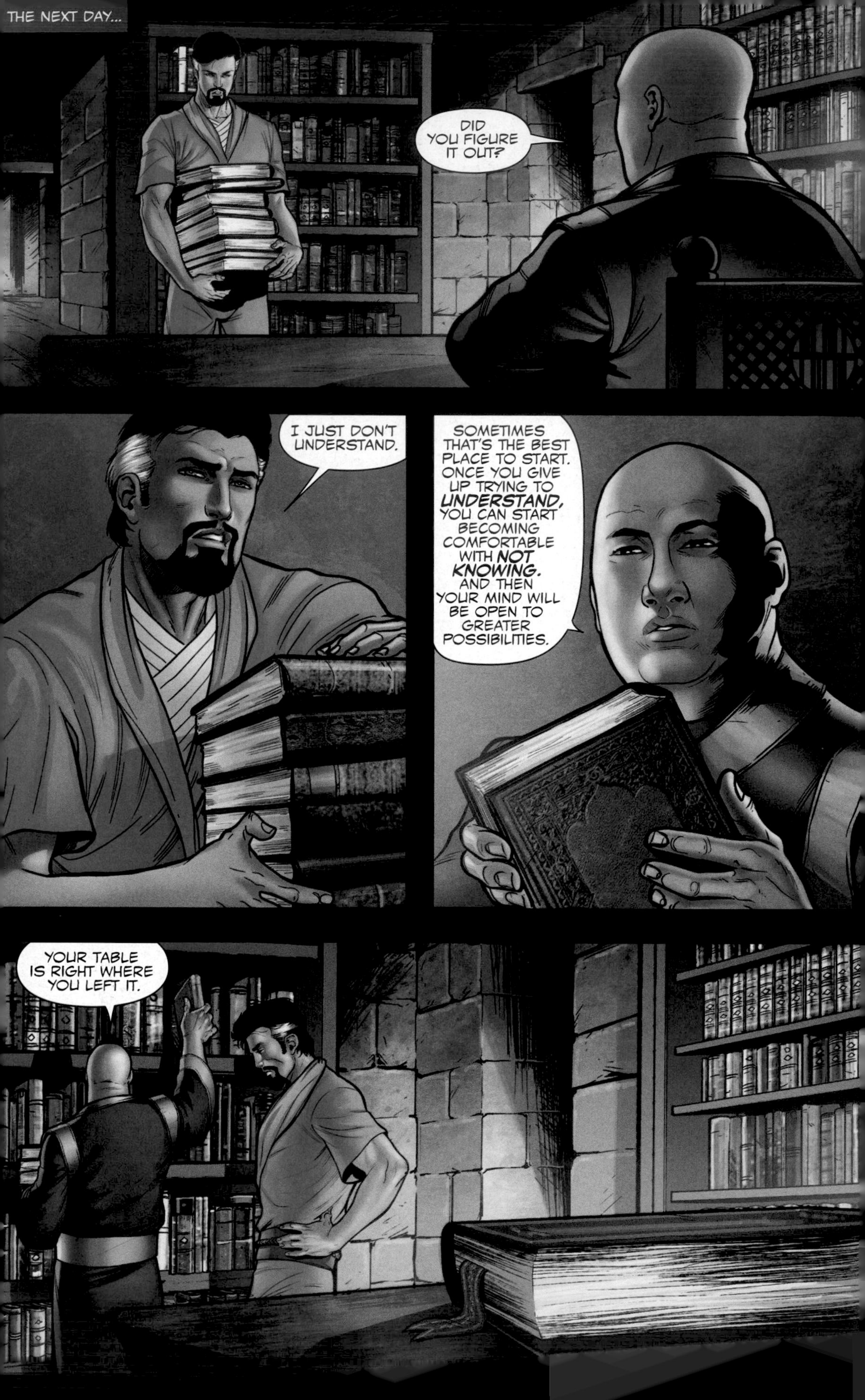
THE NEXT DAY...
DID YOU FIGURE IT OUT?
I JUST DON'T UNDERSTAND.
SOMETIMES THAT'S THE BEST PLACE TO START. ONCE YOU GIVE UP TRYING TO UNDERSTAND, YOU CAN START BECOMING COMFORTABLE WITH NOT KNOWING. AND THEN YOUR MIND WILL BE OPEN TO GREATER POSSIBILITIES.
YOUR TABLE IS RIGHT WHERE YOU LEFT IT.

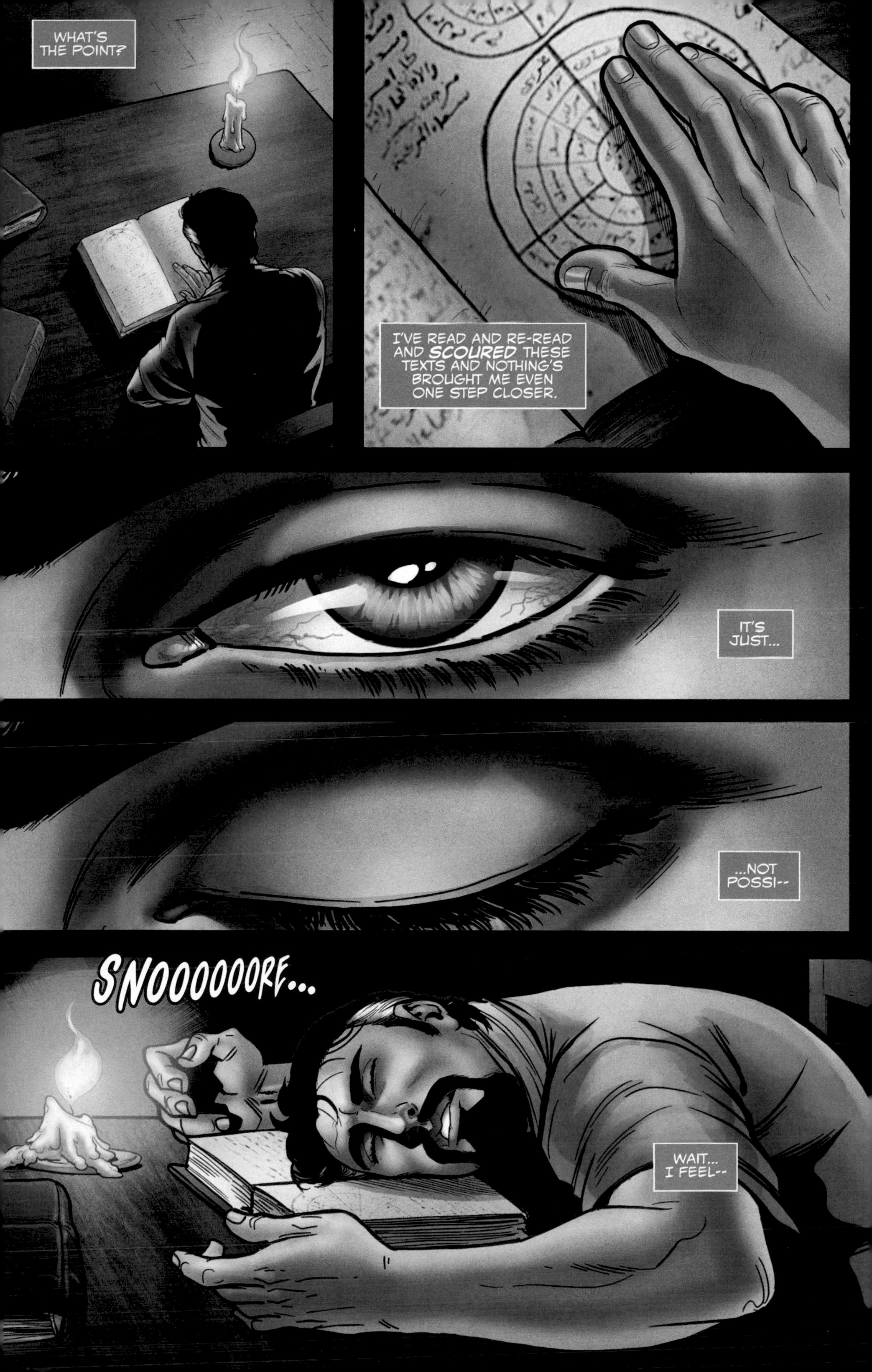
WHAT'S THE POINT?
I'VE READ AND RE-READ AND SCOURED THESE TEXTS AND NOTHING'S BROUGHT ME EVEN ONE STEP CLOSER.
IT'S JUST...
...NOT POSSI--
SNOOOOOORE...
WAIT... I FEEL--

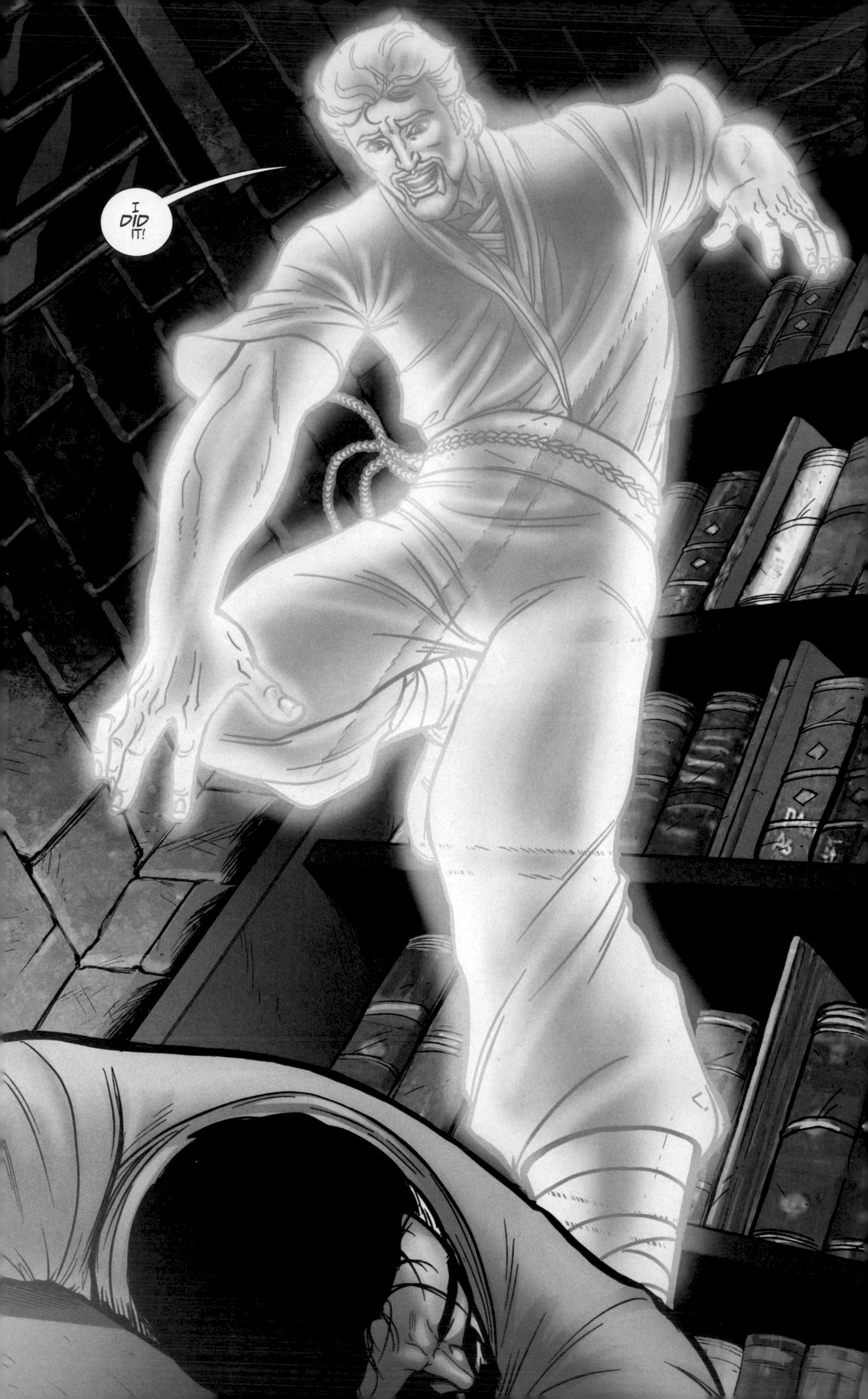
I DID IT!

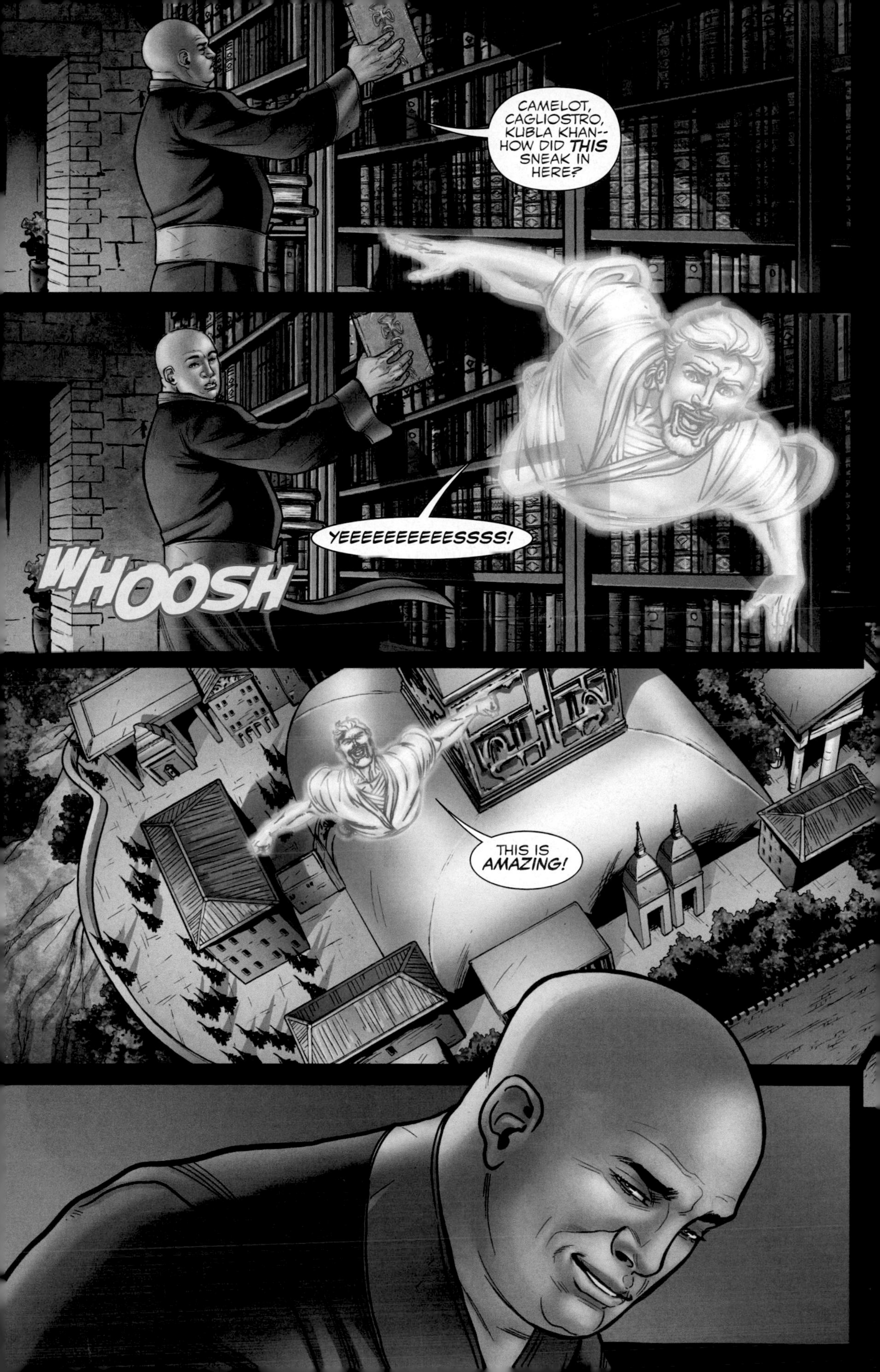
CAMELOT, CAGLIOSTRO, KUBLA KHAN-- HOW DID THIS SNEAK IN HERE?
YEEEEEEEEEEESSSS!
WHOOSH
THIS IS AMAZING!

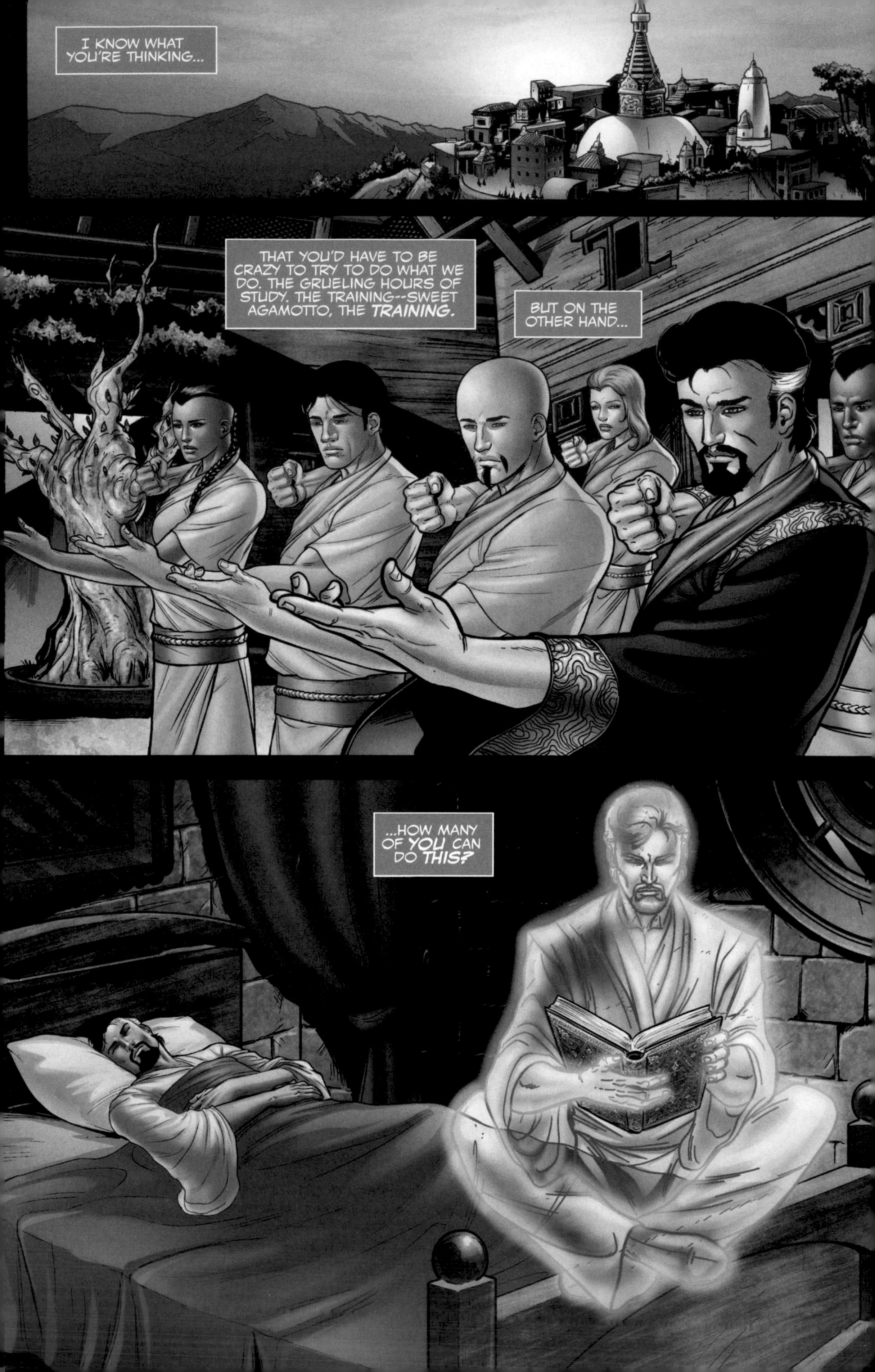
I KNOW WHAT YOU'RE THINKING...
THAT YOU'D HAVE TO BE CRAZY TO TRY TO DO WHAT WE DO. THE GRUELING HOURS OF STUDY. THE TRAINING--SWEET AGAMOTTO, THE TRAINING.
BUT ON THE OTHER HAND...
...HOW MANY OF YOU CAN DO THIS?

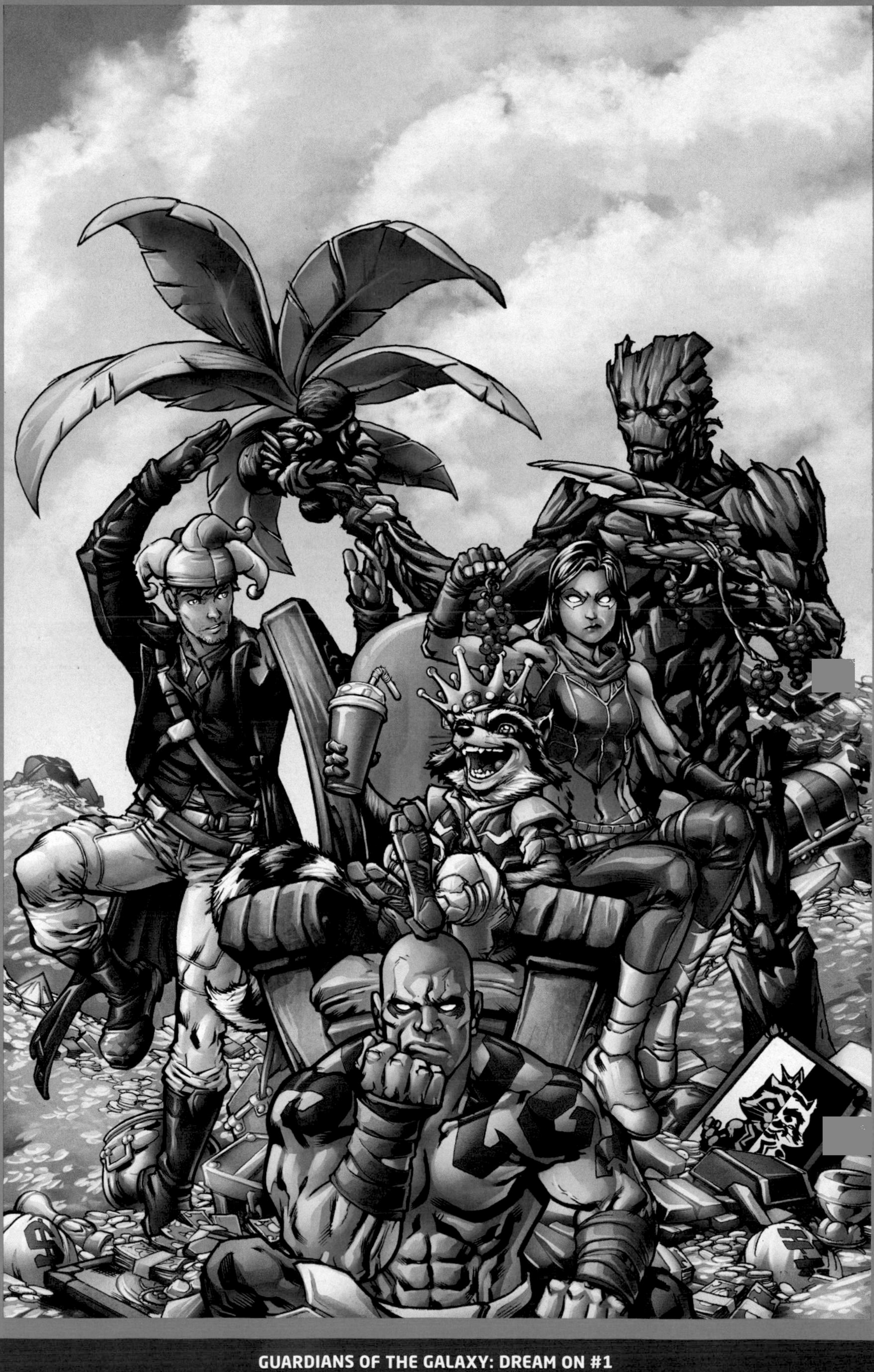

GUARDIANS OF THE GALAXY: DREAM ON #1

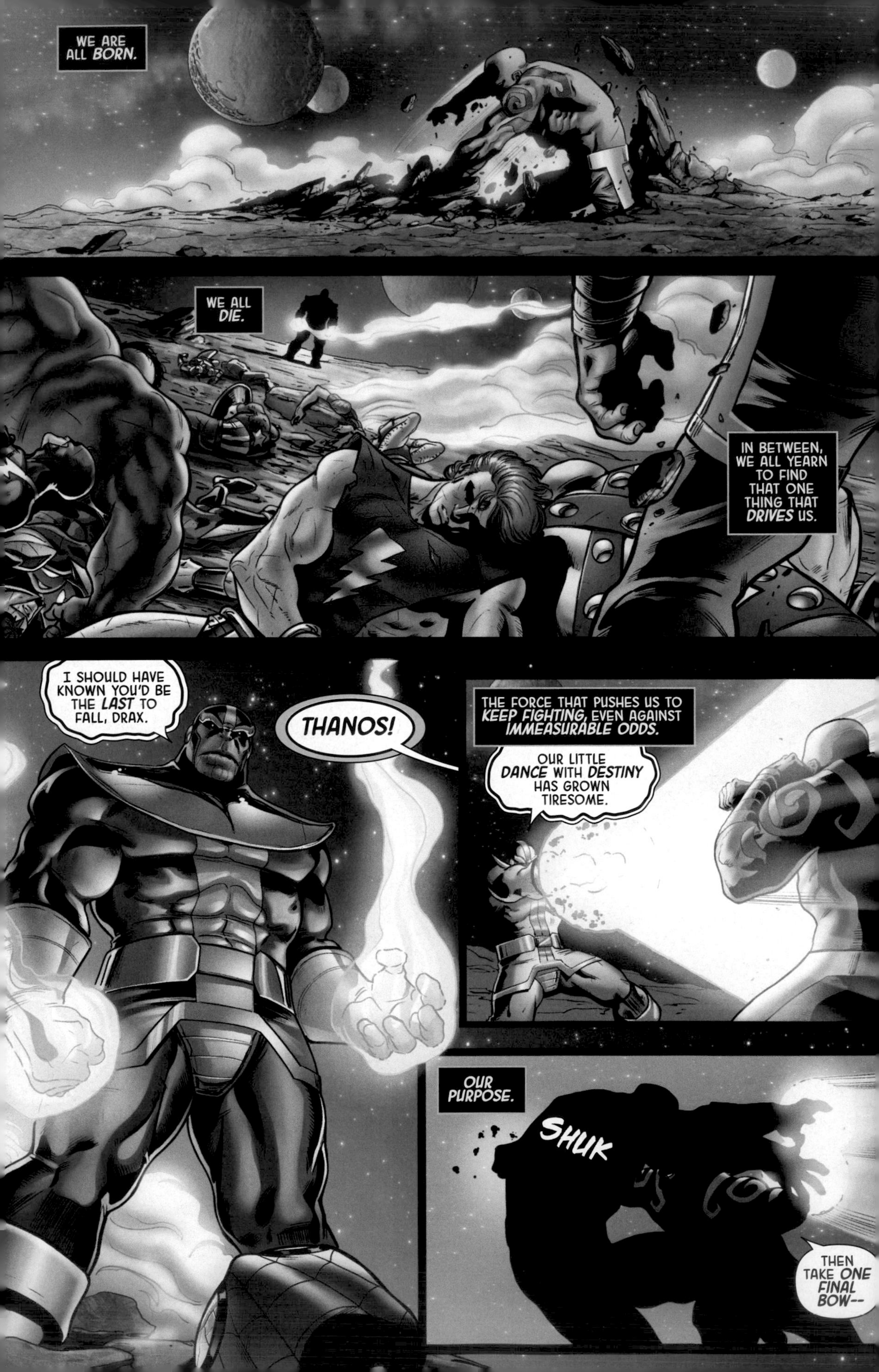
WE ARE ALL BORN.
WE ALL DIE.
IN BETWEEN, WE ALL YEARN TO FIND THAT ONE THING THAT DRIVES US.
I SHOULD HAVE KNOWN YOU'D BE THE LAST TO FALL, DRAX.
THANOS!
THE FORCE THAT PUSHES US TO KEEP FIGHTING, EVEN AGAINST IMMEASURABLE ODDS.
OUR LITTLE DANCE WITH DESTINY HAS GROWN TIRESOME.
OUR PURPOSE.
SHUK
THEN TAKE ONE FINAL BOW--

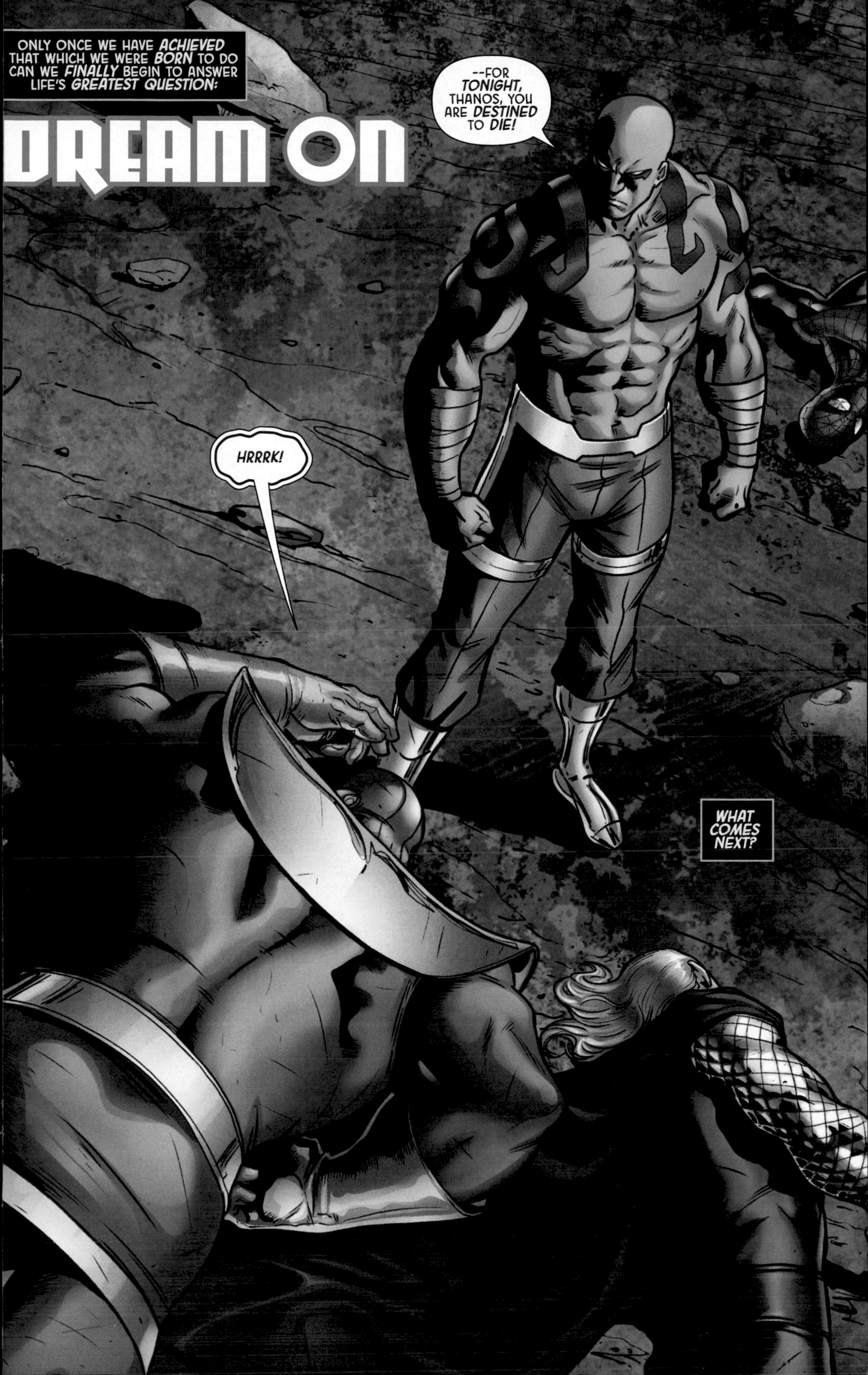
ONLY ONCE WE HAVE ACHIEVED THAT WHICH WE WERE BORN TO DO CAN WE FINALLY BEGIN TO ANSWER LIFE'S GREATEST QUESTION:
DREAM ON
--FOR TONIGHT, THANOS, YOU ARE DESTINED TO DIE!
HRRRK!
WHAT COMES NEXT?

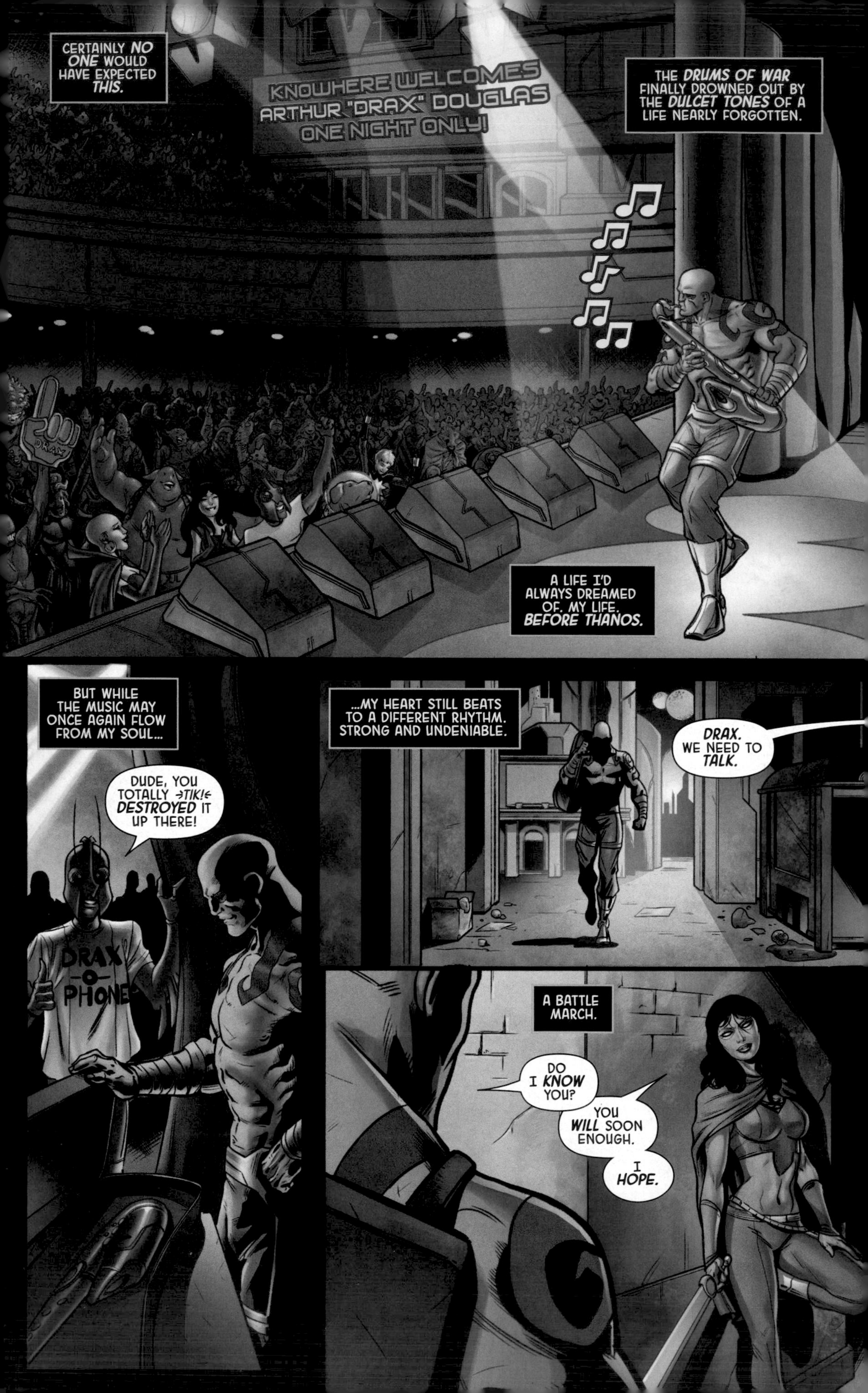

CERTAINLY NO ONE WOULD HAVE EXPECTED THIS.
KNOWHERE WELCOMES ARTHUR "DRAX" DOUGLAS ONE NIGHT ONLY!
THE DRUMS OF WAR FINALLY DROWNED OUT BY THE DULCET TONES OF A LIFE NEARLY FORGOTTEN.
DRAX
A LIFE I'D ALWAYS DREAMED OF. MY LIFE. BEFORE THANOS.
BUT WHILE THE MUSIC MAY ONCE AGAIN FLOW FROM MY SOUL...
DUDE, YOU TOTALLY →TIK!← DESTROYED IT UP THERE!
DRAX -O- PHONE
...MY HEART STILL BEATS TO A DIFFERENT RHYTHM. STRONG AND UNDENIABLE.
DRAX. WE NEED TO TALK.
A BATTLE MARCH.
DO I KNOW YOU?
YOU WILL SOON ENOUGH.
I HOPE.

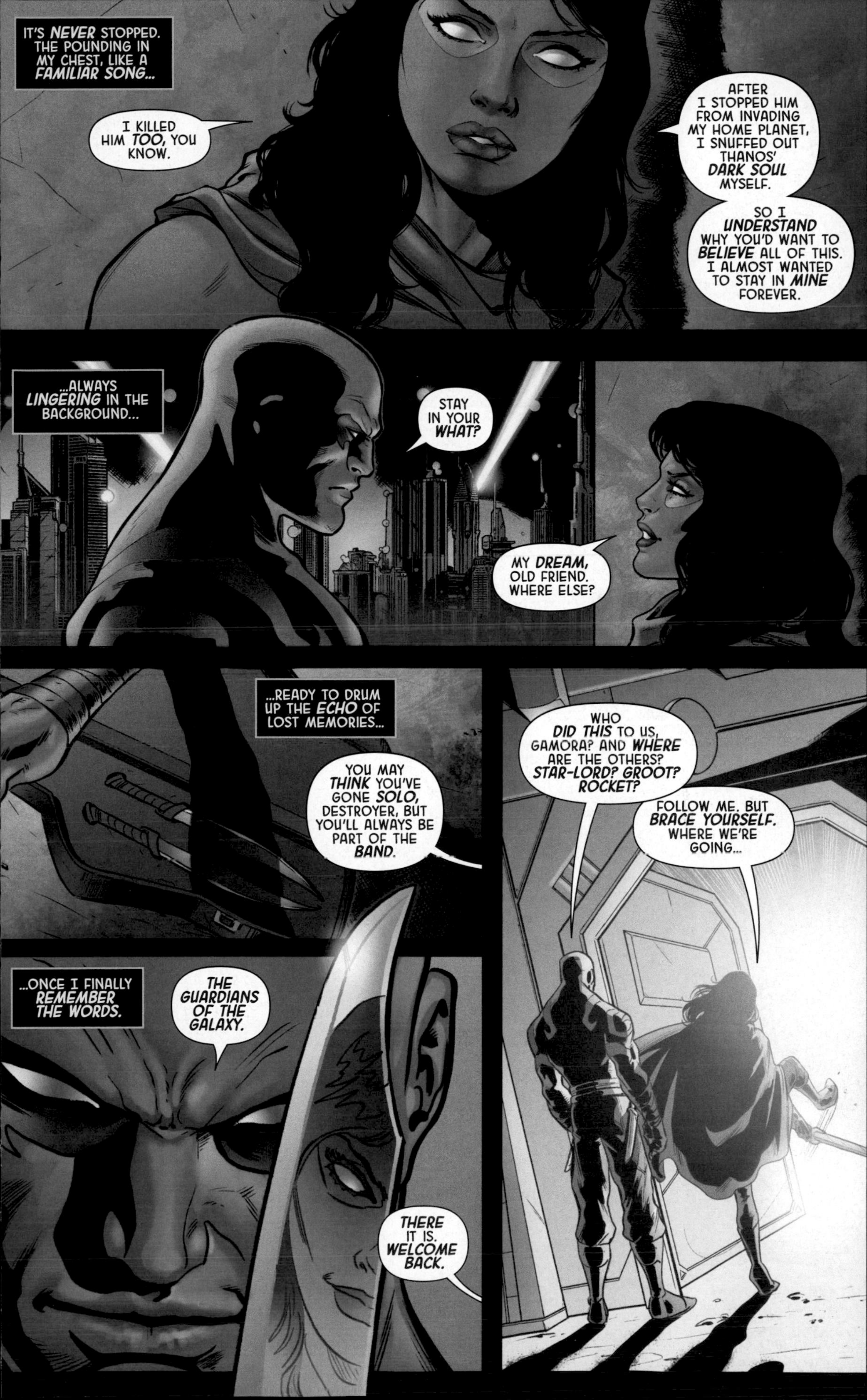
IT'S NEVER STOPPED. THE POUNDING IN MY CHEST, LIKE A FAMILIAR SONG...
I KILLED HIM TOO, YOU KNOW.
AFTER I STOPPED HIM FROM INVADING MY HOME PLANET, I SNUFFED OUT THANOS' DARK SOUL MYSELF.
SO I UNDERSTAND WHY YOU'D WANT TO BELIEVE ALL OF THIS. I ALMOST WANTED TO STAY IN MINE FOREVER.
...ALWAYS LINGERING IN THE BACKGROUND...
STAY IN YOUR WHAT?
MY DREAM, OLD FRIEND. WHERE ELSE?
...READY TO DRUM UP THE ECHO OF LOST MEMORIES...
YOU MAY THINK YOU'VE GONE SOLO, DESTROYER, BUT YOU'LL ALWAYS BE PART OF THE BAND.
...ONCE I FINALLY REMEMBER THE WORDS.
THE GUARDIANS OF THE GALAXY.
THERE IT IS. WELCOME BACK.
WHO DID THIS TO US, GAMORA? AND WHERE ARE THE OTHERS? STAR-LORD? GROOT? ROCKET?
FOLLOW ME. BUT BRACE YOURSELF. WHERE WE'RE GOING...

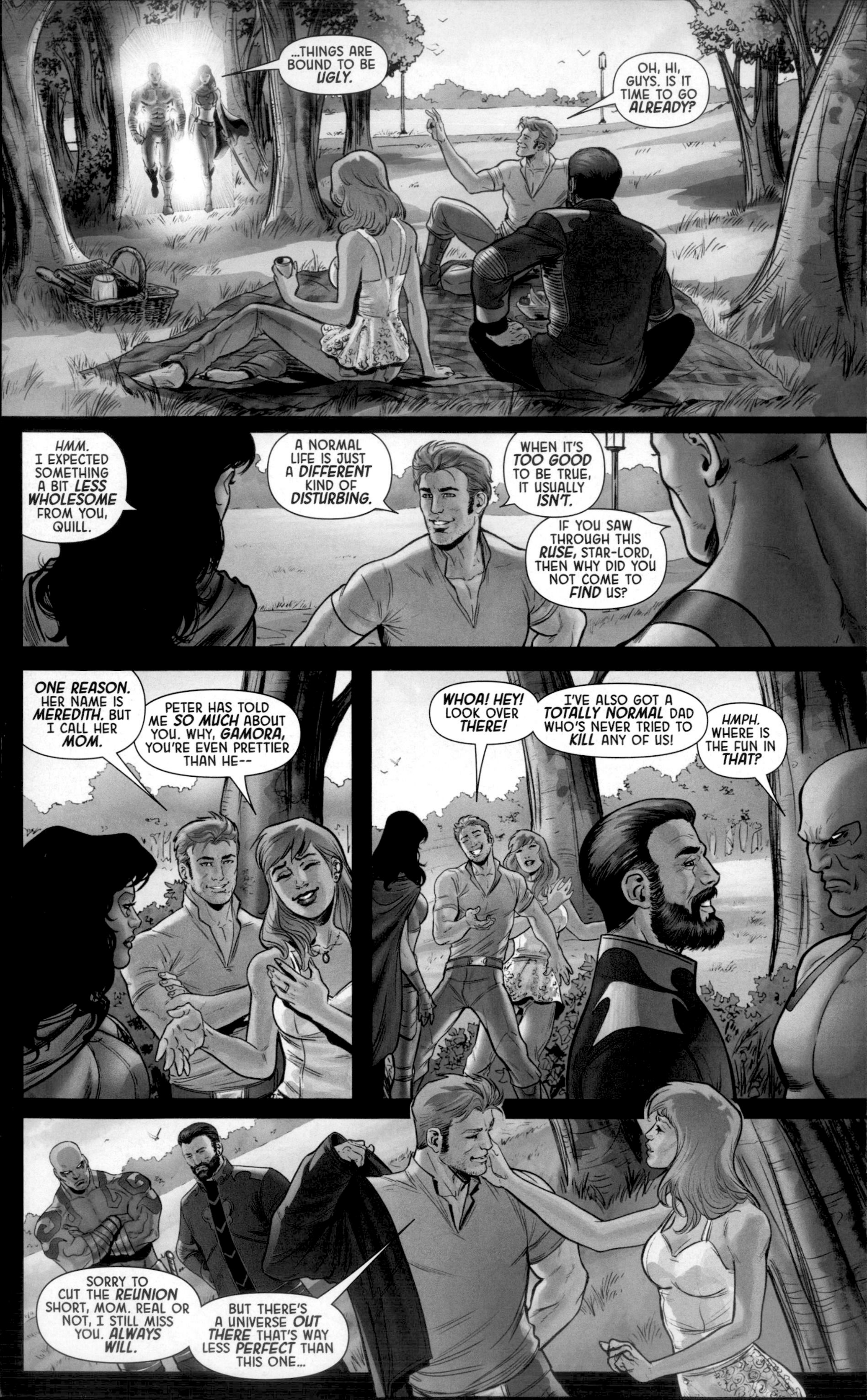
...THINGS ARE BOUND TO BE UGLY.
OH, HI, GUYS. IS IT TIME TO GO ALREADY?
HMM. I EXPECTED SOMETHING A BIT LESS WHOLESOME FROM YOU, QUILL.
A NORMAL LIFE IS JUST A DIFFERENT KIND OF DISTURBING.
WHEN IT'S TOO GOOD TO BE TRUE, IT USUALLY ISN'T.
IF YOU SAW THROUGH THIS RUSE, STAR-LORD, THEN WHY DID YOU NOT COME TO FIND US?
ONE REASON. HER NAME IS MEREDITH. BUT I CALL HER MOM.
PETER HAS TOLD ME SO MUCH ABOUT YOU. WHY, GAMORA, YOU'RE EVEN PRETTIER THAN HE--
WHOA! HEY! LOOK OVER THERE!
I'VE ALSO GOT A TOTALLY NORMAL DAD WHO'S NEVER TRIED TO KILL ANY OF US!
HMPH. WHERE IS THE FUN IN THAT?
SORRY TO CUT THE REUNION SHORT, MOM. REAL OR NOT, I STILL MISS YOU. ALWAYS WILL.
BUT THERE'S A UNIVERSE OUT THERE THAT'S WAY LESS PERFECT THAN THIS ONE...

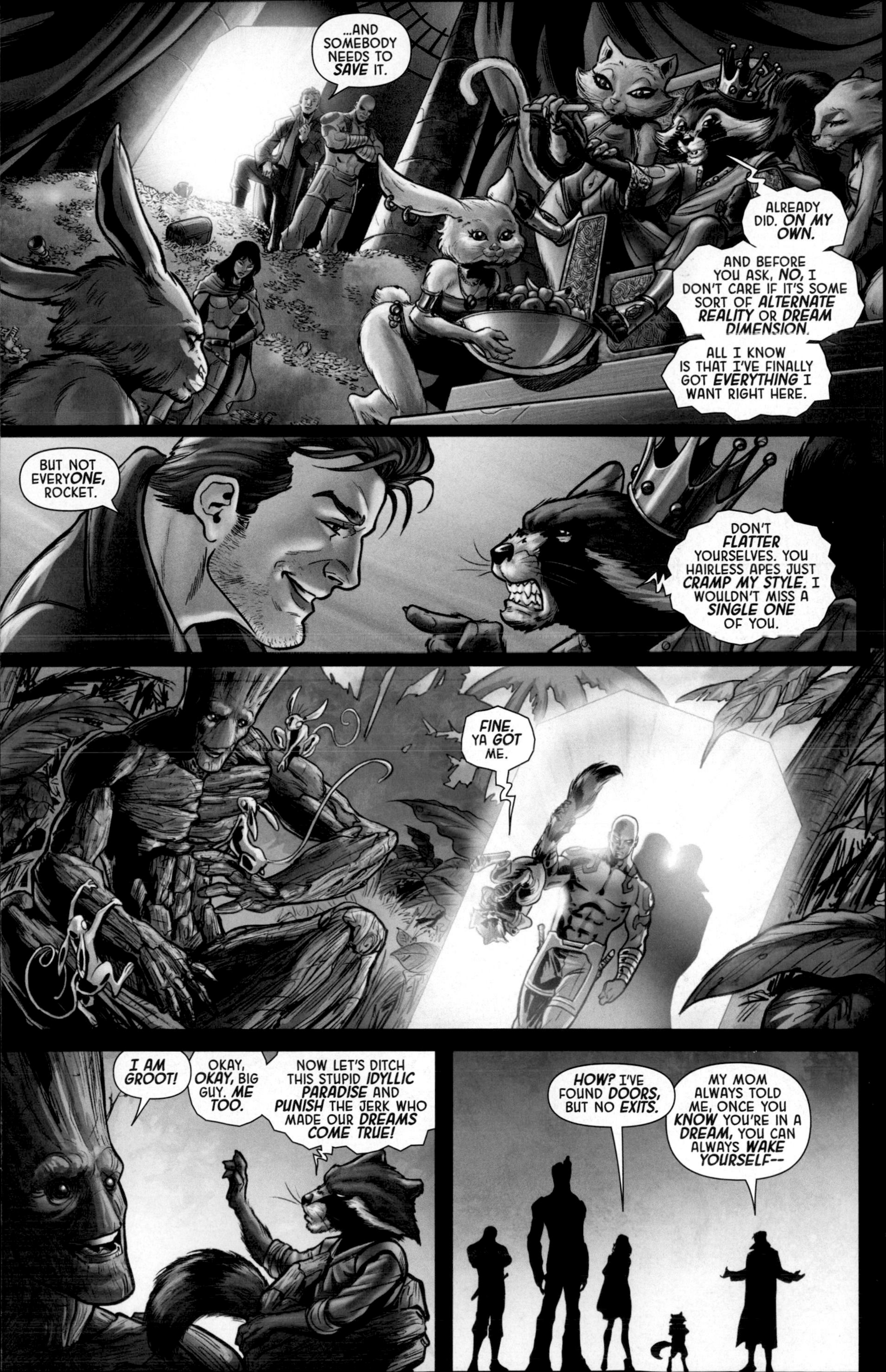
...AND SOMEBODY NEEDS TO SAVE IT.
ALREADY DID. ON MY OWN.
AND BEFORE YOU ASK, NO, I DON'T CARE IF IT'S SOME SORT OF ALTERNATE REALITY OR DREAM DIMENSION.
ALL I KNOW IS THAT I'VE FINALLY GOT EVERYTHING I WANT RIGHT HERE.
BUT NOT EVERYONE, ROCKET.
DON'T FLATTER YOURSELVES. YOU HAIRLESS APES JUST CRAMP MY STYLE. I WOULDN'T MISS A SINGLE ONE OF YOU.
FINE. YA GOT ME.
I AM GROOT!
OKAY, OKAY, BIG GUY. ME TOO.
NOW LET'S DITCH THIS STUPID IDYLLIC PARADISE AND PUNISH THE JERK WHO MADE OUR DREAMS COME TRUE!
HOW? I'VE FOUND DOORS, BUT NO EXITS.
MY MOM ALWAYS TOLD ME, ONCE YOU KNOW YOU'RE IN A DREAM, YOU CAN ALWAYS WAKE YOURSELF--

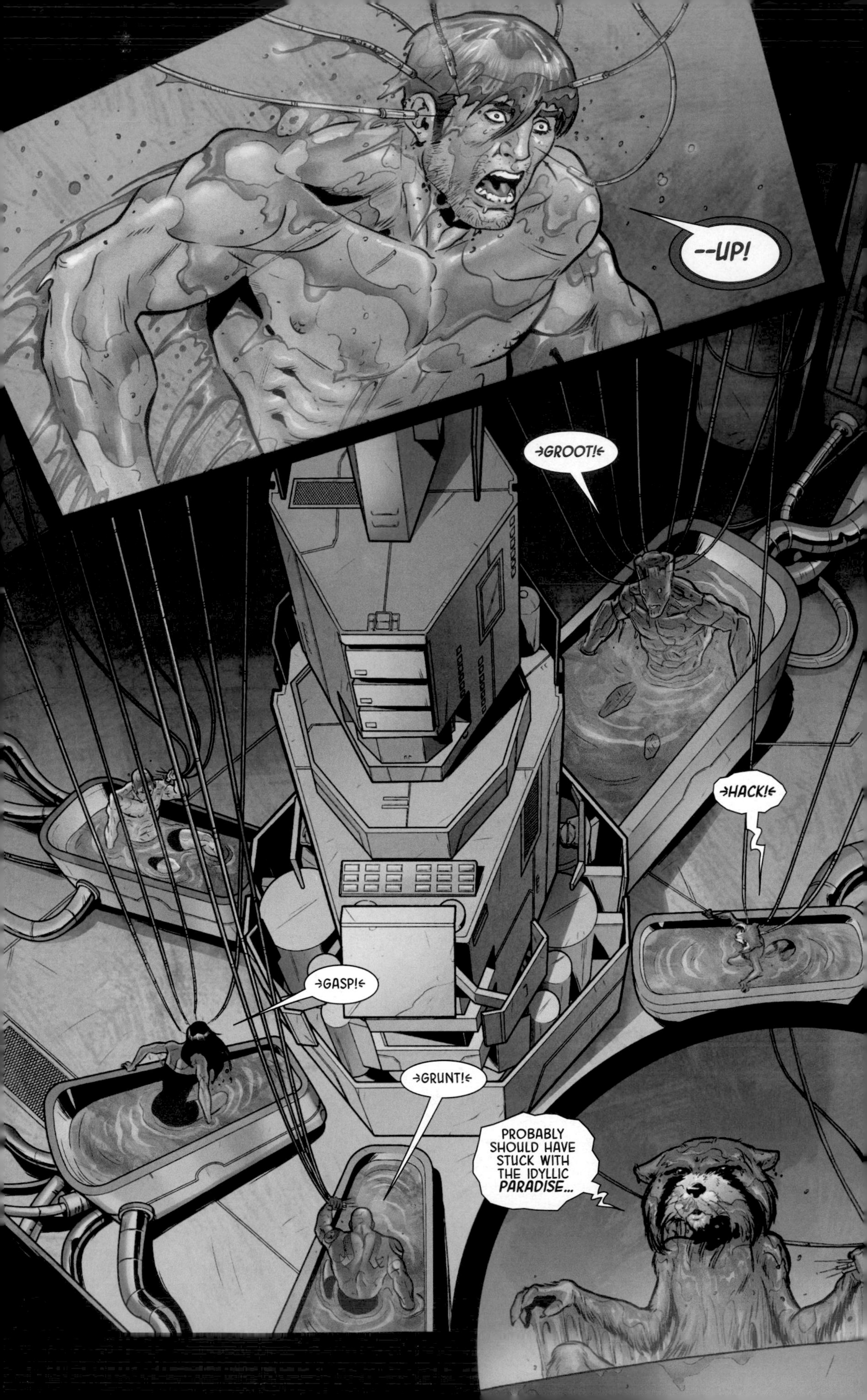
--UP!
GROOT!
HACK!
GASP!
GRUNT!
PROBABLY SHOULD HAVE STUCK WITH THE IDYLLIC *PARADISE*...

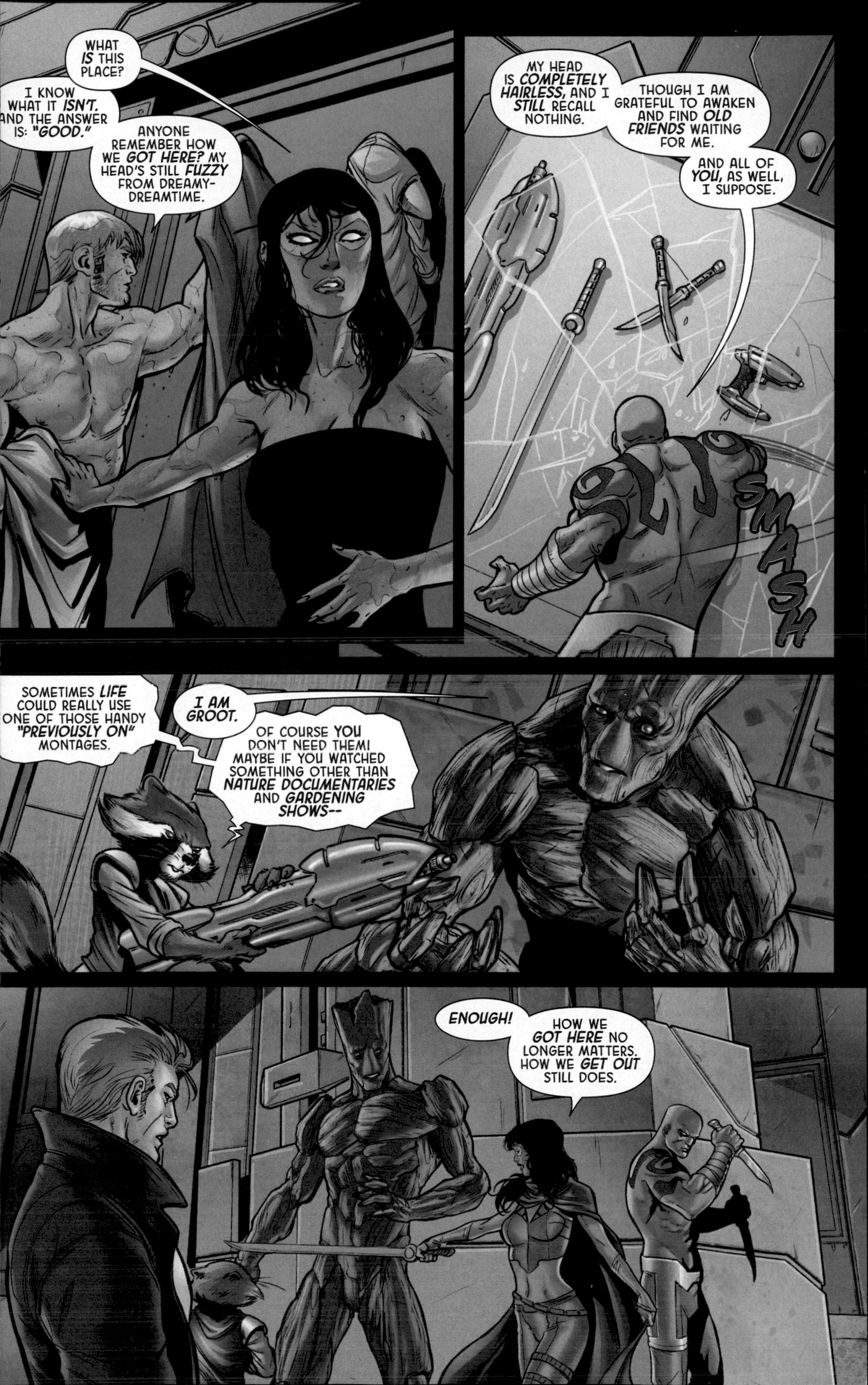
WHAT IS THIS PLACE?
I KNOW WHAT IT ISN'T. AND THE ANSWER IS: "GOOD."
ANYONE REMEMBER HOW WE GOT HERE? MY HEAD'S STILL FUZZY FROM DREAMY-DREAMTIME.
MY HEAD IS COMPLETELY HAIRLESS, AND I STILL RECALL NOTHING.
THOUGH I AM GRATEFUL TO AWAKEN AND FIND OLD FRIENDS WAITING FOR ME.
AND ALL OF YOU, AS WELL, I SUPPOSE.
SMASH
SOMETIMES LIFE COULD REALLY USE ONE OF THOSE HANDY "PREVIOUSLY ON" MONTAGES.
I AM GROOT.
OF COURSE YOU DON'T NEED THEM! MAYBE IF YOU WATCHED SOMETHING OTHER THAN NATURE DOCUMENTARIES AND GARDENING SHOWS--
ENOUGH!
HOW WE GOT HERE NO LONGER MATTERS. HOW WE GET OUT STILL DOES.

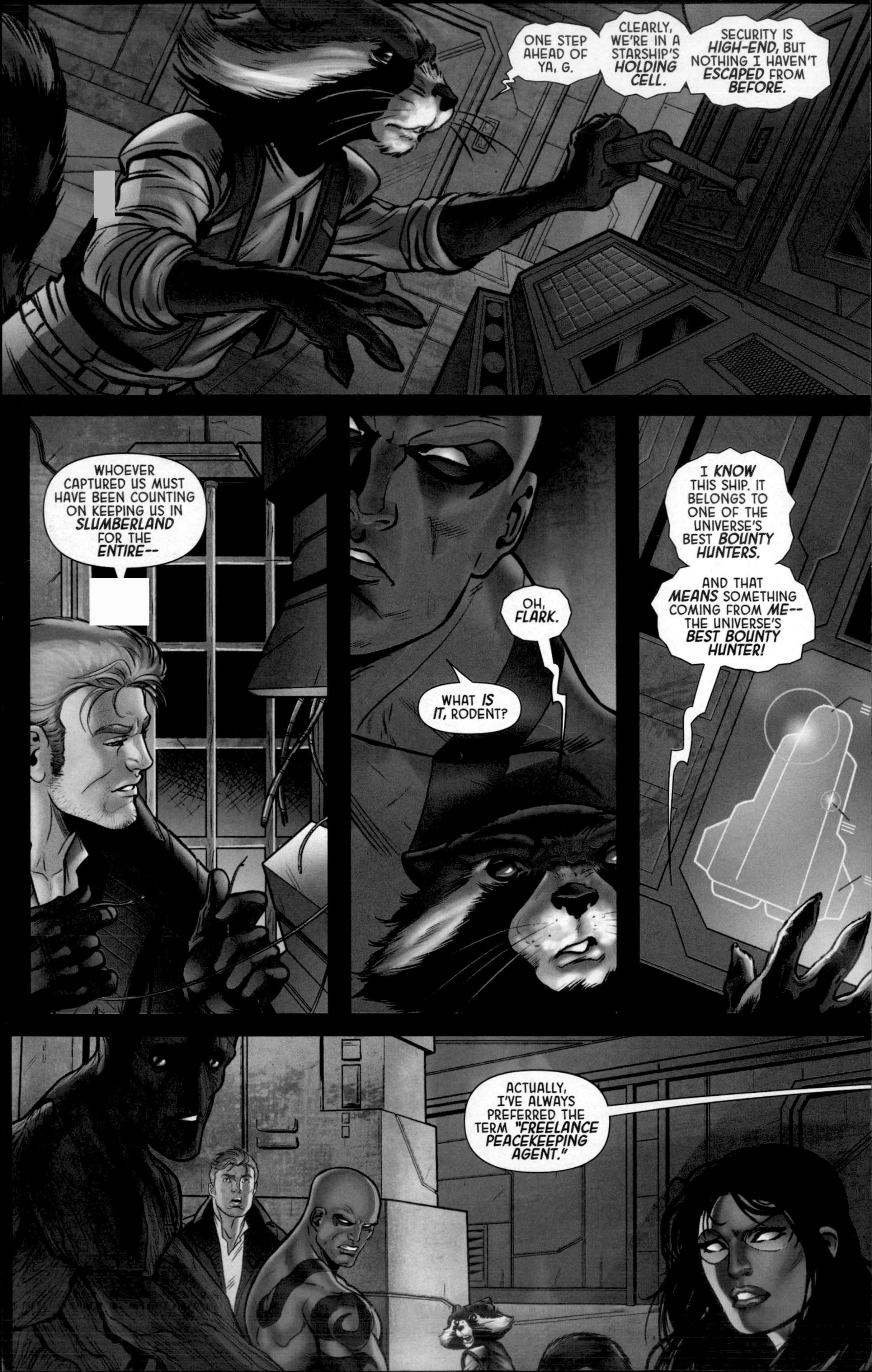

ONE STEP AHEAD OF YA, G.
CLEARLY, WE'RE IN A STARSHIP'S HOLDING CELL.
SECURITY IS HIGH-END, BUT NOTHING I HAVEN'T ESCAPED FROM BEFORE.
WHOEVER CAPTURED US MUST HAVE BEEN COUNTING ON KEEPING US IN SLUMBERLAND FOR THE ENTIRE--
OH, FLARK.
WHAT IS IT, RODENT?
I KNOW THIS SHIP. IT BELONGS TO ONE OF THE UNIVERSE'S BEST BOUNTY HUNTERS.
AND THAT MEANS SOMETHING COMING FROM ME-- THE UNIVERSE'S BEST BOUNTY HUNTER!
ACTUALLY, I'VE ALWAYS PREFERRED THE TERM "FREELANCE PEACEKEEPING AGENT."

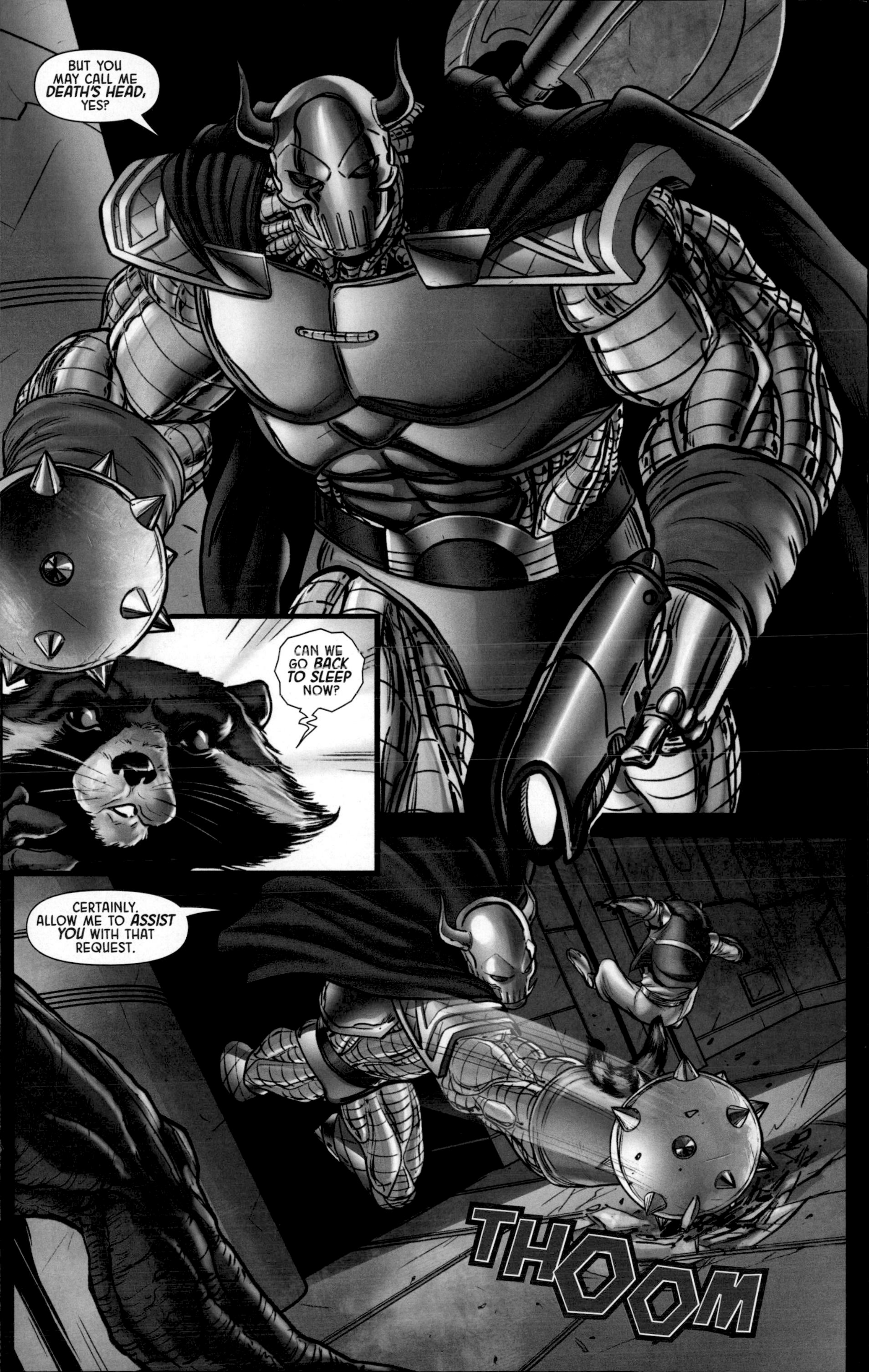
BUT YOU MAY CALL ME DEATH'S HEAD, YES?
CAN WE GO BACK TO SLEEP NOW?
CERTAINLY. ALLOW ME TO ASSIST YOU WITH THAT REQUEST.
THOOM

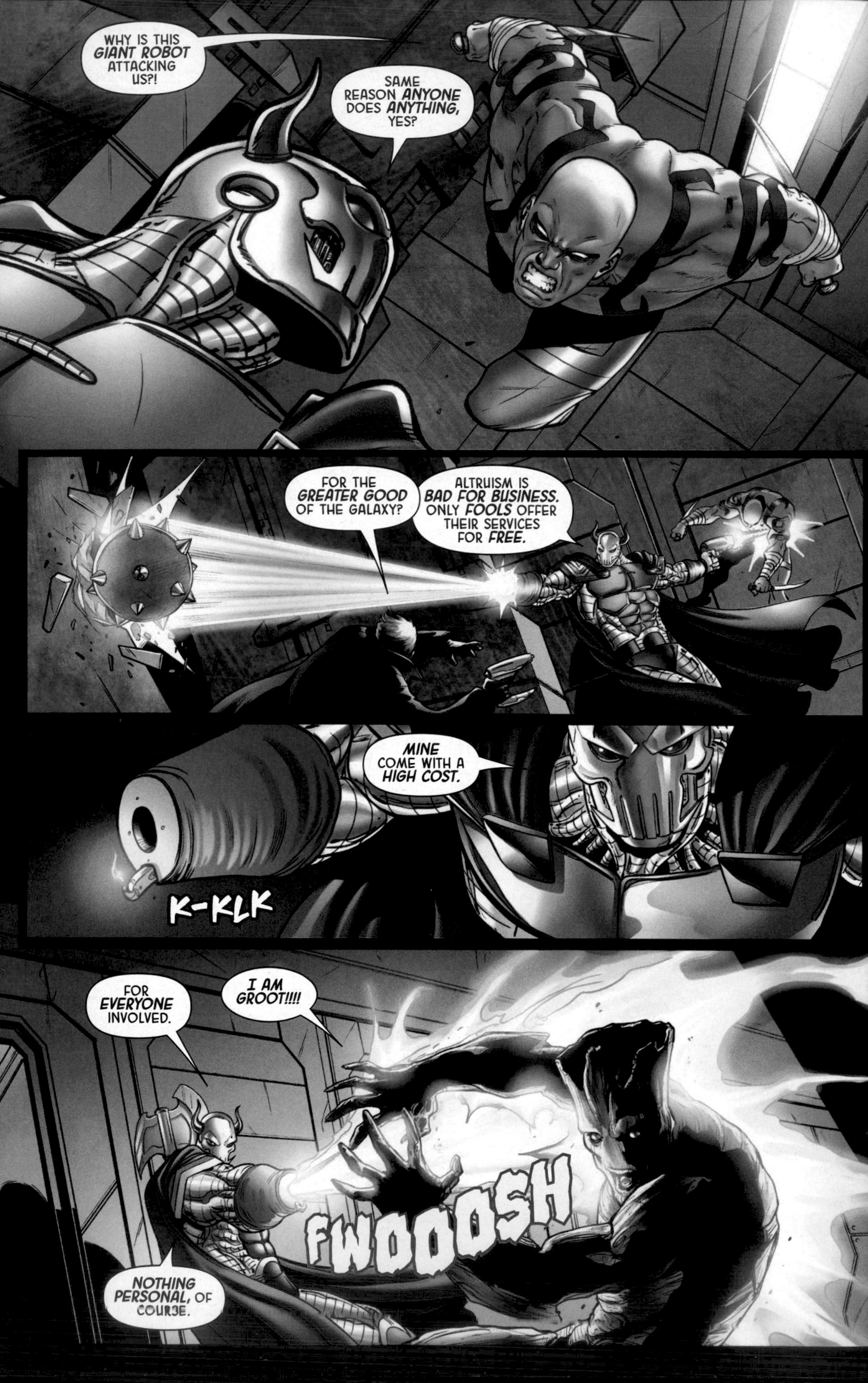
WHY IS THIS GIANT ROBOT ATTACKING US?!
SAME REASON ANYONE DOES ANYTHING, YES?
FOR THE GREATER GOOD OF THE GALAXY?
ALTRUISM IS BAD FOR BUSINESS. ONLY FOOLS OFFER THEIR SERVICES FOR FREE.
MINE COME WITH A HIGH COST.
K-KLK
FOR EVERYONE INVOLVED.
I AM GROOT!!!!
FWOOOSH
NOTHING PERSONAL, OF COURSE.

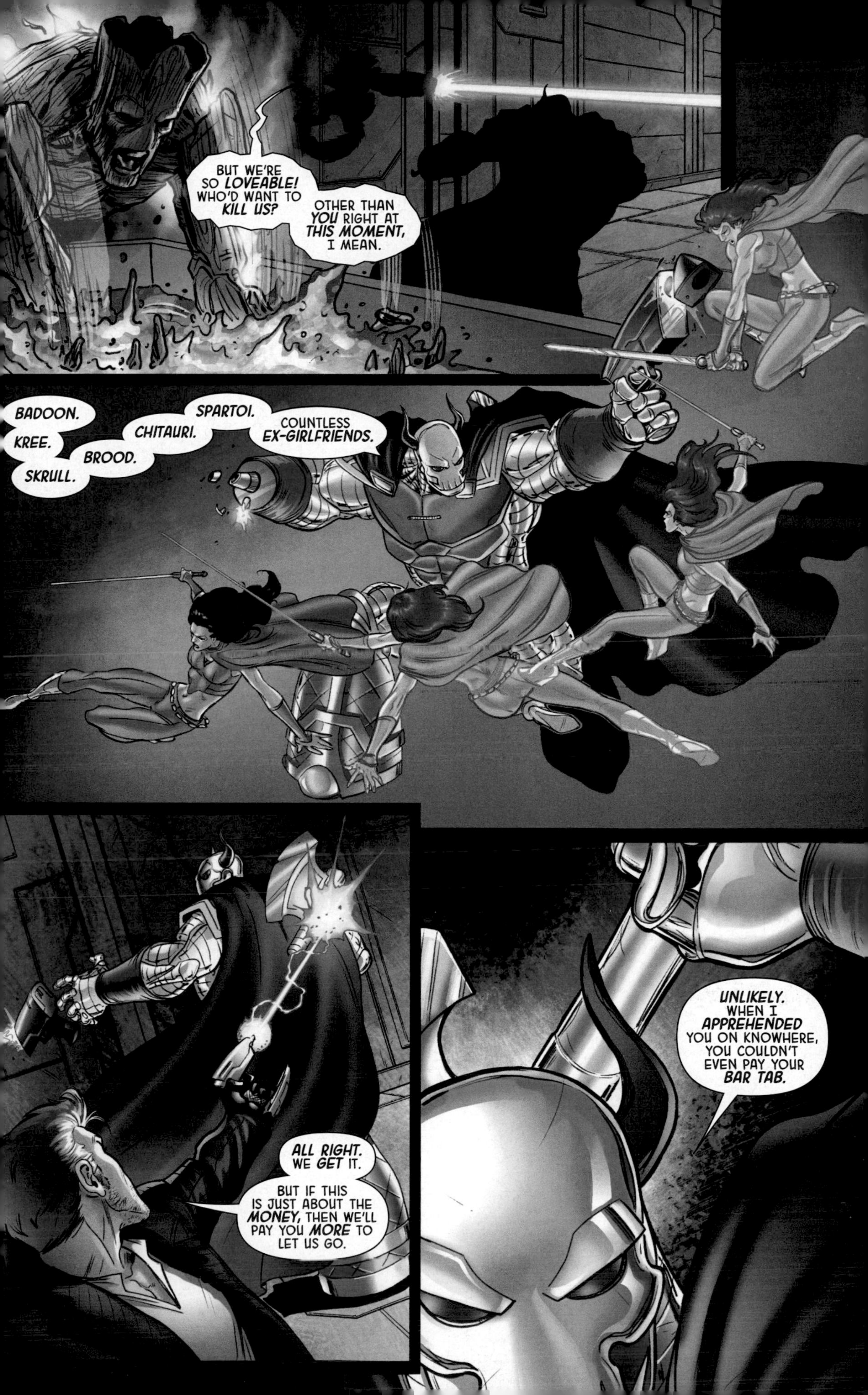
BUT WE'RE SO LOVEABLE! WHO'D WANT TO KILL US?
OTHER THAN YOU RIGHT AT THIS MOMENT, I MEAN.
BADOON.
KREE.
SKRULL.
BROOD.
CHITAURI.
SPARTOI.
COUNTLESS EX-GIRLFRIENDS.
ALL RIGHT. WE GET IT.
BUT IF THIS IS JUST ABOUT THE MONEY, THEN WE'LL PAY YOU MORE TO LET US GO.
UNLIKELY. WHEN I APPREHENDED YOU ON KNOWHERE, YOU COULDN'T EVEN PAY YOUR BAR TAB.

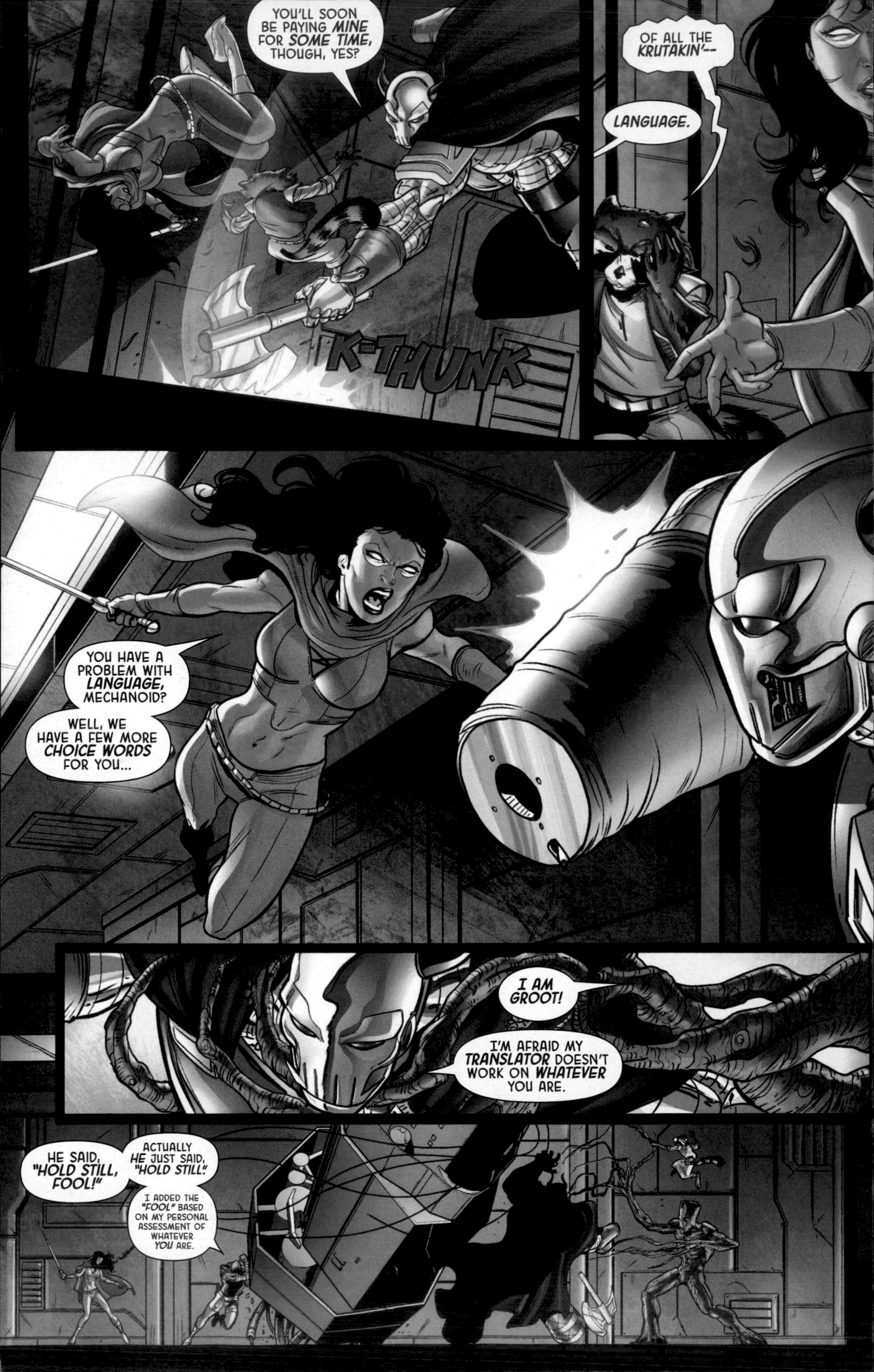
YOU'LL SOON BE PAYING MINE FOR SOME TIME, THOUGH, YES?
K-THUNK
OF ALL THE KRUTAKIN'--
LANGUAGE.
YOU HAVE A PROBLEM WITH LANGUAGE, MECHANOID?
WELL, WE HAVE A FEW MORE CHOICE WORDS FOR YOU...
I AM GROOT!
I'M AFRAID MY TRANSLATOR DOESN'T WORK ON WHATEVER YOU ARE.
HE SAID, "HOLD STILL, FOOL!"
ACTUALLY HE JUST SAID, "HOLD STILL."
I ADDED THE "FOOL" BASED ON MY PERSONAL ASSESSMENT OF WHATEVER YOU ARE.

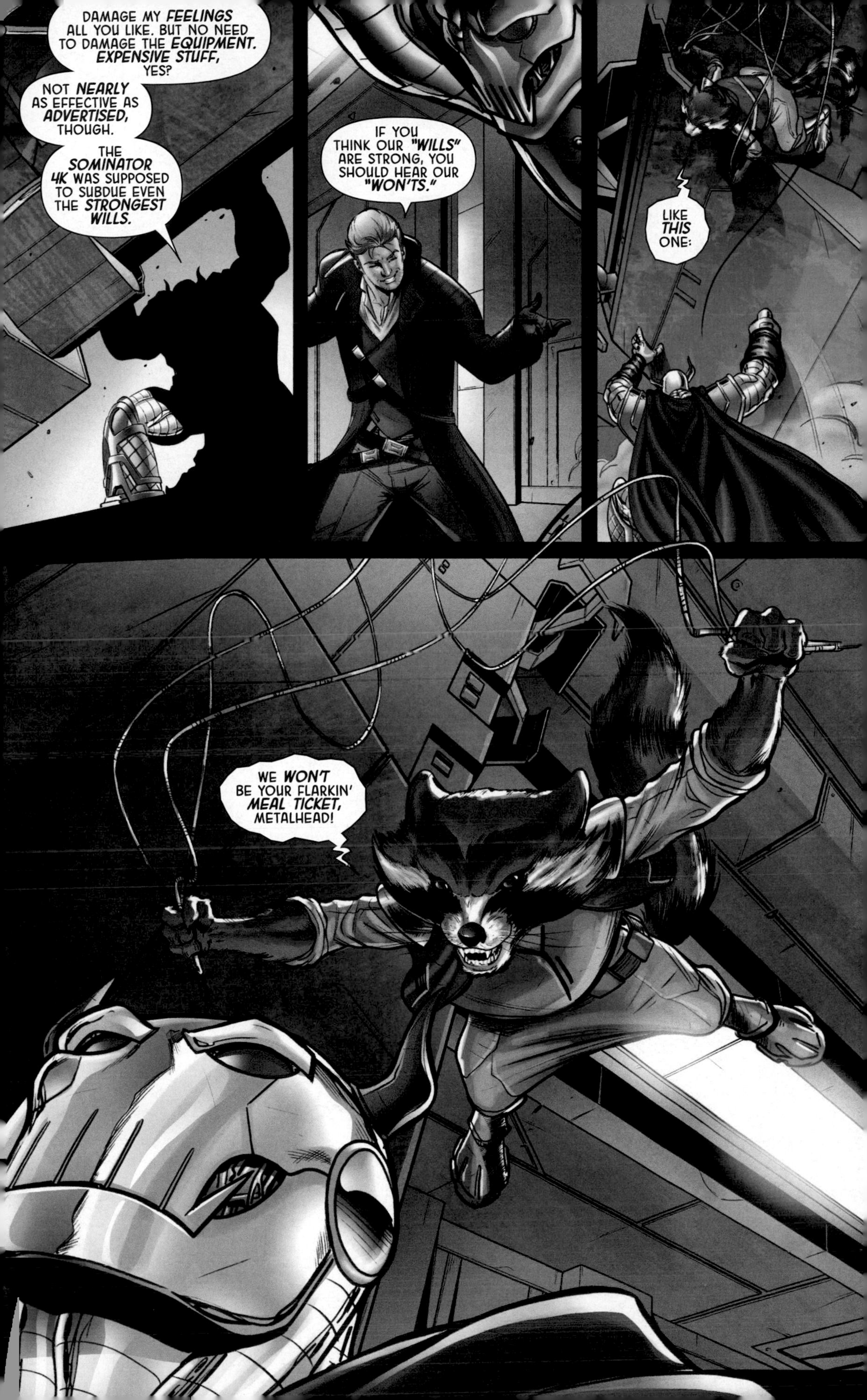
DAMAGE MY FEELINGS ALL YOU LIKE. BUT NO NEED TO DAMAGE THE EQUIPMENT. EXPENSIVE STUFF, YES?
NOT NEARLY AS EFFECTIVE AS ADVERTISED, THOUGH.
THE SOMINATOR 4K WAS SUPPOSED TO SUBDUE EVEN THE STRONGEST WILLS.
IF YOU THINK OUR "WILLS" ARE STRONG, YOU SHOULD HEAR OUR "WON'TS."
LIKE THIS ONE:
WE WON'T BE YOUR FLARKIN' MEAL TICKET, METALHEAD!

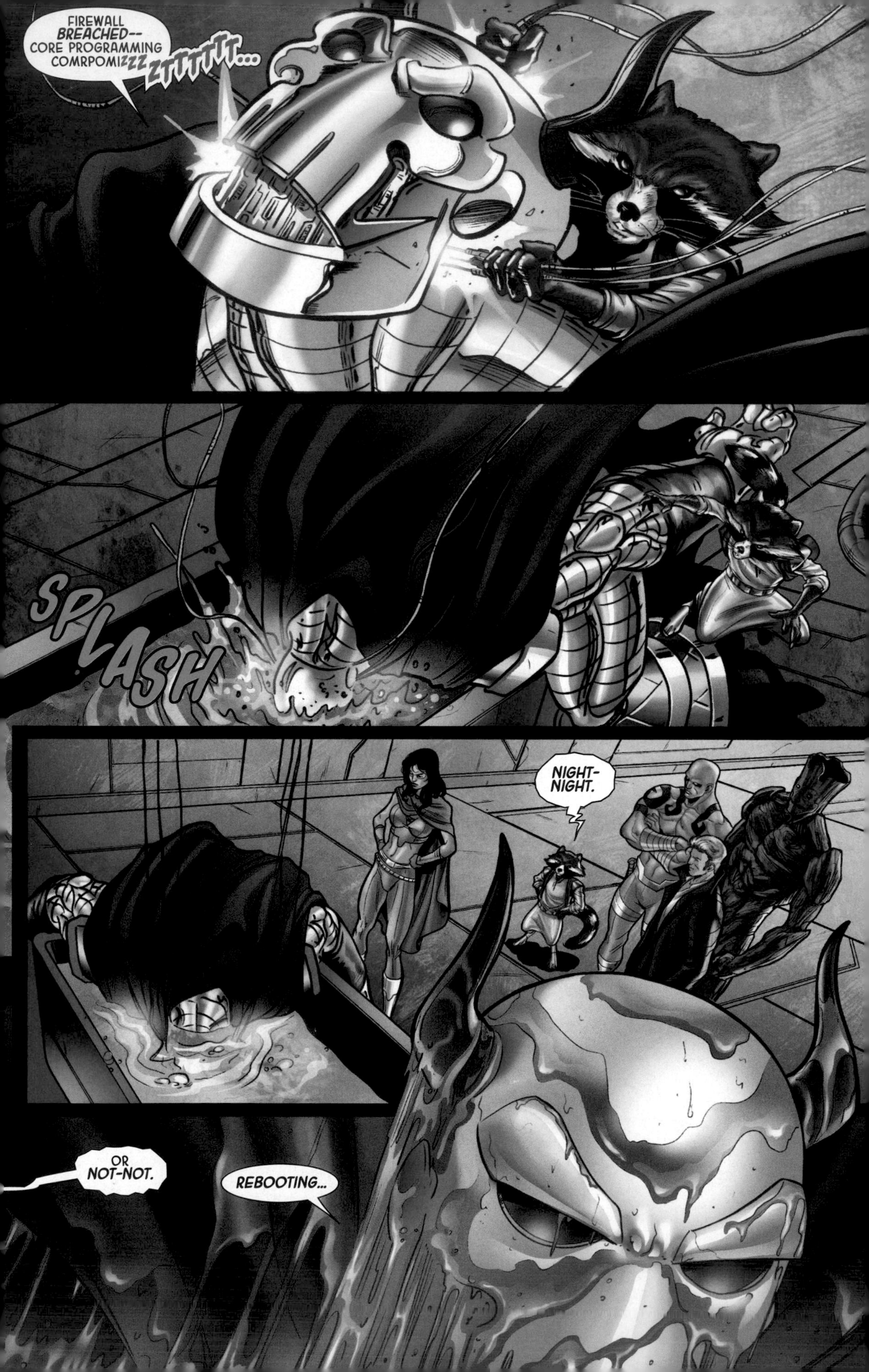
FIREWALL BREACHED-- CORE PROGRAMMING COMRPOMIZZZ
ZTTTTTTT...
SPLASH
NIGHT-NIGHT.
OR NOT-NOT.
REBOOTING...

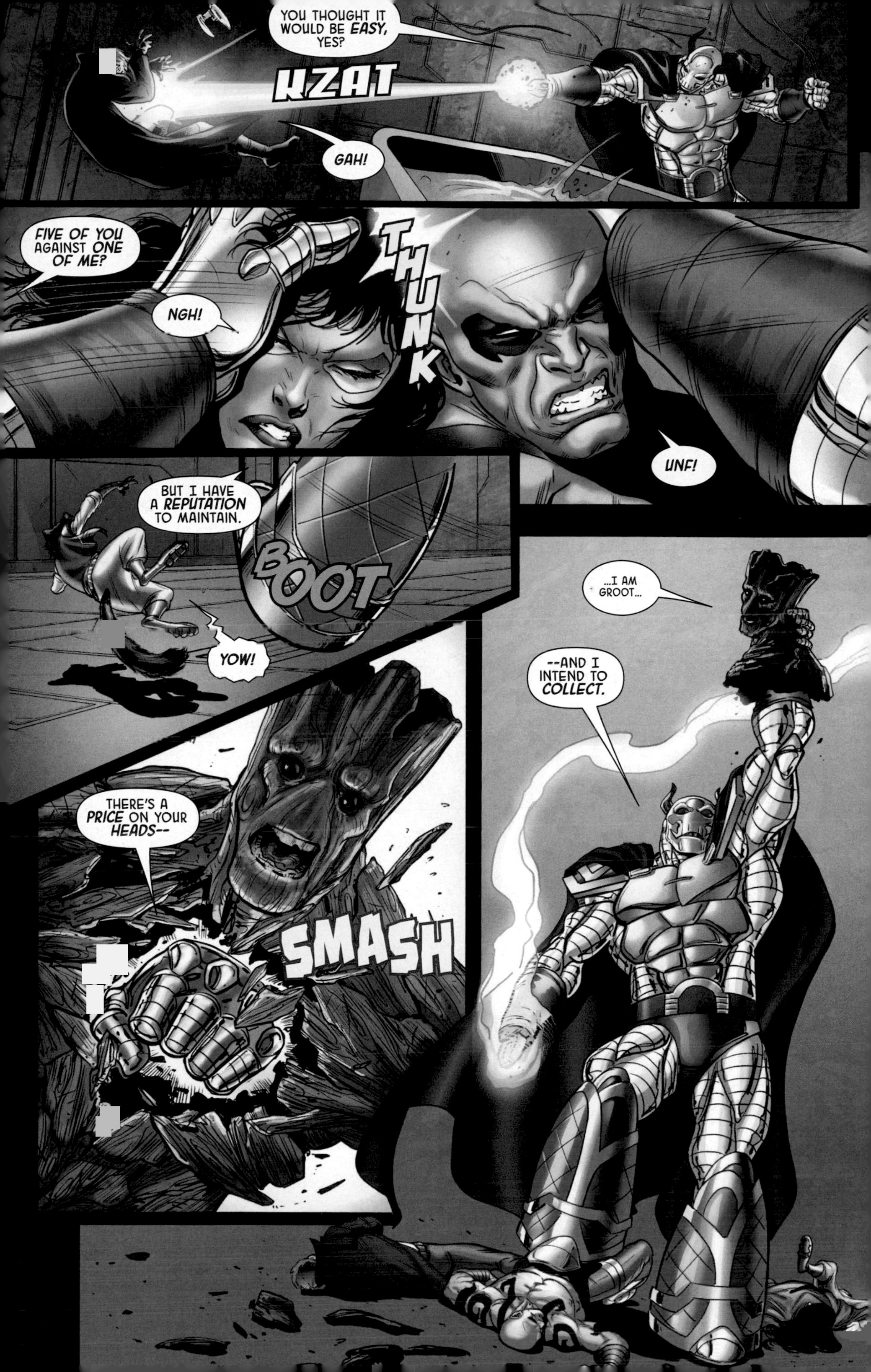
YOU THOUGHT IT WOULD BE *EASY,* YES?
KZAT
GAH!
FIVE OF YOU AGAINST *ONE* OF *ME?*
NGH!
THUNK
UNF!
BUT I HAVE A *REPUTATION* TO MAINTAIN.
BOOT
YOW!
THERE'S A *PRICE* ON YOUR *HEADS--*
SMASH
...I AM GROOT...
--AND I INTEND TO *COLLECT.*

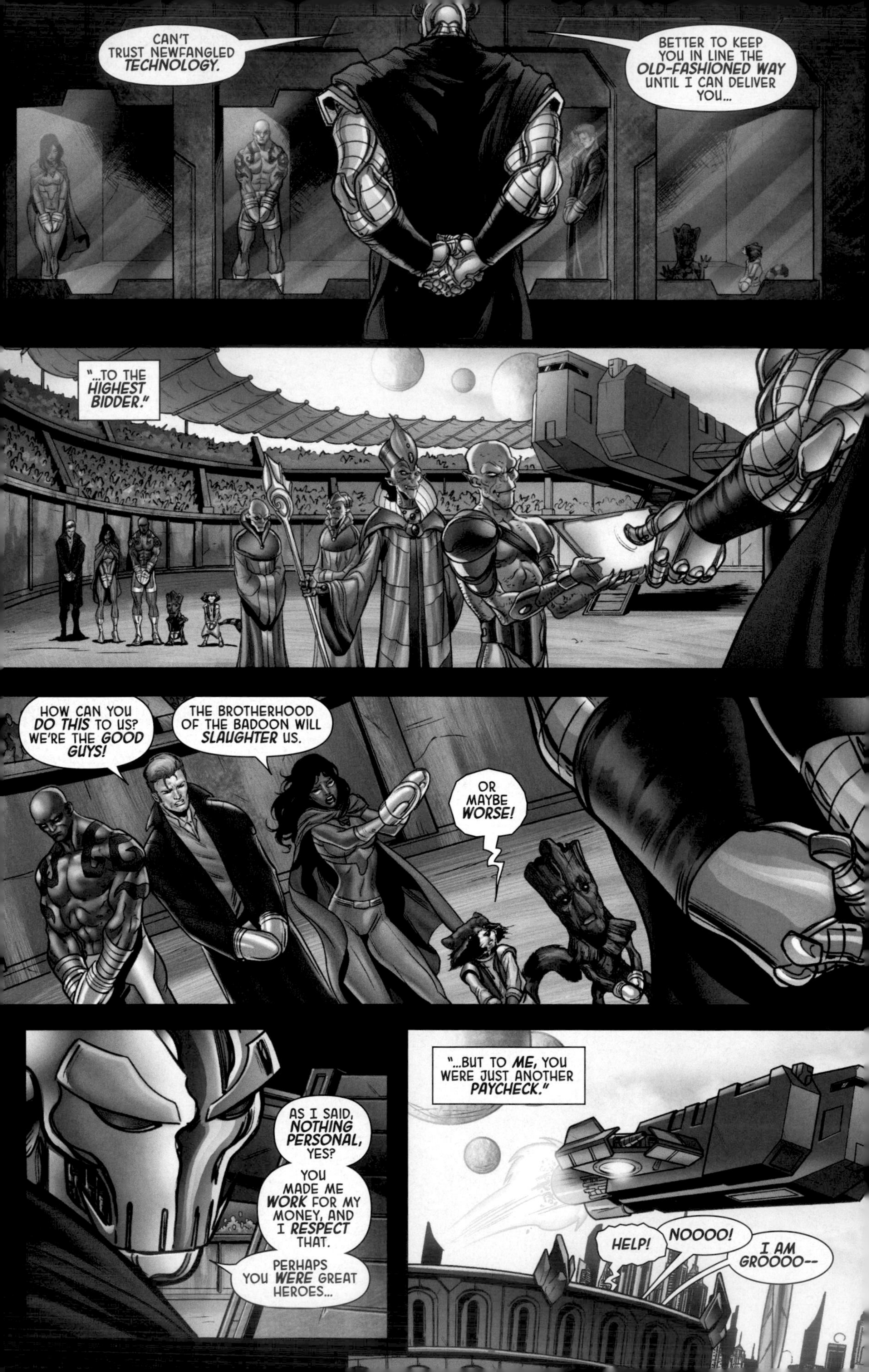
CAN'T TRUST NEWFANGLED TECHNOLOGY.
BETTER TO KEEP YOU IN LINE THE OLD-FASHIONED WAY UNTIL I CAN DELIVER YOU...
"...TO THE HIGHEST BIDDER."
HOW CAN YOU DO THIS TO US? WE'RE THE GOOD GUYS!
THE BROTHERHOOD OF THE BADOON WILL SLAUGHTER US.
OR MAYBE WORSE!
AS I SAID, NOTHING PERSONAL, YES?
YOU MADE ME WORK FOR MY MONEY, AND I RESPECT THAT.
PERHAPS YOU WERE GREAT HEROES...
"...BUT TO ME, YOU WERE JUST ANOTHER PAYCHECK."
HELP!
NOOOO!
I AM GROOOO--

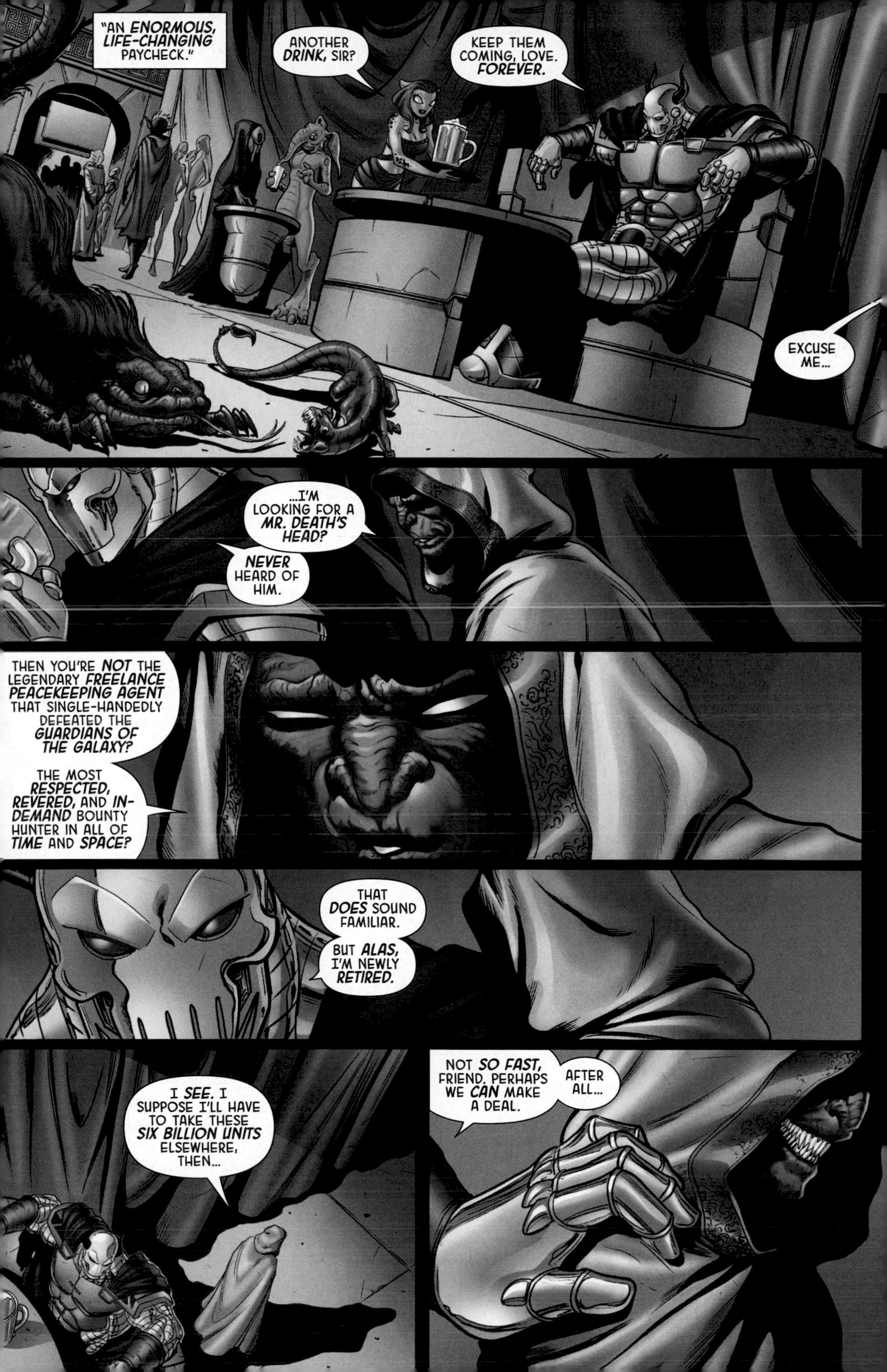
"AN ENORMOUS, LIFE-CHANGING PAYCHECK."
ANOTHER DRINK, SIR?
KEEP THEM COMING, LOVE. FOREVER.
EXCUSE ME...
...I'M LOOKING FOR A MR. DEATH'S HEAD?
NEVER HEARD OF HIM.
THEN YOU'RE NOT THE LEGENDARY FREELANCE PEACEKEEPING AGENT THAT SINGLE-HANDEDLY DEFEATED THE GUARDIANS OF THE GALAXY?
THE MOST RESPECTED, REVERED, AND IN-DEMAND BOUNTY HUNTER IN ALL OF TIME AND SPACE?
THAT DOES SOUND FAMILIAR.
BUT ALAS, I'M NEWLY RETIRED.
I SEE. I SUPPOSE I'LL HAVE TO TAKE THESE SIX BILLION UNITS ELSEWHERE, THEN...
NOT SO FAST, FRIEND. PERHAPS WE CAN MAKE A DEAL.
AFTER ALL...

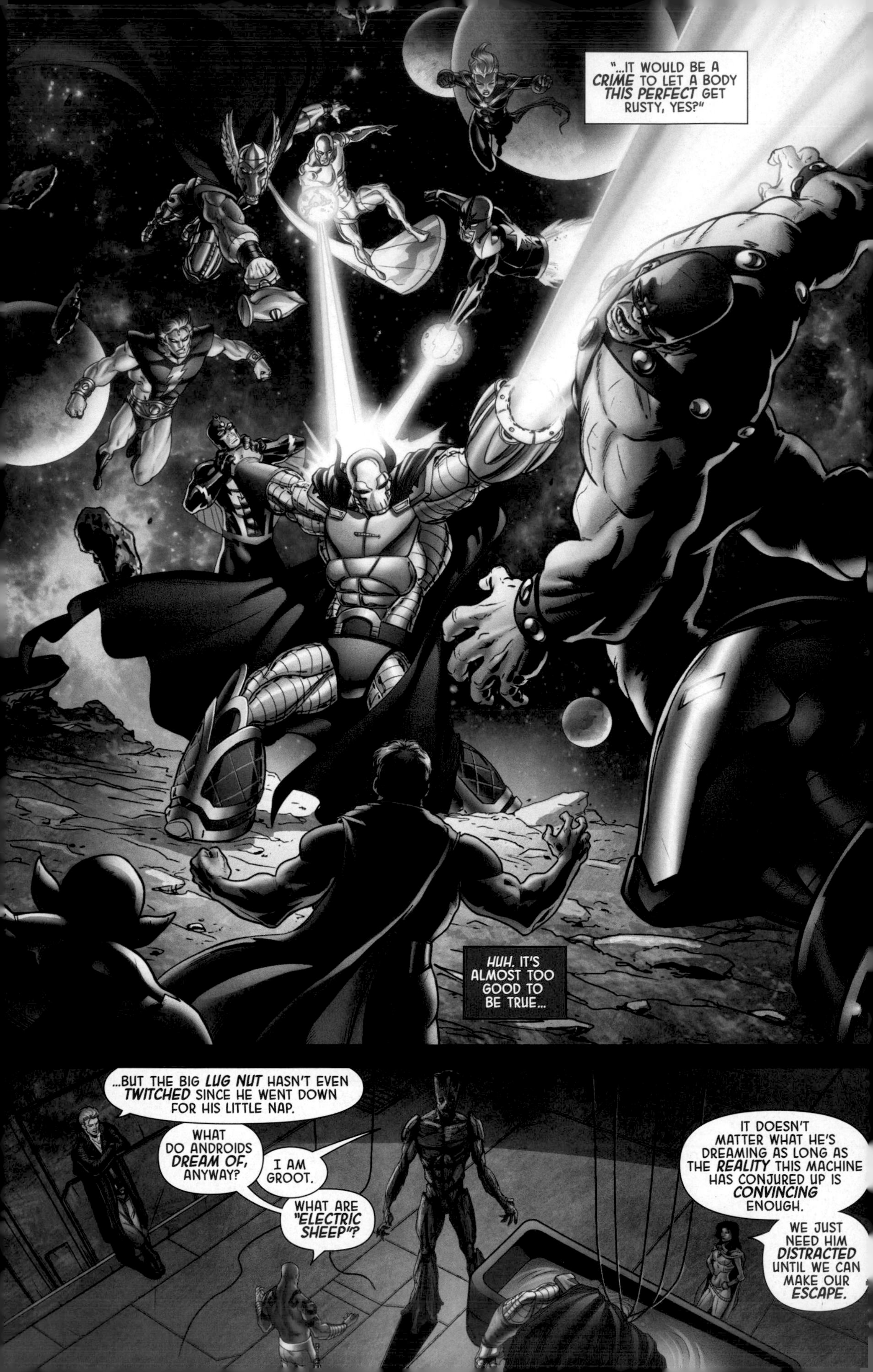
"...IT WOULD BE A CRIME TO LET A BODY THIS PERFECT GET RUSTY, YES?"
HUH. IT'S ALMOST TOO GOOD TO BE TRUE...
...BUT THE BIG LUG NUT HASN'T EVEN TWITCHED SINCE HE WENT DOWN FOR HIS LITTLE NAP.
WHAT DO ANDROIDS DREAM OF, ANYWAY?
I AM GROOT.
WHAT ARE "ELECTRIC SHEEP"?
IT DOESN'T MATTER WHAT HE'S DREAMING AS LONG AS THE REALITY THIS MACHINE HAS CONJURED UP IS CONVINCING ENOUGH.
WE JUST NEED HIM DISTRACTED UNTIL WE CAN MAKE OUR ESCAPE.

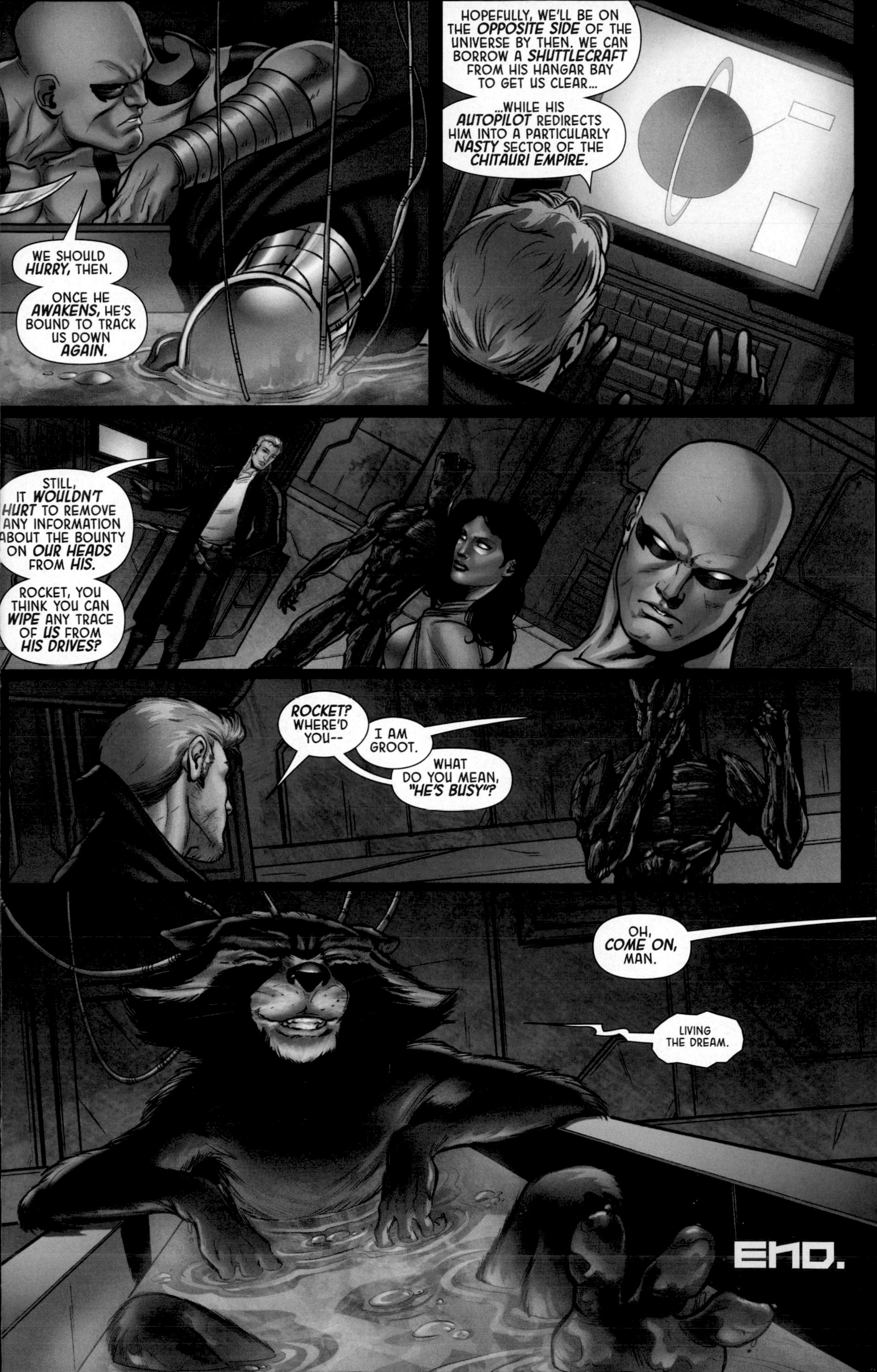
WE SHOULD HURRY, THEN.
ONCE HE AWAKENS, HE'S BOUND TO TRACK US DOWN AGAIN.
HOPEFULLY, WE'LL BE ON THE OPPOSITE SIDE OF THE UNIVERSE BY THEN. WE CAN BORROW A SHUTTLECRAFT FROM HIS HANGAR BAY TO GET US CLEAR...
...WHILE HIS AUTOPILOT REDIRECTS HIM INTO A PARTICULARLY NASTY SECTOR OF THE CHITAURI EMPIRE.
STILL, IT WOULDN'T HURT TO REMOVE ANY INFORMATION ABOUT THE BOUNTY ON OUR HEADS FROM HIS.
ROCKET, YOU THINK YOU CAN WIPE ANY TRACE OF US FROM HIS DRIVES?
ROCKET? WHERE'D YOU--
I AM GROOT.
WHAT DO YOU MEAN, "HE'S BUSY"?
OH, COME ON, MAN.
LIVING THE DREAM.
END.

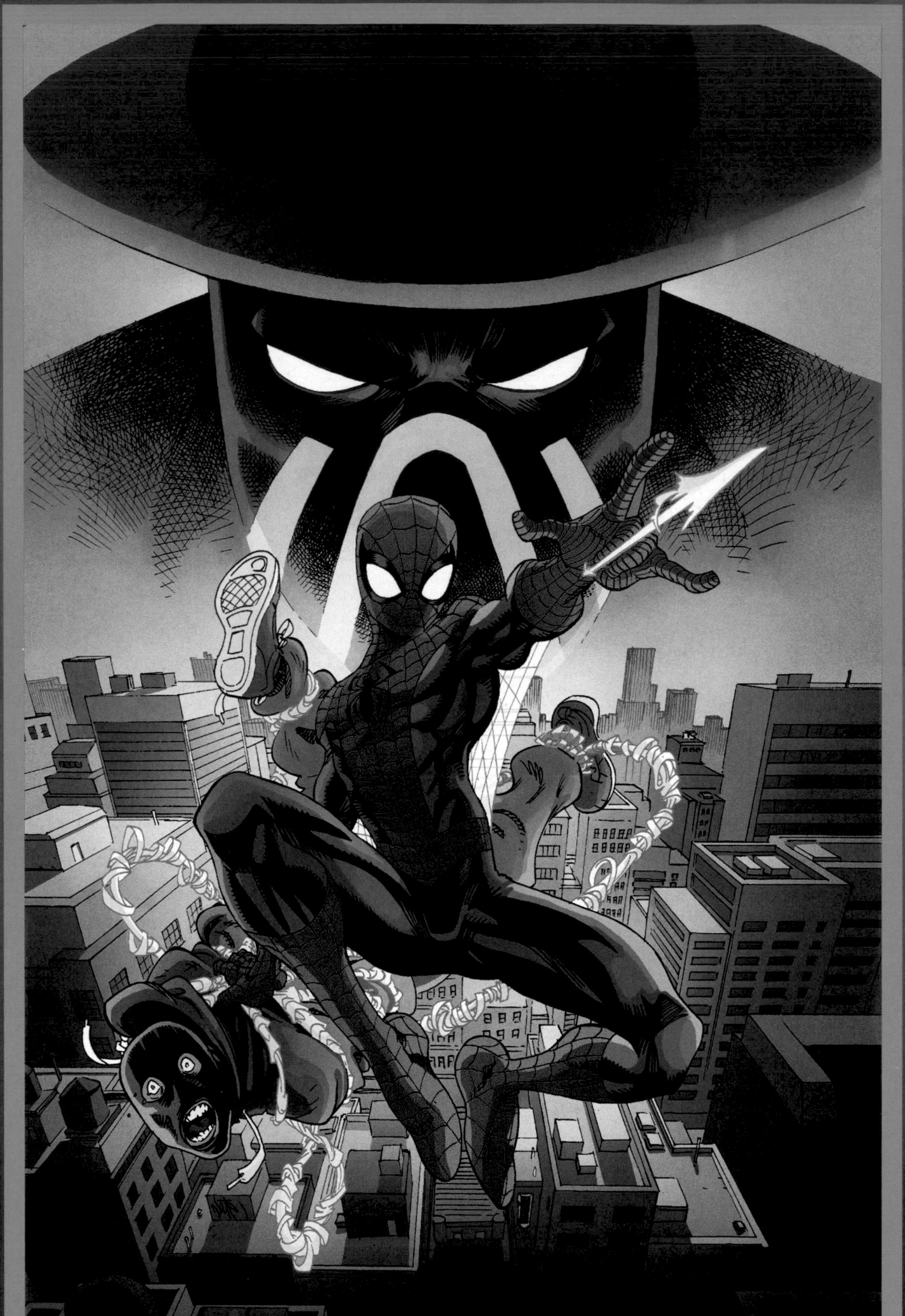

SPIDER-MAN: MASTER PLAN #1

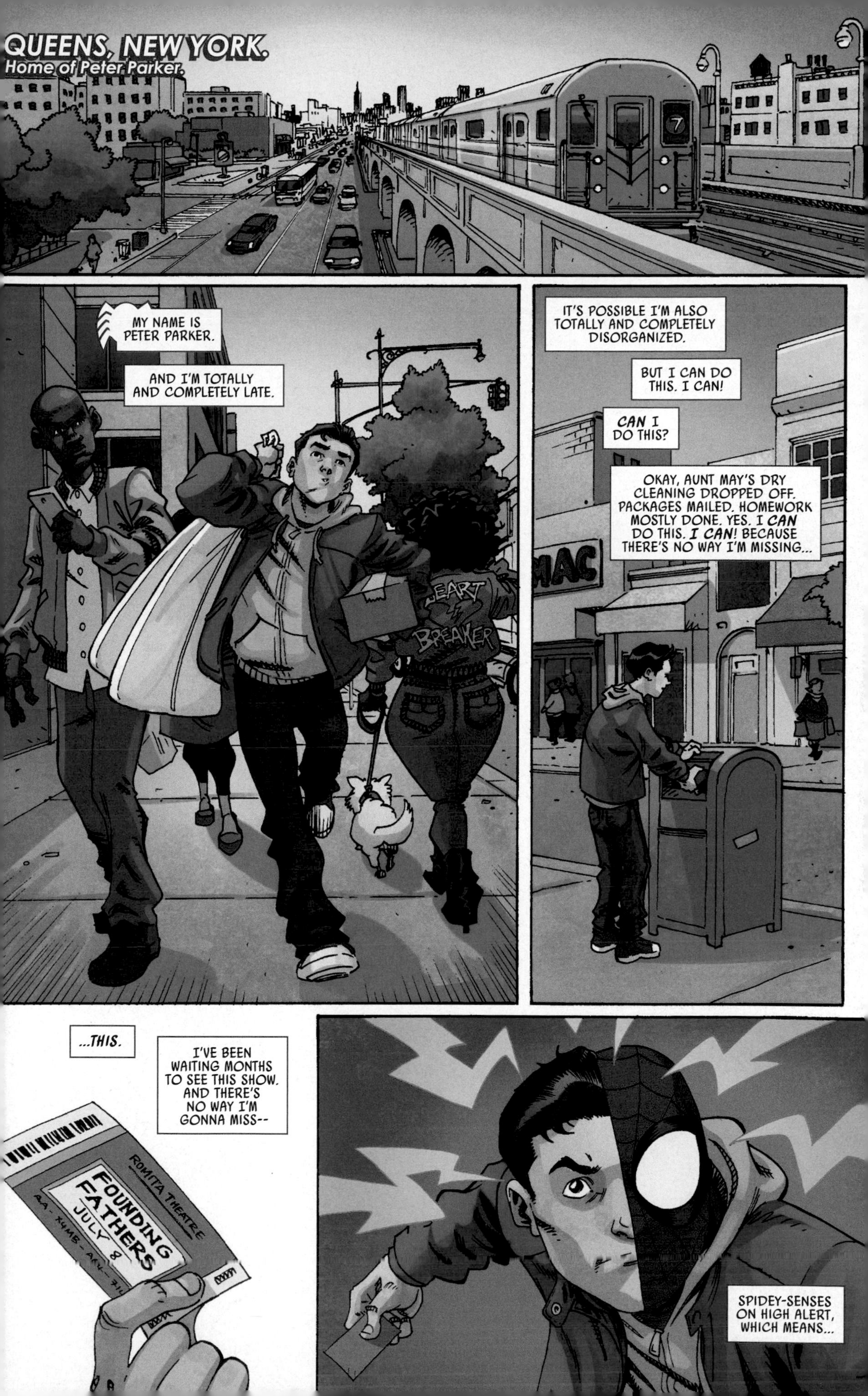
QUEENS, NEW YORK.
Home of Peter Parker.
MY NAME IS PETER PARKER.
AND I'M TOTALLY AND COMPLETELY LATE.
HEART BREAKER
IT'S POSSIBLE I'M ALSO TOTALLY AND COMPLETELY DISORGANIZED.
BUT I CAN DO THIS. I CAN!
CAN I DO THIS?
OKAY, AUNT MAY'S DRY CLEANING DROPPED OFF. PACKAGES MAILED. HOMEWORK MOSTLY DONE. YES. I CAN DO THIS. I CAN! BECAUSE THERE'S NO WAY I'M MISSING...
...THIS.
I'VE BEEN WAITING MONTHS TO SEE THIS SHOW. AND THERE'S NO WAY I'M GONNA MISS--
ROMITA THEATRE
FOUNDING FATHERS
JULY 8
SPIDEY-SENSES ON HIGH ALERT, WHICH MEANS...

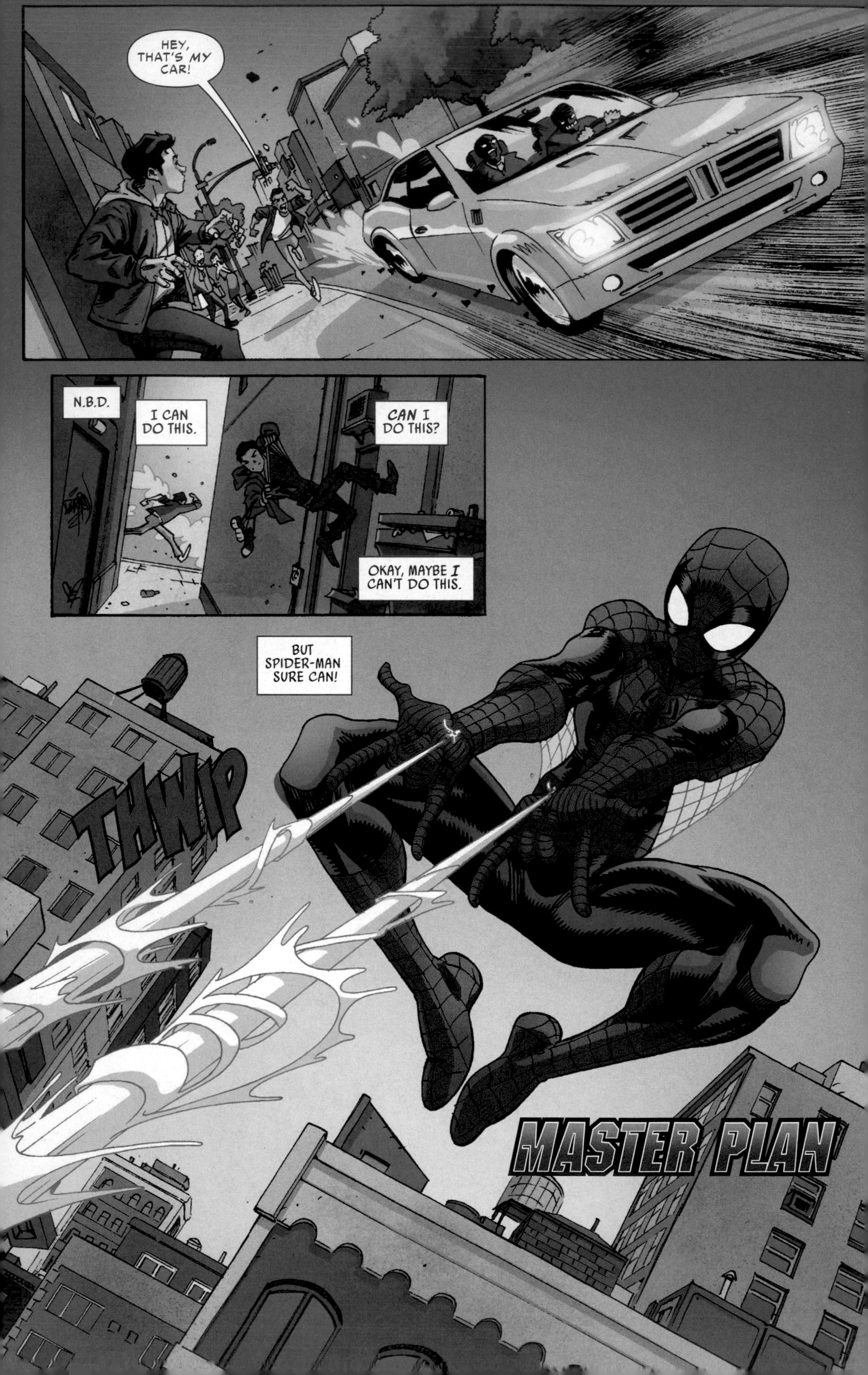
HEY, THAT'S MY CAR!
N.B.D.
I CAN DO THIS.
CAN I DO THIS?
OKAY, MAYBE I CAN'T DO THIS.
BUT SPIDER-MAN SURE CAN!
THWIP
MASTER PLAN

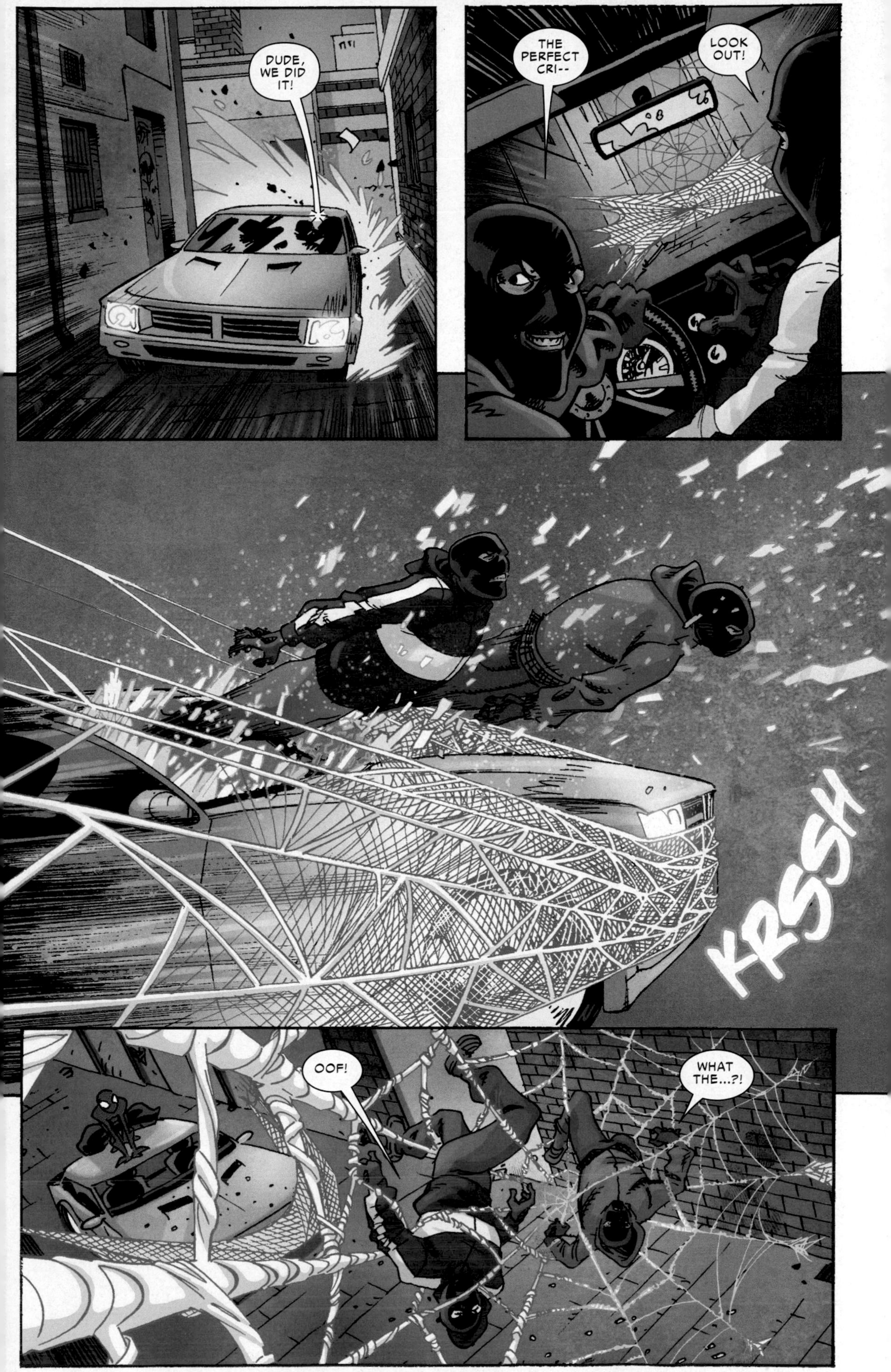
DUDE, WE DID IT!
THE PERFECT CRI--
LOOK OUT!
KRSSH
OOF!
WHAT THE...?!

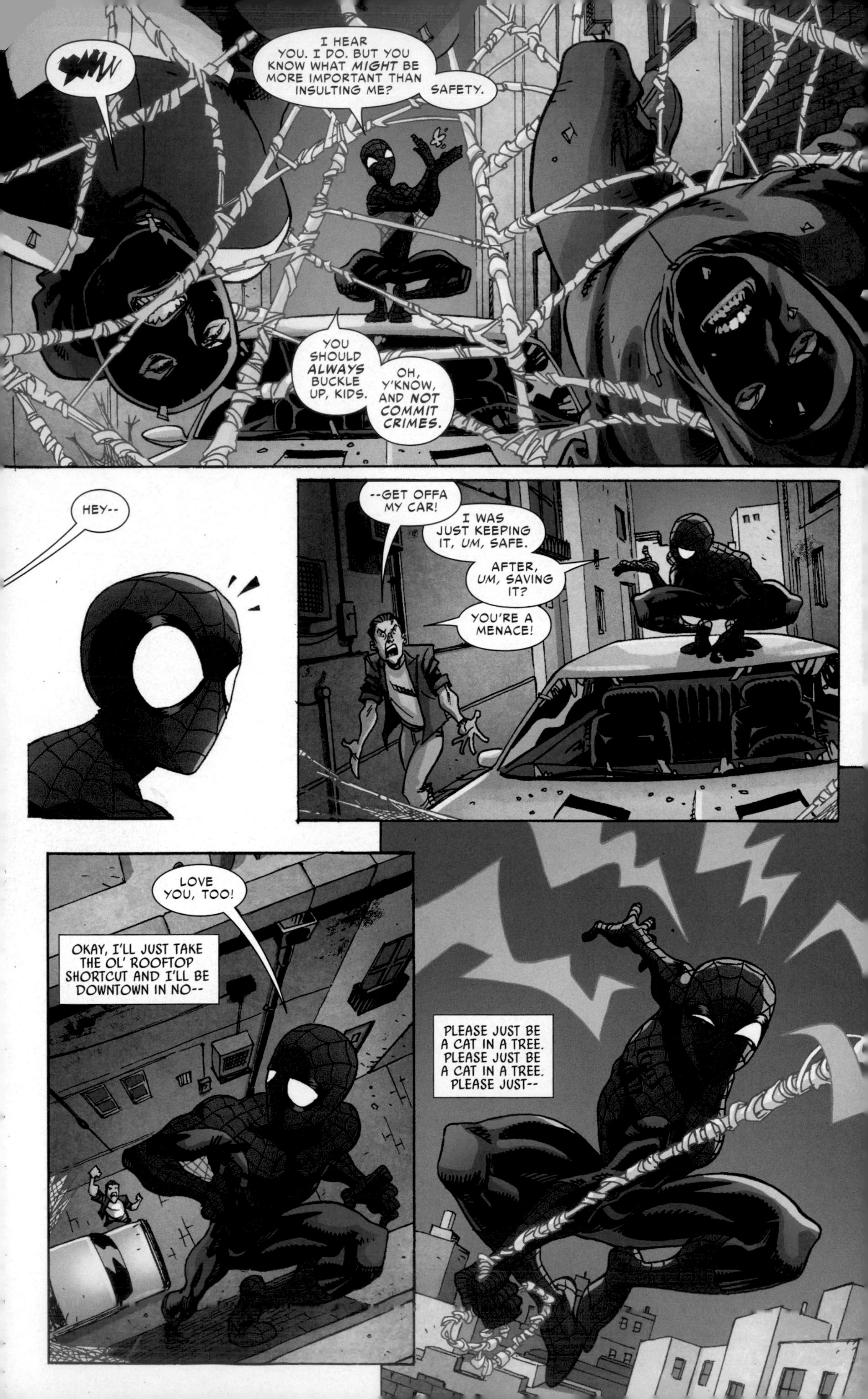
I HEAR YOU. I DO. BUT YOU KNOW WHAT *MIGHT* BE MORE IMPORTANT THAN INSULTING ME?
SAFETY.
YOU SHOULD *ALWAYS* BUCKLE UP, KIDS.
OH, Y'KNOW, AND *NOT COMMIT CRIMES*.
HEY--
--GET OFFA MY CAR!
I WAS JUST KEEPING IT, *UM*, SAFE.
AFTER, *UM*, SAVING IT?
YOU'RE A MENACE!
LOVE YOU, TOO!
OKAY, I'LL JUST TAKE THE OL' ROOFTOP SHORTCUT AND I'LL BE DOWNTOWN IN NO--
PLEASE JUST BE A CAT IN A TREE. PLEASE JUST BE A CAT IN A TREE. PLEASE JUST--

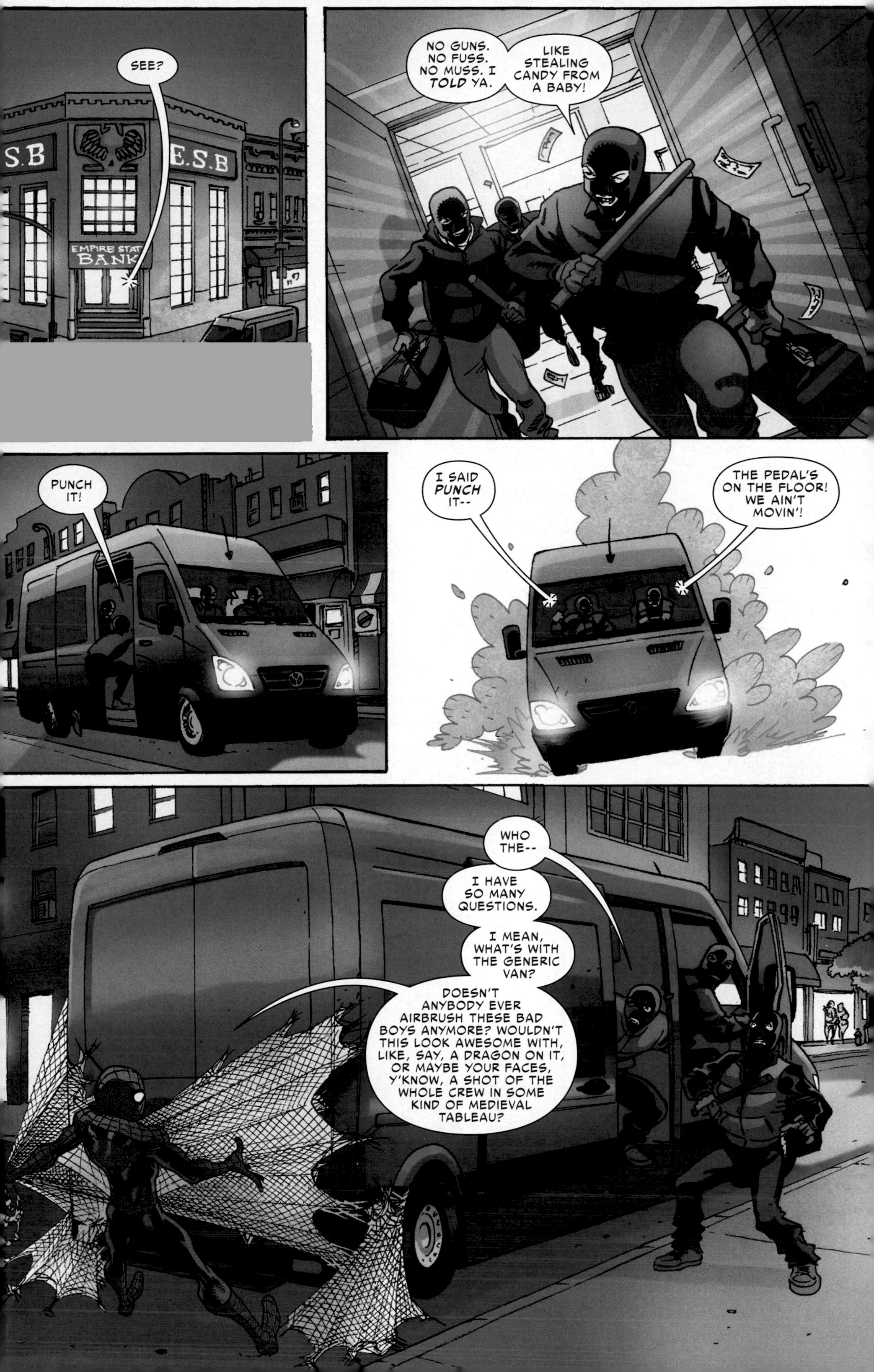
SEE?
E.S.B
EMPIRE STAT
BANK
NO GUNS. NO FUSS. NO MUSS. I *TOLD* YA.
LIKE STEALING CANDY FROM A BABY!
PUNCH IT!
I SAID *PUNCH* IT--
THE PEDAL'S ON THE FLOOR! WE AIN'T MOVIN'!
WHO THE--
I HAVE SO MANY QUESTIONS.
I MEAN, WHAT'S WITH THE GENERIC VAN?
DOESN'T ANYBODY EVER AIRBRUSH THESE BAD BOYS ANYMORE? WOULDN'T THIS LOOK AWESOME WITH, LIKE, SAY, A DRAGON ON IT, OR MAYBE YOUR FACES, Y'KNOW, A SHOT OF THE WHOLE CREW IN SOME KIND OF MEDIEVAL TABLEAU?

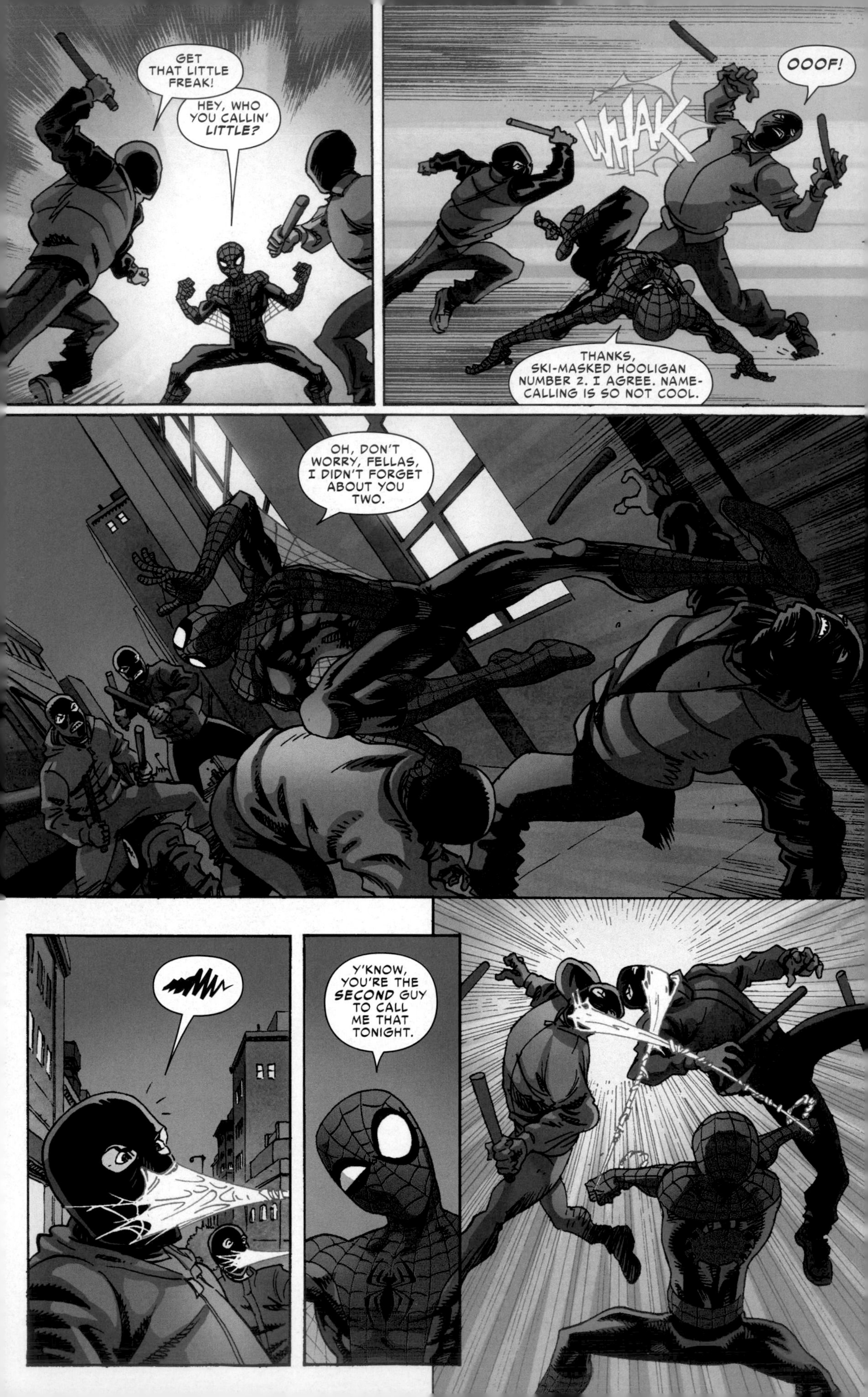
GET THAT LITTLE FREAK!
HEY, WHO YOU CALLIN' *LITTLE?*
OOOF!
WHAK
THANKS, SKI-MASKED HOOLIGAN NUMBER 2. I AGREE. NAME-CALLING IS SO NOT COOL.
OH, DON'T WORRY, FELLAS, I DIDN'T FORGET ABOUT YOU TWO.
Y'KNOW, YOU'RE THE *SECOND* GUY TO CALL ME THAT TONIGHT.

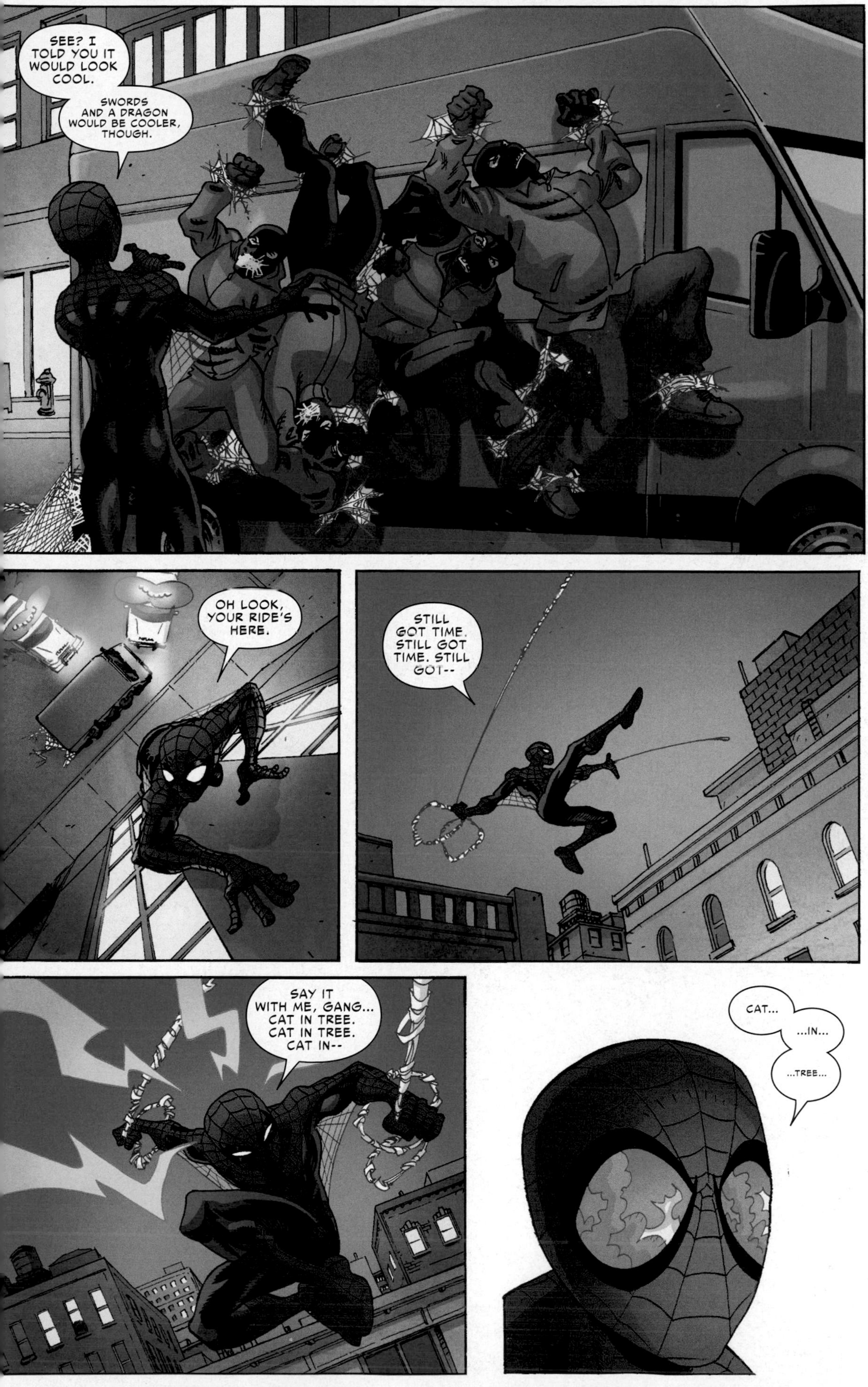
SEE? I TOLD YOU IT WOULD LOOK COOL.
SWORDS AND A DRAGON WOULD BE COOLER, THOUGH.
OH LOOK, YOUR RIDE'S HERE.
STILL GOT TIME. STILL GOT TIME. STILL GOT--
SAY IT WITH ME, GANG... CAT IN TREE. CAT IN TREE. CAT IN--
CAT...
...IN...
...TREE...

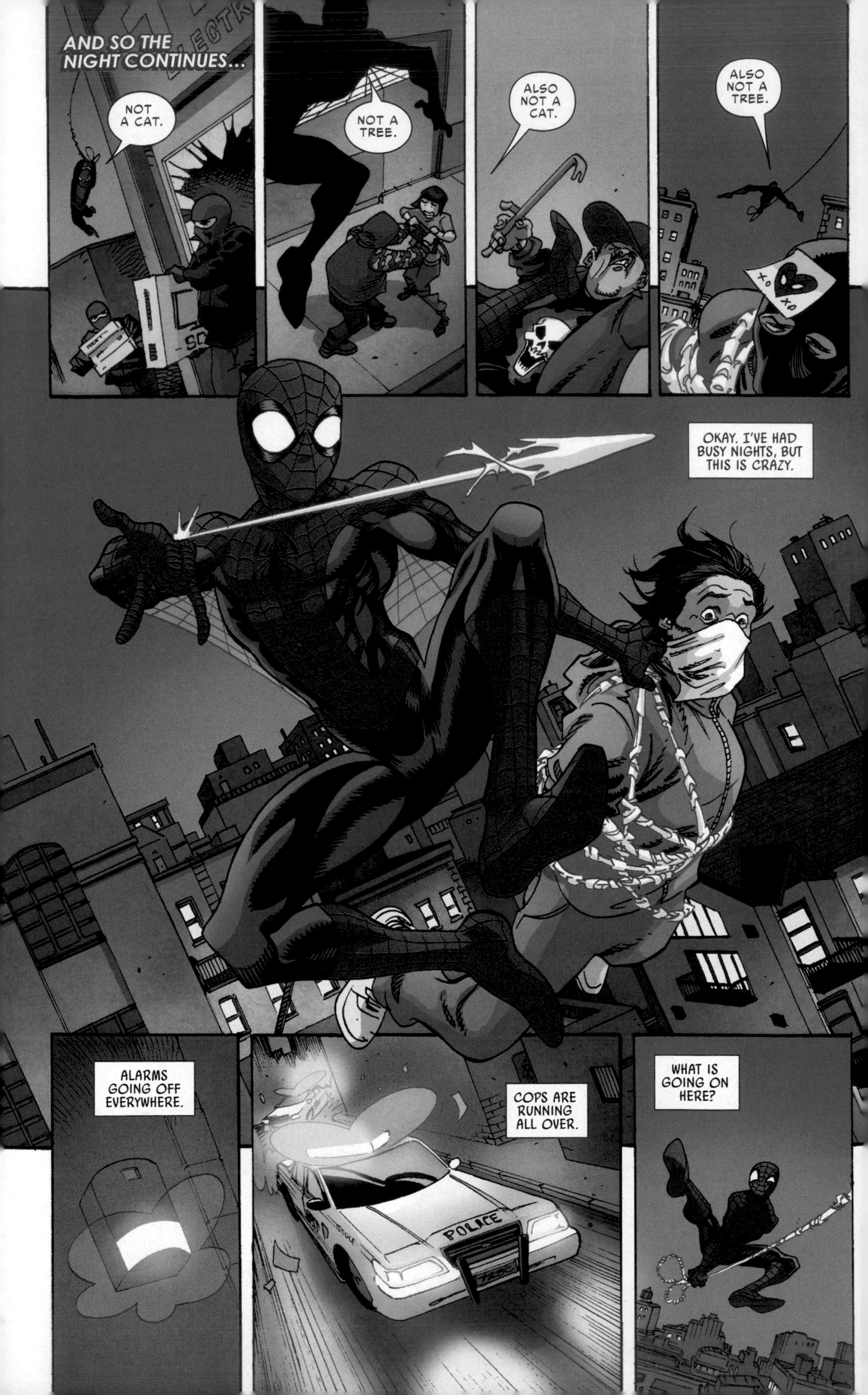
AND SO THE NIGHT CONTINUES...
NOT A CAT.
NOT A TREE.
ALSO NOT A CAT.
ALSO NOT A TREE.
OKAY. I'VE HAD BUSY NIGHTS, BUT THIS IS CRAZY.
ALARMS GOING OFF EVERYWHERE.
COPS ARE RUNNING ALL OVER.
WHAT IS GOING ON HERE?
POLICE

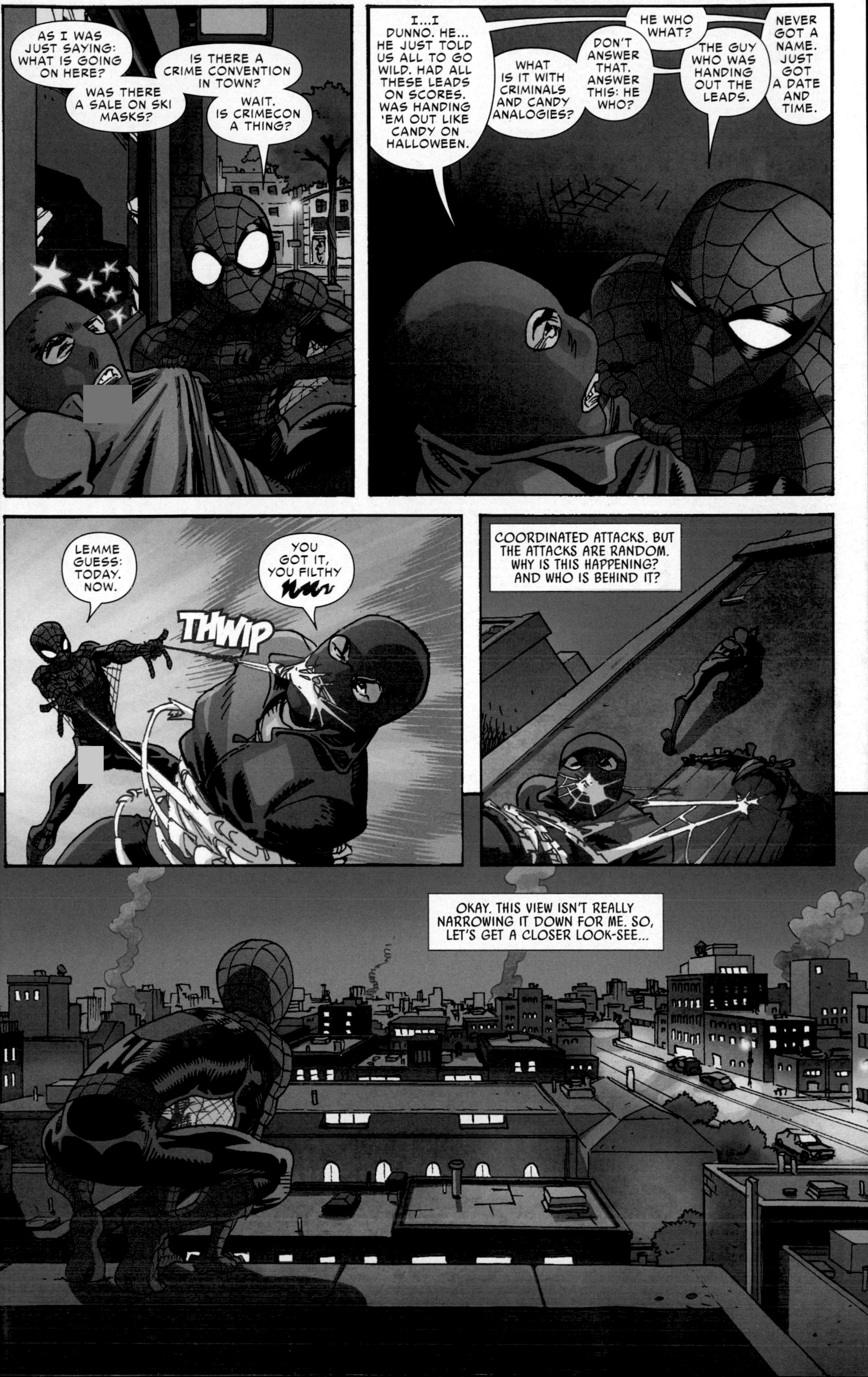

AS I WAS JUST SAYING: WHAT IS GOING ON HERE?
WAS THERE A SALE ON SKI MASKS?
IS THERE A CRIME CONVENTION IN TOWN?
WAIT. IS CRIMECON A THING?
I...I DUNNO. HE... HE JUST TOLD US ALL TO GO WILD. HAD ALL THESE LEADS ON SCORES. WAS HANDING 'EM OUT LIKE CANDY ON HALLOWEEN.
WHAT IS IT WITH CRIMINALS AND CANDY ANALOGIES?
DON'T ANSWER THAT. ANSWER THIS: HE WHO?
HE WHO WHAT?
THE GUY WHO WAS HANDING OUT THE LEADS.
NEVER GOT A NAME. JUST GOT A DATE AND TIME.
LEMME GUESS: TODAY. NOW.
YOU GOT IT, YOU FILTHY
THWIP
COORDINATED ATTACKS. BUT THE ATTACKS ARE RANDOM. WHY IS THIS HAPPENING? AND WHO IS BEHIND IT?
OKAY. THIS VIEW ISN'T REALLY NARROWING IT DOWN FOR ME. SO, LET'S GET A CLOSER LOOK-SEE...

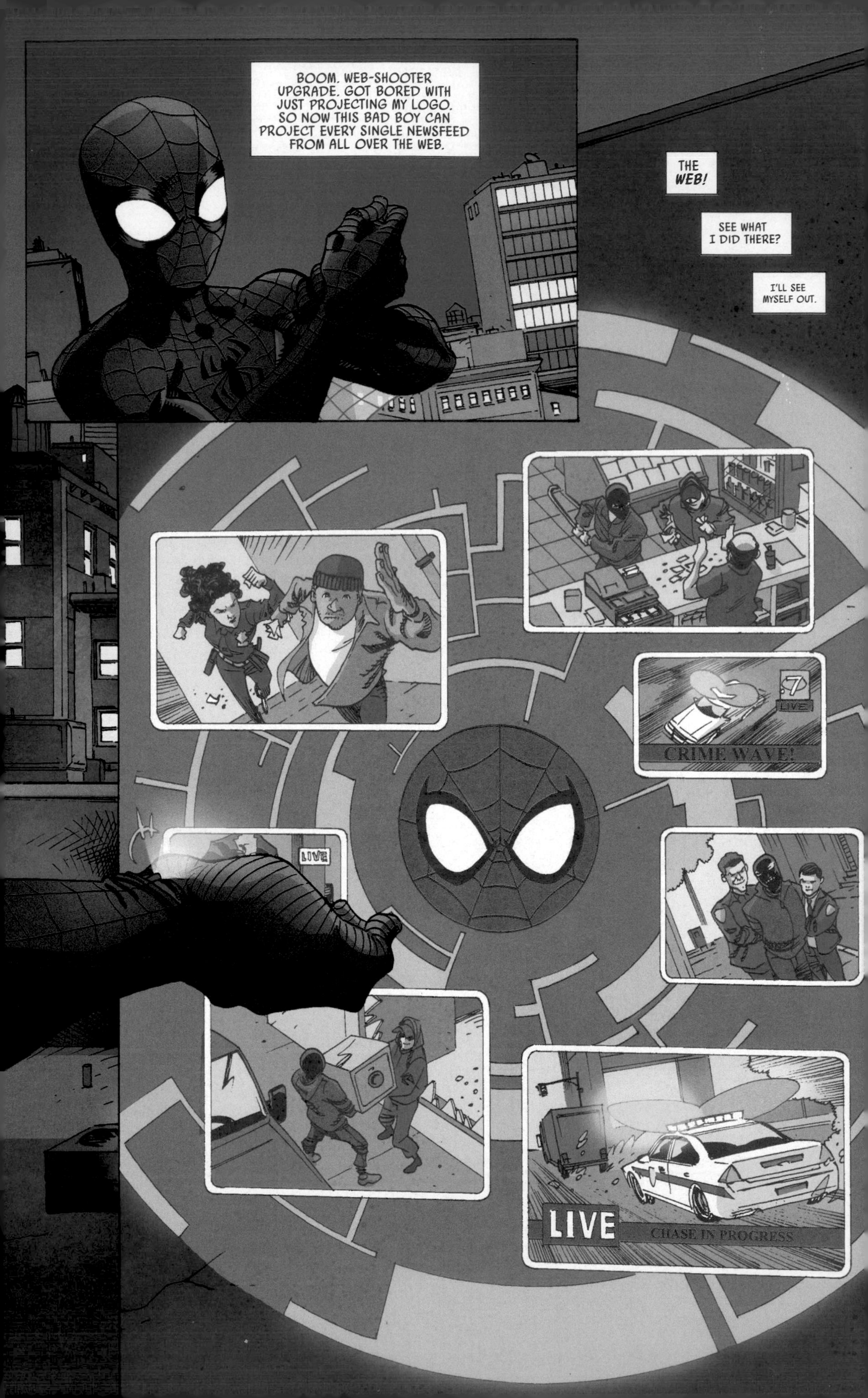
BOOM. WEB-SHOOTER UPGRADE. GOT BORED WITH JUST PROJECTING MY LOGO. SO NOW THIS BAD BOY CAN PROJECT EVERY SINGLE NEWSFEED FROM ALL OVER THE WEB.
THE WEB!
SEE WHAT I DID THERE?
I'LL SEE MYSELF OUT.
7
LIVE
CRIME WAVE!
LIVE
LIVE
CHASE IN PROGRESS

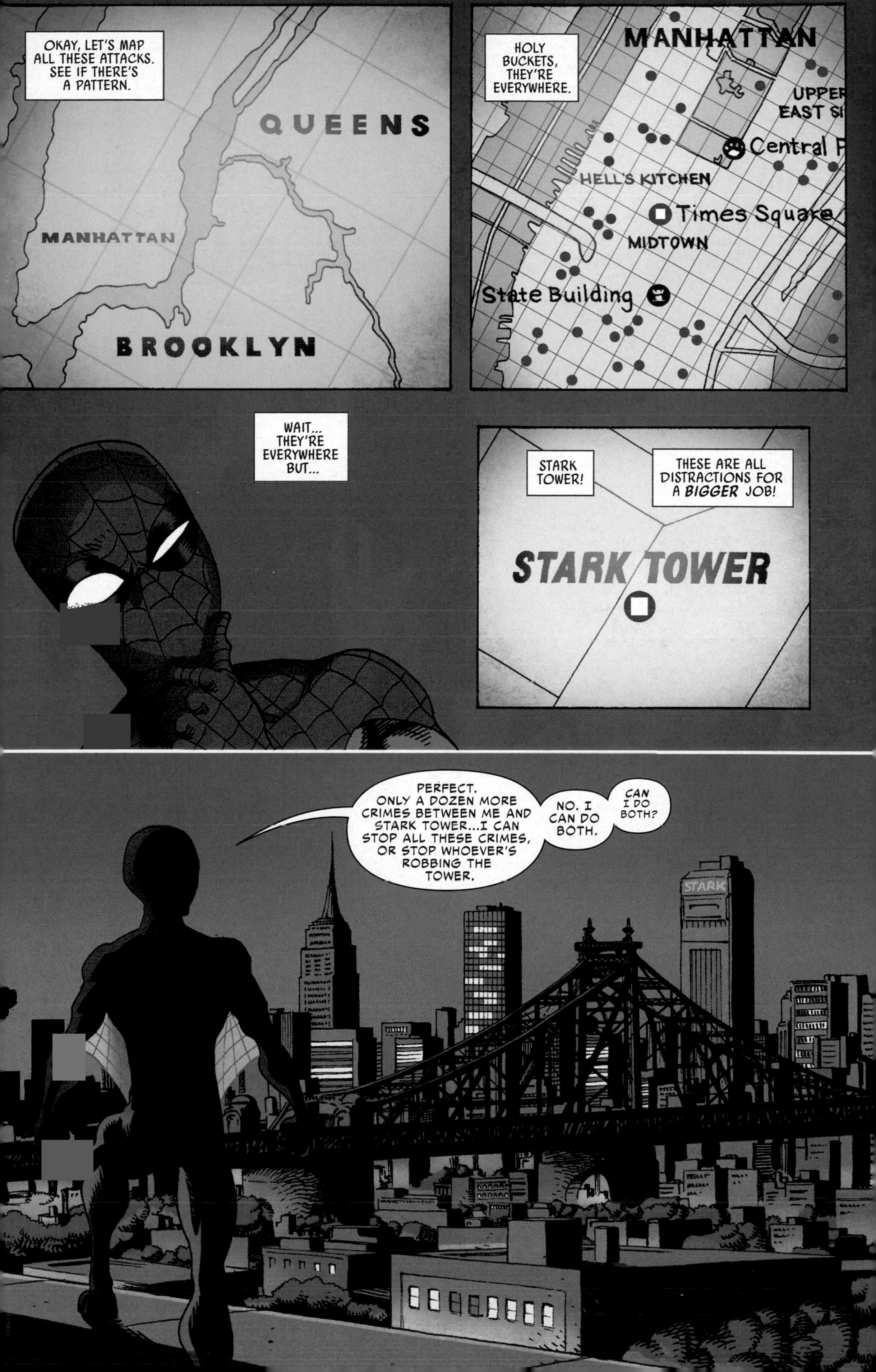
OKAY, LET'S MAP ALL THESE ATTACKS. SEE IF THERE'S A PATTERN.
QUEENS
MANHATTAN
BROOKLYN
HOLY BUCKETS, THEY'RE EVERYWHERE.
MANHATTAN
UPPER EAST SI
Central P
HELL'S KITCHEN
Times Square
MIDTOWN
State Building
WAIT... THEY'RE EVERYWHERE BUT...
STARK TOWER!
THESE ARE ALL DISTRACTIONS FOR A *BIGGER* JOB!
STARK TOWER
PERFECT. ONLY A DOZEN MORE CRIMES BETWEEN ME AND STARK TOWER...I CAN STOP ALL THESE CRIMES, OR STOP WHOEVER'S ROBBING THE TOWER.
NO. I CAN DO BOTH.
CAN I DO BOTH?
STARK

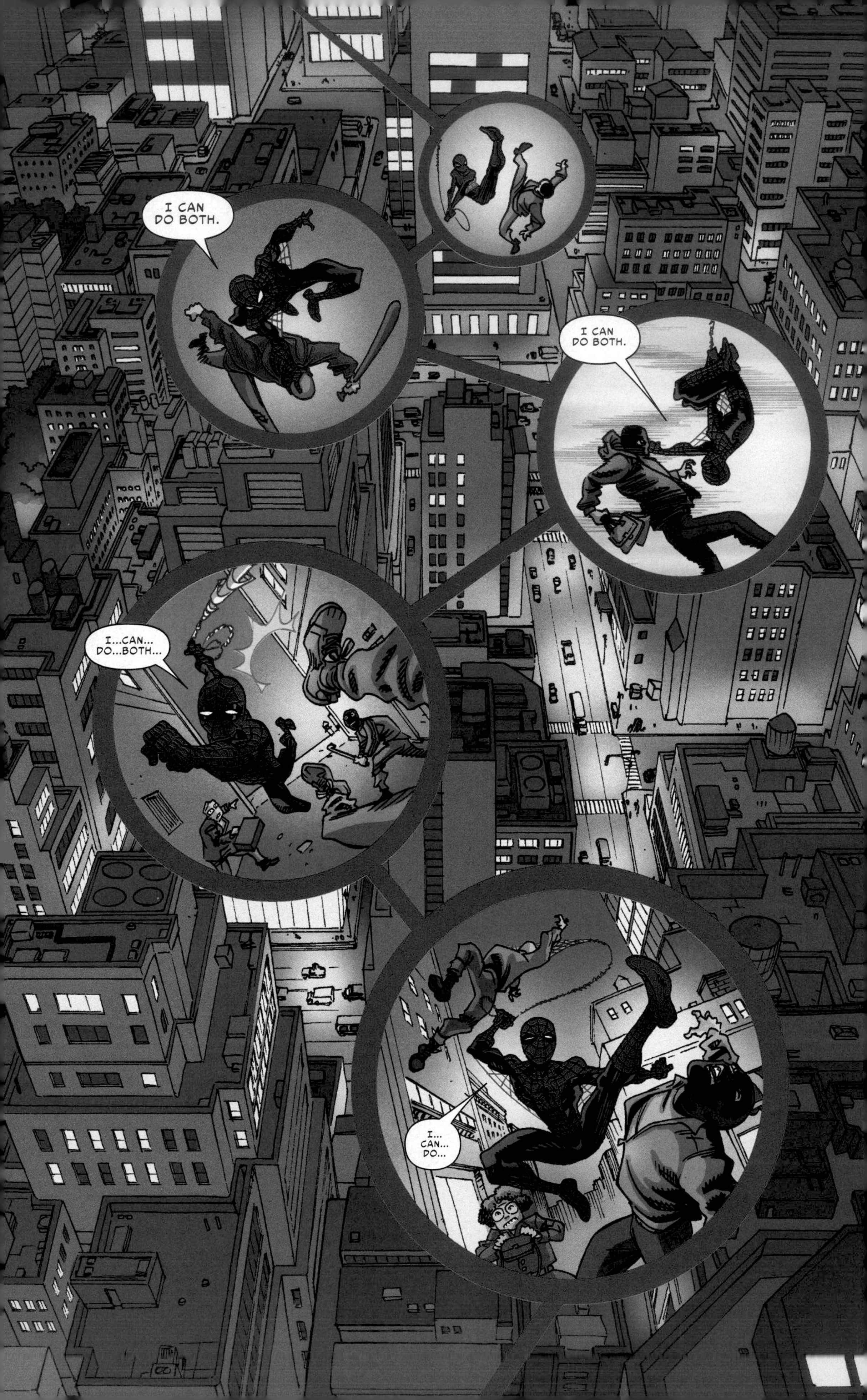
I CAN DO BOTH.
I CAN DO BOTH.
I...CAN... DO...BOTH...
I... CAN... DO...

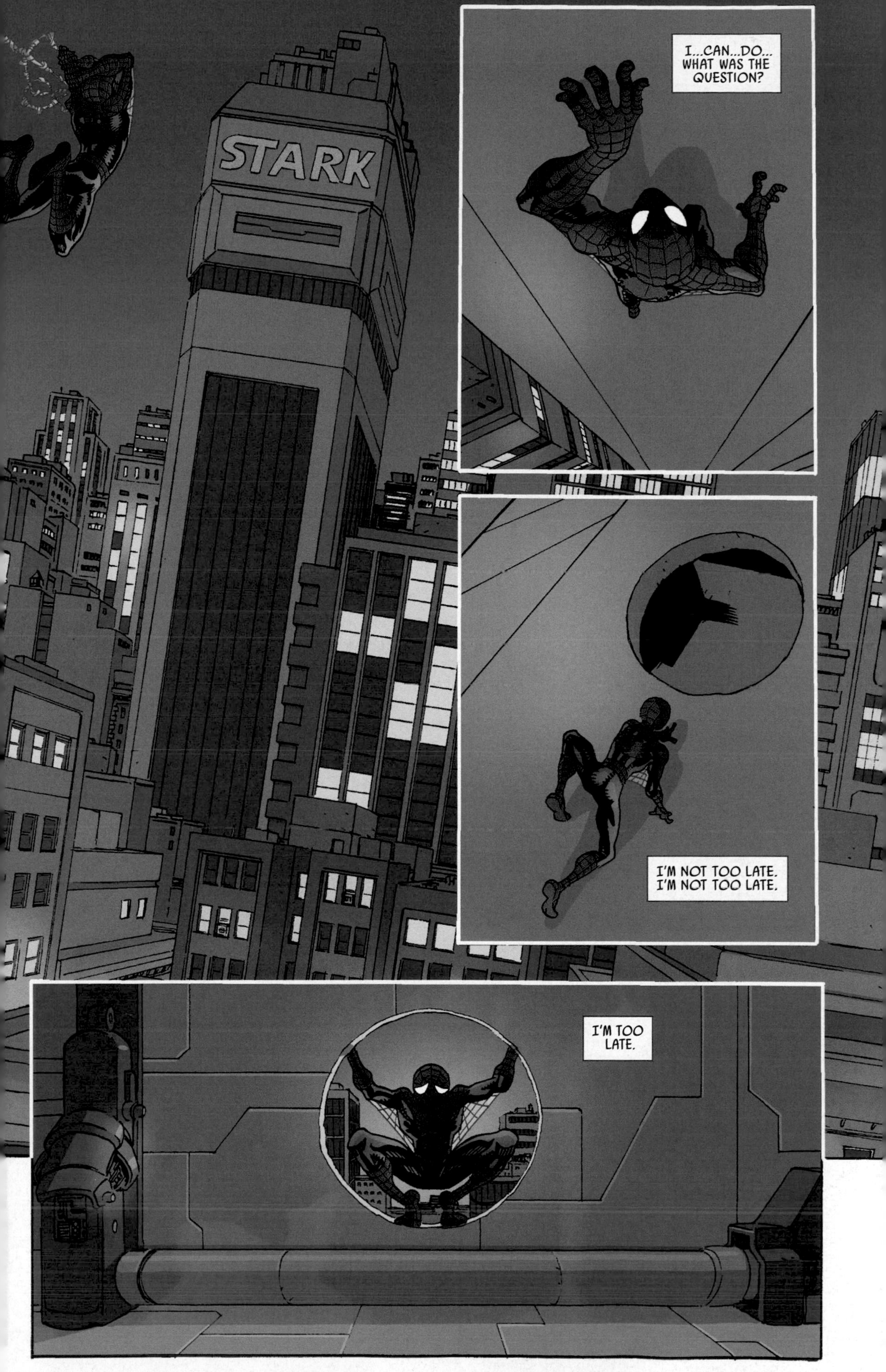
STARK
I...CAN...DO...
WHAT WAS THE
QUESTION?
I'M NOT TOO LATE.
I'M NOT TOO LATE.
I'M TOO
LATE.

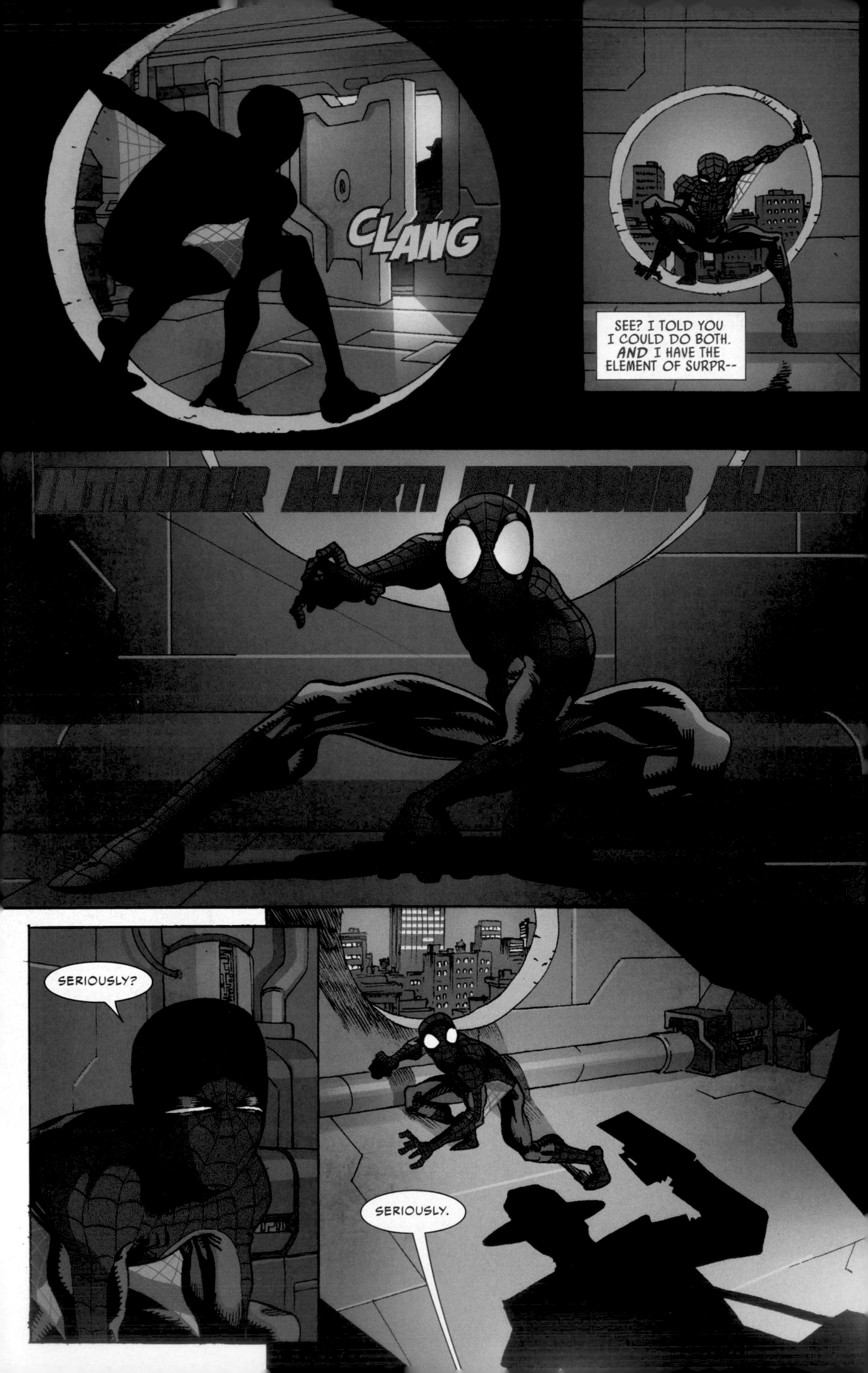
CLANG
SEE? I TOLD YOU I COULD DO BOTH. AND I HAVE THE ELEMENT OF SURPR--
INTRUDER ALERT
SERIOUSLY?
SERIOUSLY.

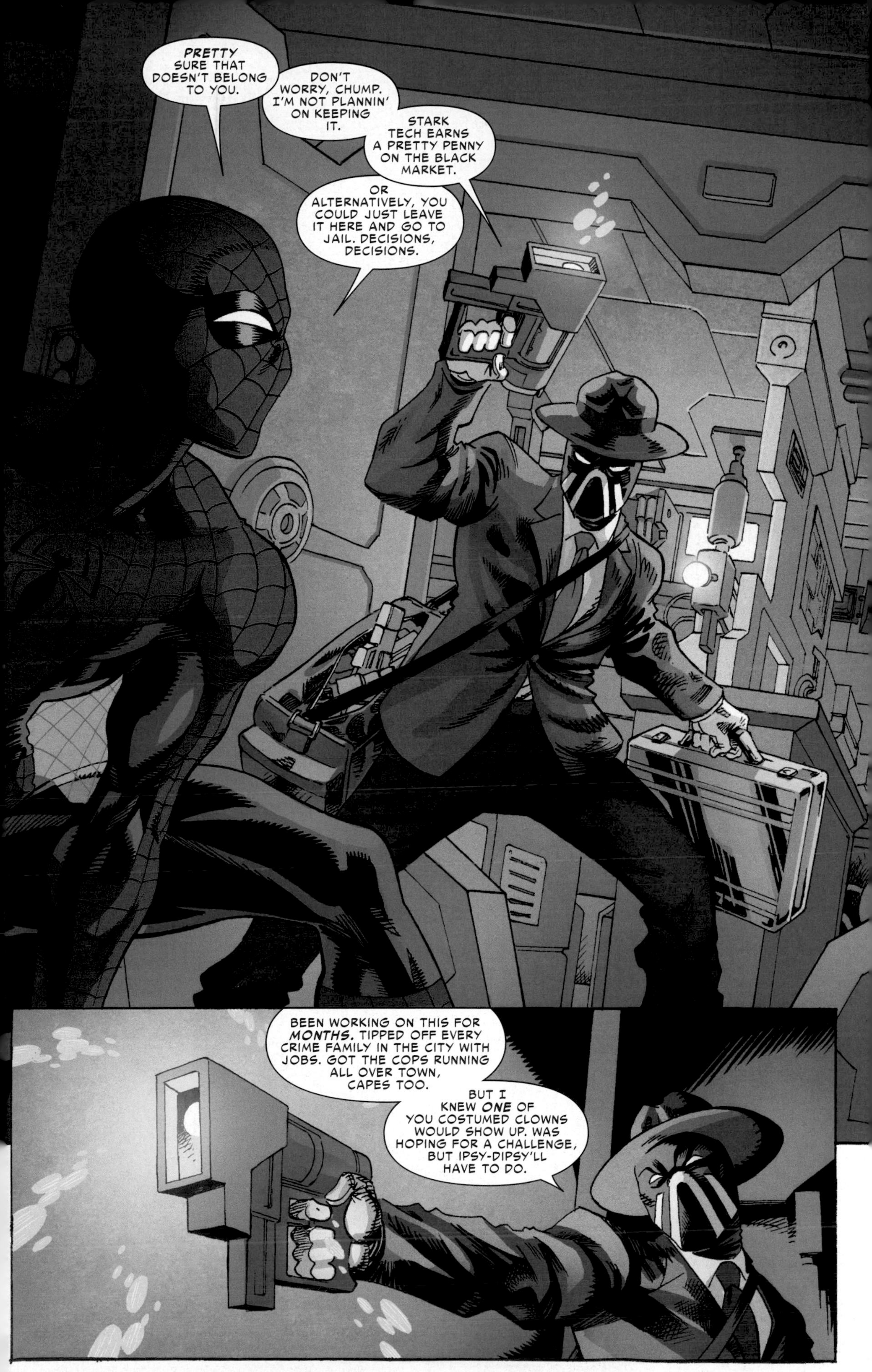
PRETTY SURE THAT DOESN'T BELONG TO YOU.
DON'T WORRY, CHUMP. I'M NOT PLANNIN' ON KEEPING IT.
STARK TECH EARNS A PRETTY PENNY ON THE BLACK MARKET.
OR ALTERNATIVELY, YOU COULD JUST LEAVE IT HERE AND GO TO JAIL. DECISIONS, DECISIONS.
BEEN WORKING ON THIS FOR MONTHS. TIPPED OFF EVERY CRIME FAMILY IN THE CITY WITH JOBS. GOT THE COPS RUNNING ALL OVER TOWN, CAPES TOO.
BUT I KNEW ONE OF YOU COSTUMED CLOWNS WOULD SHOW UP. WAS HOPING FOR A CHALLENGE, BUT IPSY-DIPSY'LL HAVE TO DO.

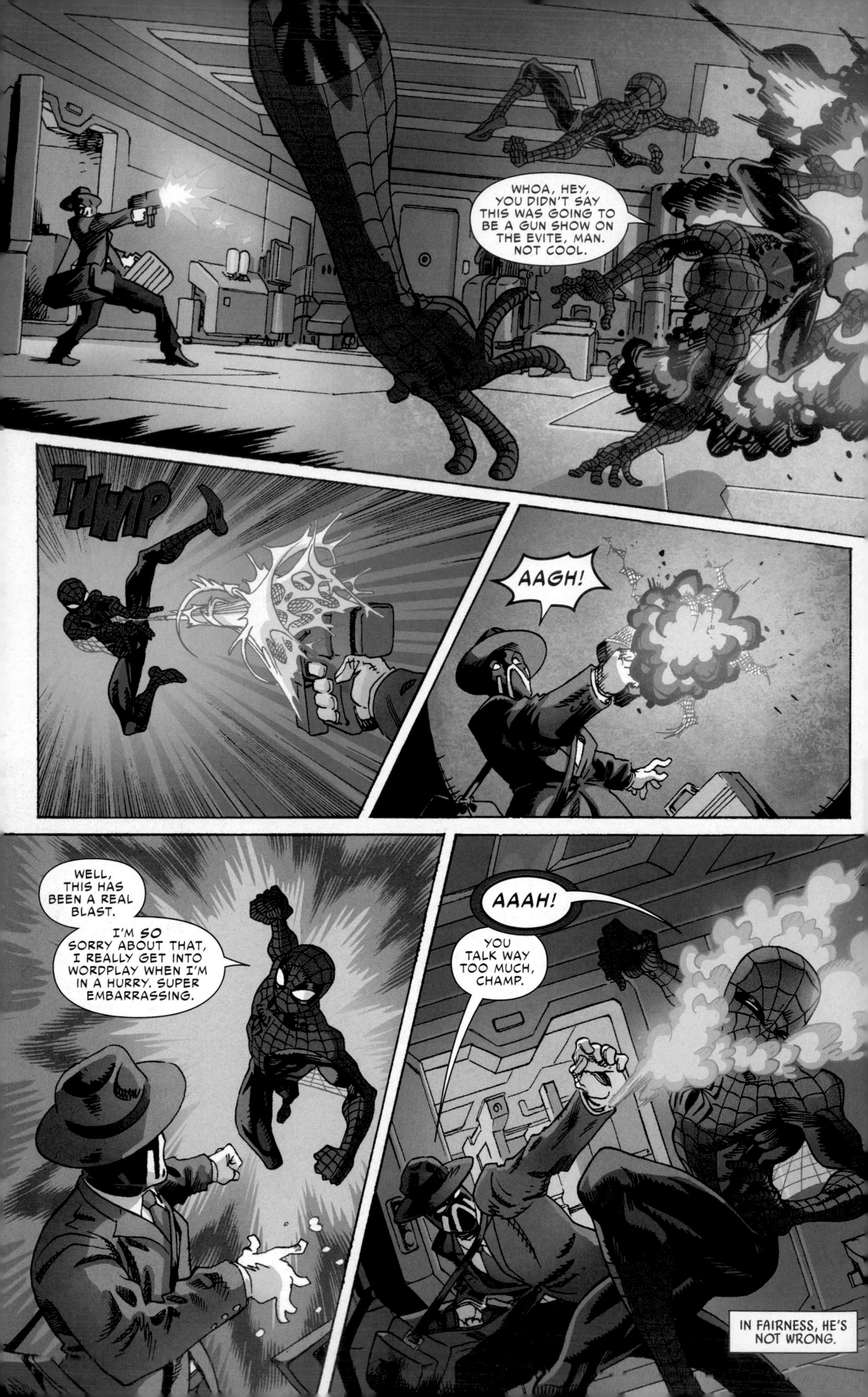
WHOA, HEY, YOU DIDN'T SAY THIS WAS GOING TO BE A GUN SHOW ON THE EVITE, MAN. NOT COOL.
THWIP
AAGH!
WELL, THIS HAS BEEN A REAL BLAST.
I'M SO SORRY ABOUT THAT, I REALLY GET INTO WORDPLAY WHEN I'M IN A HURRY. SUPER EMBARRASSING.
AAAH!
YOU TALK WAY TOO MUCH, CHAMP.
IN FAIRNESS, HE'S NOT WRONG.

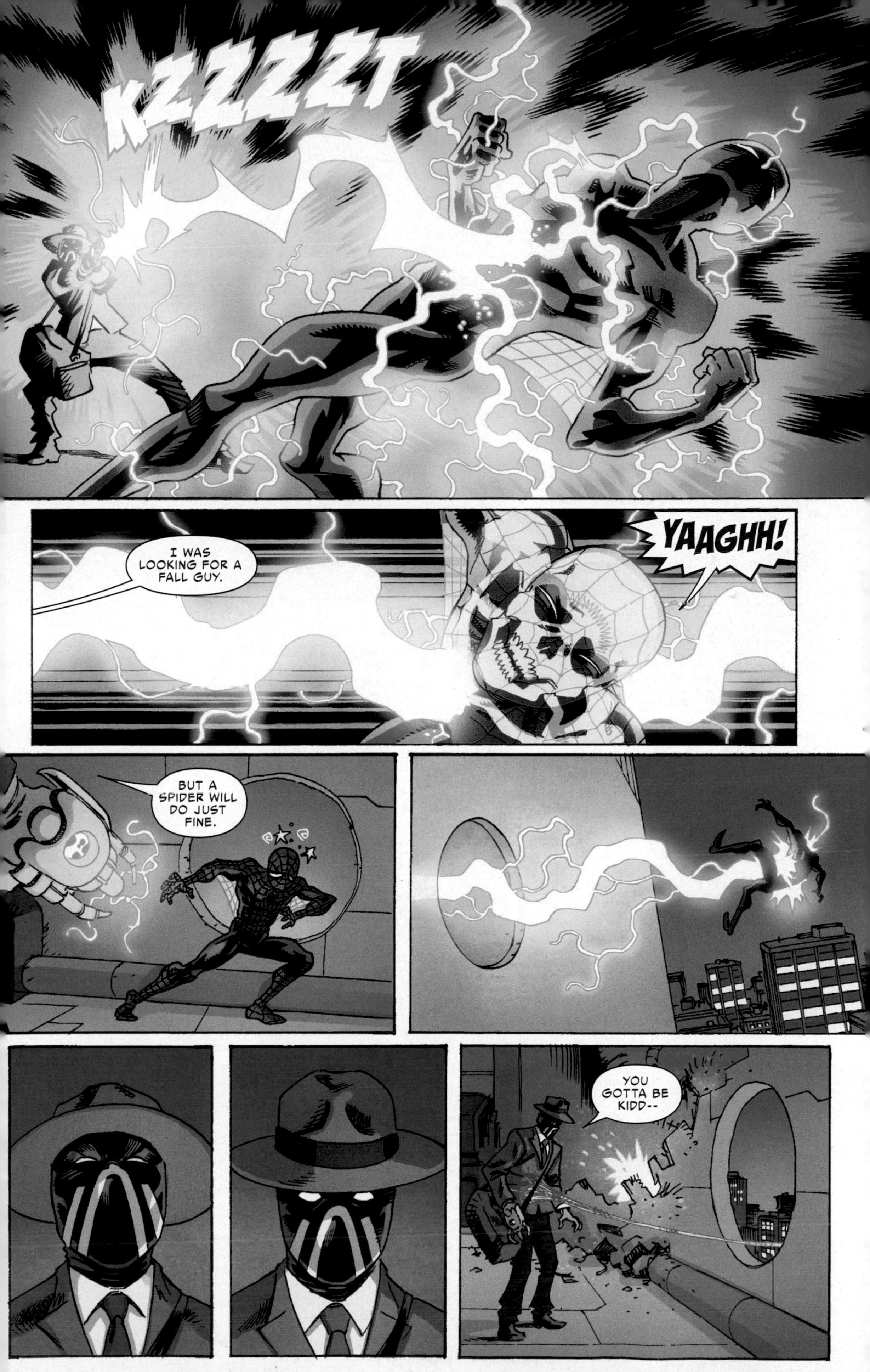
KZZZZZT
I WAS LOOKING FOR A FALL GUY.
YAAGHH!
BUT A SPIDER WILL DO JUST FINE.
YOU GOTTA BE KIDD--

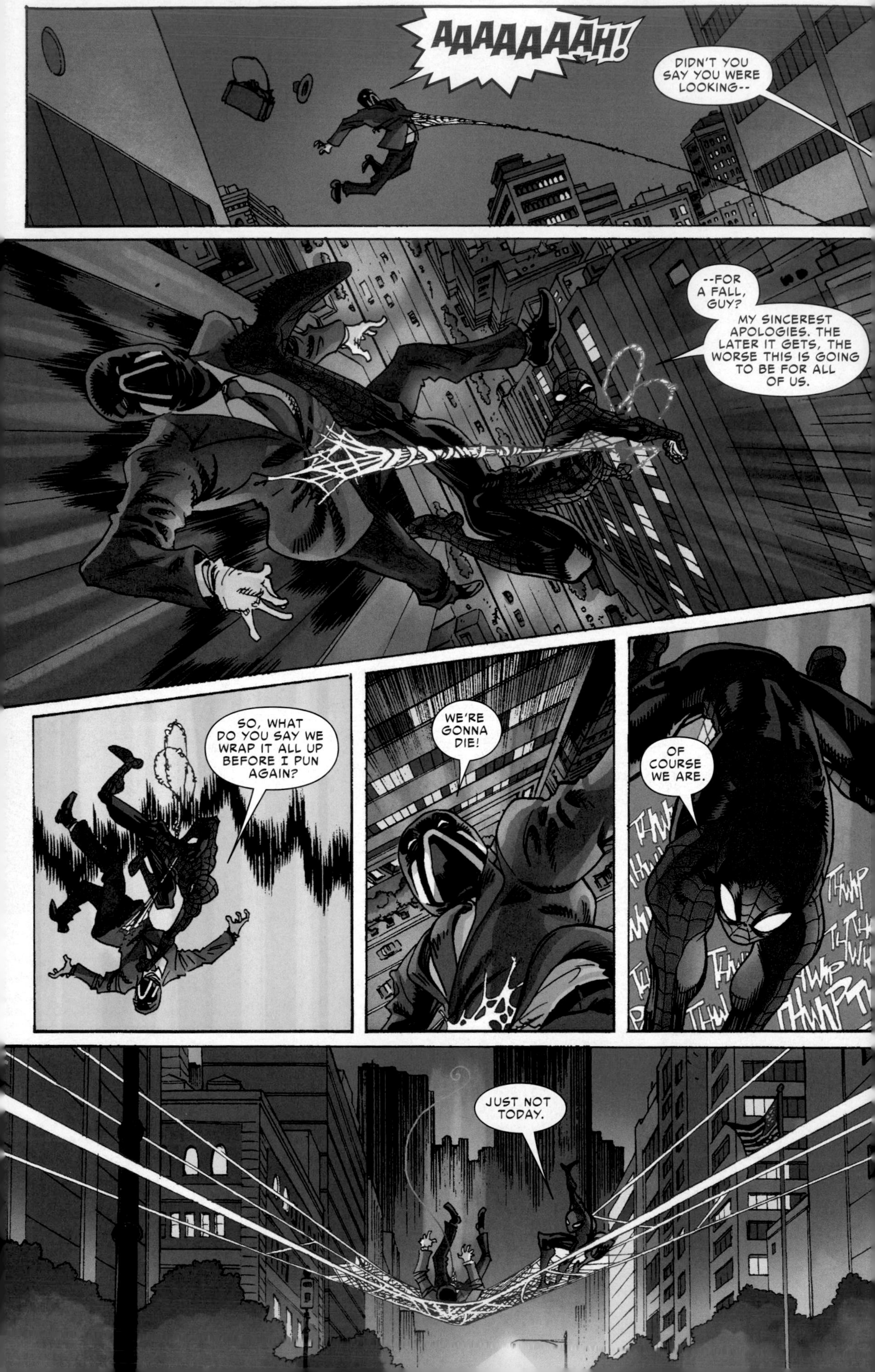
AAAAAAAH!
DIDN'T YOU SAY YOU WERE LOOKING--
--FOR A FALL, GUY?
MY SINCEREST APOLOGIES. THE LATER IT GETS, THE WORSE THIS IS GOING TO BE FOR ALL OF US.
SO, WHAT DO YOU SAY WE WRAP IT ALL UP BEFORE I PUN AGAIN?
WE'RE GONNA DIE!
OF COURSE WE ARE.
JUST NOT TODAY.

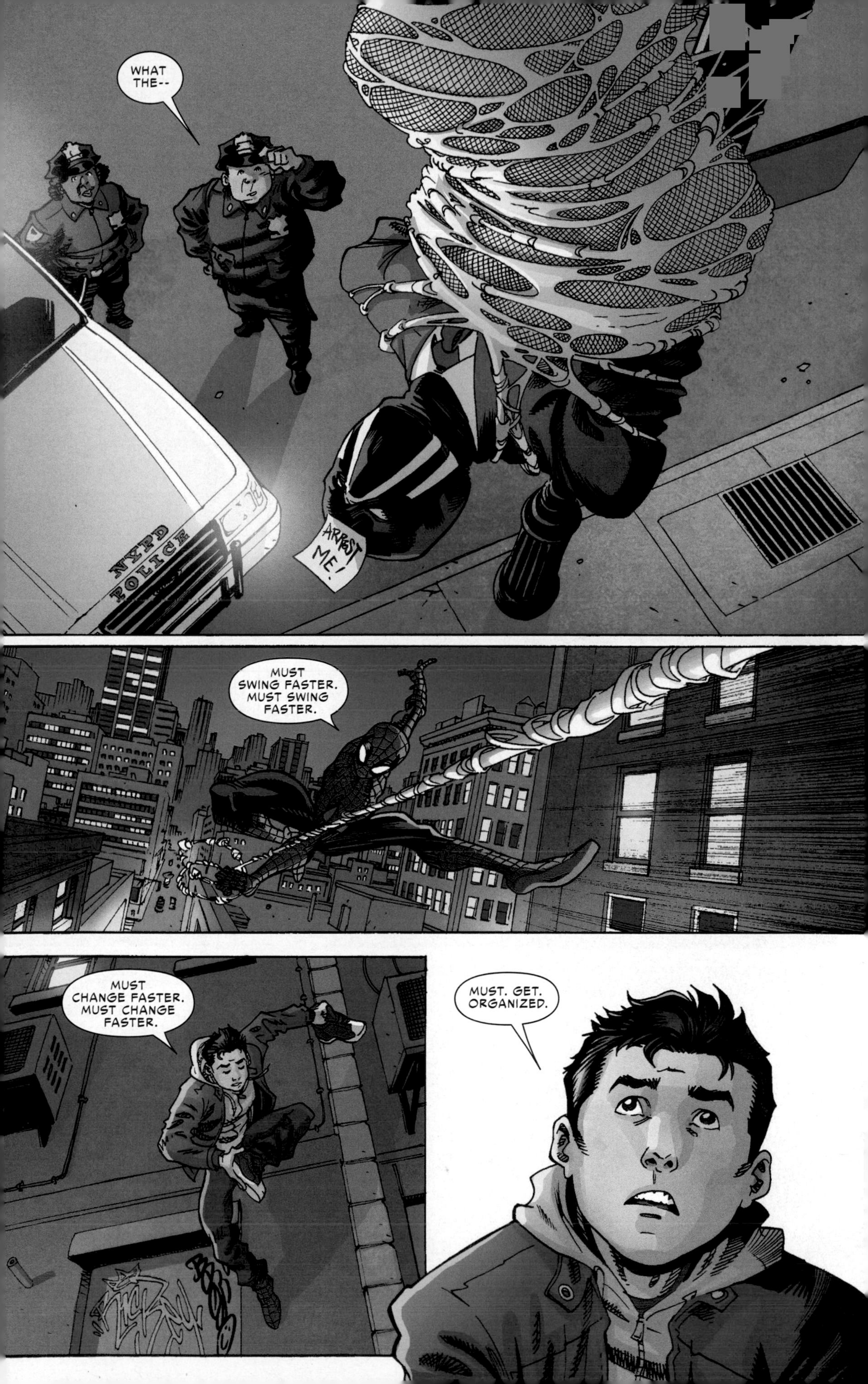
WHAT THE--
NYPD
POLICE
ARREST ME!
MUST SWING FASTER. MUST SWING FASTER.
MUST CHANGE FASTER. MUST CHANGE FASTER.
MUST. GET. ORGANIZED.

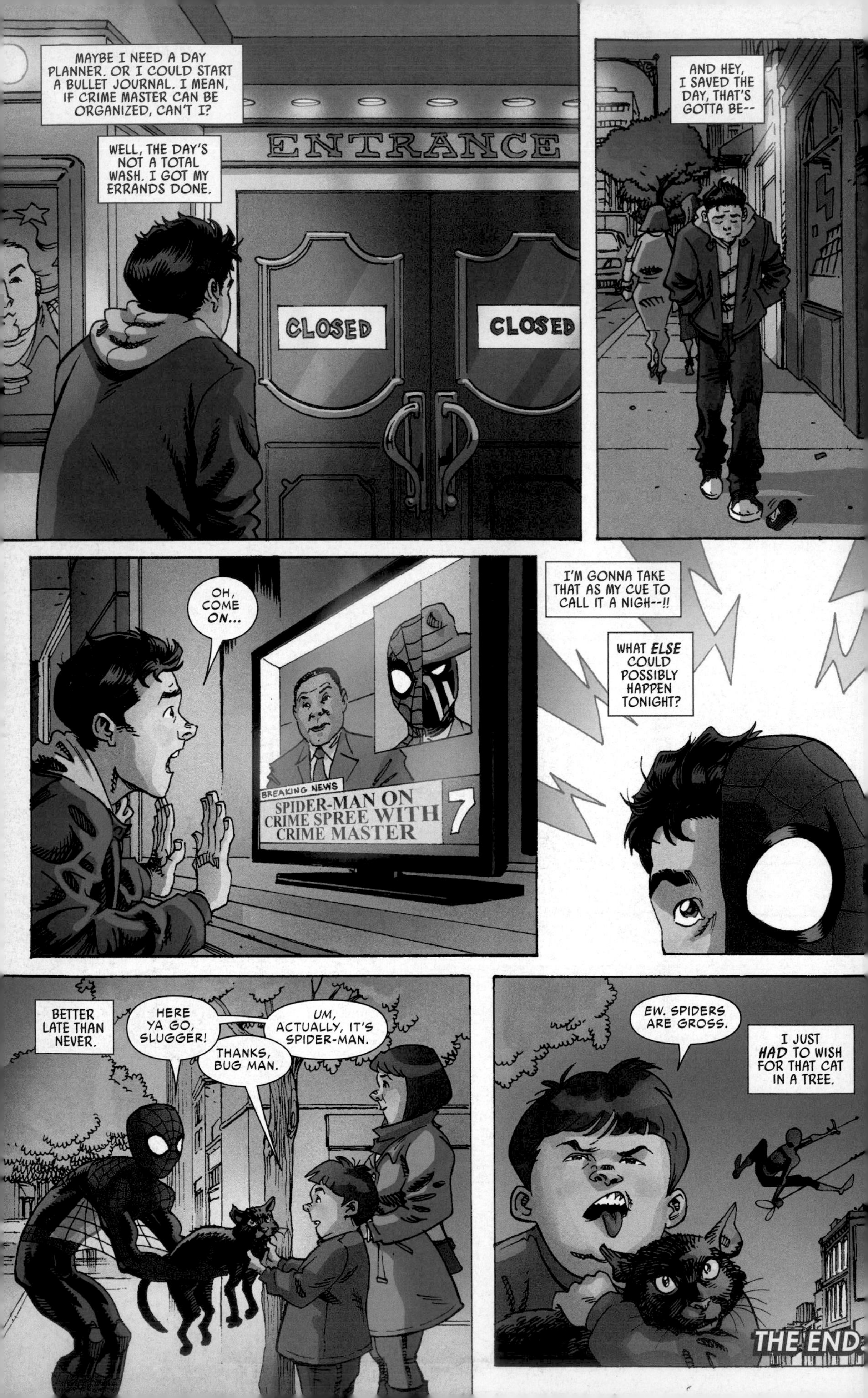
MAYBE I NEED A DAY PLANNER. OR I COULD START A BULLET JOURNAL. I MEAN, IF CRIME MASTER CAN BE ORGANIZED, CAN'T I?
WELL, THE DAY'S NOT A TOTAL WASH. I GOT MY ERRANDS DONE.
ENTRANCE
CLOSED
CLOSED
AND HEY, I SAVED THE DAY, THAT'S GOTTA BE--
OH, COME ON...
BREAKING NEWS
SPIDER-MAN ON CRIME SPREE WITH CRIME MASTER
7
I'M GONNA TAKE THAT AS MY CUE TO CALL IT A NIGH--!!
WHAT ELSE COULD POSSIBLY HAPPEN TONIGHT?
BETTER LATE THAN NEVER.
HERE YA GO, SLUGGER!
THANKS, BUG MAN.
UM, ACTUALLY, IT'S SPIDER-MAN.
EW. SPIDERS ARE GROSS.
I JUST HAD TO WISH FOR THAT CAT IN A TREE.
THE END.

DOCTOR STRANGE: MYSTIC APPRENTICE #1
VARIANT BY TODD NAUCK
& RACHELLE ROSENBERG

DOCTOR STRANGE: MYSTIC APPRENTICE #1
VARIANT BY RON LIM
& RACHELLE ROSENBERG

DOCTOR STRANGE: MYSTIC APPRENTICE #1
VARIANT BY CHRISTIAN WARD

SPIDER-MAN: MASTER PLAN #1
VARIANT BY **RON LIM, SCOTT HANNA**
& CHRIS SOTOMAYOR

SPIDER-MAN: MASTER PLAN #1
VARIANT BY **GIUSEPPE CAMUNCOLI**
& DANIELE ORLANDINI

GUARDIANS OF THE GALAXY: DREAM ON #1
VARIANT BY **TODD NAUCK**
& RACHELLE ROSENBERG